Unlawful Sex

Offences, Victims and Offenders in the Criminal Justice System of England and Wales

THE REPORT OF A HOWARD LEAGUE WORKING PARTY

WATERLOW PUBLISHERS LIMITED

This report has been approved for publication
by the Council of the Howard League.

The Council wishes to record its gratitude to
Lucilla Butler for bearing the costs of producing the report.

First Edition 1985

Waterlow Publishers Limited
Maxwell House
74 Worship Street
London EC2A 2EN
A member of the British Printing & Communication Corporation PLC

ISBN 0 08 039220 2

British Library Cataloguing in Publication Data

Howard League for Penal Reform
Unlawful sex: offences victims and offenders in the criminal justice system of England and Wales.—(Waterlow's legal and social policy library)
1. Sex crimes—England 2. Law reform—England
I. Title
344.205'253 KD7975

Printed in Great Britain by
A. Wheaton & Co. Ltd., Exeter

The Committee

Chairman

JANE WILLIAMS, J.P.
Parole Board Member 1979–1983

Secretary

DR DONALD J. WEST
Professor of Clinical Criminology, Cambridge University

Members

LUCILLA BUTLER
Chairman, London Union of Youth Clubs

DR DAVID COOK
Consultant Senior Lecturer in Mental Health, Department of Mental Health, Bristol University

CHARLES FOX
Avon Probation and After-Care Service

DR T.C.N. GIBBENS, C.B.E. (died in October 1983)
Emeritus Professor of Forensic Psychiatry, London University

DERMOT GRUBB
Prison Governor (retired)

DR D.E. PERKINS
Principal Psychologist, H.M. Prison, Winson Green, Birmingham

PAUL SIEGHART
Barrister

DR FAITH SPICER, O.B.E.
Medical Director, London Youth Advisory Centre

Observer

ROY WALMSLEY
Research and Planning Unit, Home Office

Contents

Preface

This working party was set up under the auspices of the Howard League for Penal Reform to consider the problems of sex offending in relation to the criminal justice system of England and Wales, and to make recommendations.

Our aim has been to describe, plainly but as frankly as possible, what is known today about offences, victims and offenders in this field, and to explore the many varieties of deviant sexual behaviour in order to consider how the problems which they present might be better handled, both in and out of the penal system. This is a subject that calls for regular review and reappraisal in the light of changing social and political attitudes. We have tried not to reflect views that might be held by one or another minority group, but rather what should be acceptable to public opinion generally. If this book can help to allay some of the anxiety and concern so deeply and understandably felt about sex offences and their victims, our task will not have been in vain.

The working party met 15 times over a period of three years from 1981, and received written and oral comments from many organisations and individuals, some of whom generously gave up their time to attend our meetings. We have paid a number of visits, either in groups or individually, to people and establishments relevant to the subject of our enquiry. We wish to record our gratitude for the welcome we received on all these visits, for the information and assistance generously provided, and for the concern and interest shown in what we were trying to do in relation to these complicated and emotive issues.

One of our members, Professor Trevor Gibbens, died in October 1983. Despite failing health, he attended our meetings almost until his death. He brought with him a breadth of vision, a compassion and an understanding of both victim and offender that was the result of his long and distinguished career as a forensic psychiatrist and criminologist. We have greatly missed his presence among us and we should like to pay tribute to his generous contribution to our work.

We should also like to record particular thanks to Roy Walmsley of the Home Office Research and Planning Unit who served as an observer on the working party, attending all our meetings and supplying valuable up-to-date statistics and information.

All our members have taken an active and constructive part in the work. Paul Sieghart has been of special help on matters of law, and in the drafting of our recommendations in that area. We are also most grateful to Mary Percival for preparing the Appendix summarising the sexual offences known to the law of England and Wales.

Professor Donald West, Director of the Cambridge Institute of Criminology, has acted throughout both as a member and as Secretary to the working party. He has collected and collated much of the material in this book, and been responsible for most of the drafting and editing. His untiring contribution has been unique in enabling us to bring our work to completion, and we owe him a deep debt of gratitude.

Jane Williams
Chairman

Acknowledgements

Throughout our work we have had the benefit of collaboration with the Director of the Howard League, Martin Wright until 1982, and since then David Jenkins.

The Working Group corresponded with and sought advice or comment from a large number of individuals, too many to name them all, but they included the persons listed below, none of whom is in any way responsible for any of the material or opinions contained in our Report. Those who attended sessions of the Group to give evidence in person are marked with an asterisk.

* David Atkinson	Formerly Prison Governor I, now Home Office, P2 Division
Cyril S. Bagshaw	Asst Chief Probation Officer, Essex
Dr Brian J. Barrett	Sen Medical Officer, H.M. Prison, Grendon
Dr Arnon Bentovim	Consultant Psychiatrist, Gt Ormond St Hospital for Sick Children
Professor (Emer) Ruth Bowden O.B.E.	London University, Royal Free Hospital Medical School
Thomas Burke, O.B.E.	Chief Probation Officer, Middx
J. Michael Cartwright-Sharp	Barrister. Formerly secretary of the Law Commission
Dr Christine Cooper, O.B.E.	Consultant Paediatrician, Newcastle-upon-Tyne
* Professor Ingrid Cooper	McGill University, School of Social Work, Montreal
Miss Joan Court	Independent Social Worker
Albin Crook O.B.E.	Chief Probation Officer, Mid Glamorgan
Alan Croston	Chief Probation Officer, Somerset
A. William Driscoll, Q.G.M.	Commandant, Prison Service College, Wakefield
Colin J. Edwards	Chief Probation Officer, Nottingham
Dr O.W.S. Fitzgerald	Consultant psychiatrist, formerly visiting psychotherapist, H.M. Prison, Dartmoor (retired)

Adrian Fulford	Barrister
Ralph W. Harris,	Chief Probation Officer, Staffordshire
Dr Neville Gittleson	Consultant Psychiatrist, Middlewood Hospital, Sheffield
Professor Cyril Greenland	Dept of Social Work, McMaster University, Hamilton, Ontario
Anthony Grey	Sexual Law Reform Society
Paul Griffiths	Nottingham Social Services
Professor John Gunn	Forensic Psychiatry Dept, London University Institute of Psychiatry
Michael W. Halford	Chief Probation Officer, Norfolk
* Dr Ronald Ingrey-Senn	Formerly Director, Prison Medical Service
Dr Marjory Jones, J.P.	
Dr R.L. Jillet (deceased)	Formerly Governor of H.M. Prison, Grendon
Lady (Jane) Lloyd	Psychotherapist
* Sir John Nightingale, C.B.E., Q.P.M.	Formerly Chief Constable of Essex
Robert Norman, O.B.E.	Formerly Chief Probation Officer, Buckinghamshire
Tim Owen	Co-ordinator, Radical Alternatives to Prison
Dr Elizabeth Parker	Special Hospitals Case Register
Peter Ralphs	Chief Probation Officer, Kent
Stanley Ratcliffe	Deputy Chief Probation Officer for Inner London
Ms Helen Reeves	National Association of Victim Support Schemes
Roger Shaw	Senior Probation Officer, Leicester
Dr Anthony Storr	Consultant Psychiatrist, Warneford Hospital, Oxford
Dr T. Gavin Tennent	Medical Director, St Andrew's Hospital, Northampton
Dr David A. Thomas	Lecturer in Criminology, University of Cambridge
Miss D.J. Tibbits, O.B.E.	Formerly Chief Probation Officer, Surrey
* Dennis J. Trevelyan, C.B.	Formerly Director General, Prison Service
His Hon Judge Stephen Tumin	Circuit Judge
Merfyn Turner	Founder of Norman Houses for ex-prisoners

Detective Chief Inspector Thelma Wagstaff	Scotland Yard
Nigel D. Walker, C.B.E.	Wolfson Professor of Criminology, University of Cambridge
Rt Hon Lord Justice Waller, O.B.E.	Lord Justice of Appeal
Deputy Asst Commissioner Richard Wells	Director of Information, Scotland Yard
Peter Warburton	Chief Probation Officer, Durham County
Mrs Angela Willans	Journalist

CHAPTER 1

Introduction

1.1 Hardly any other category of criminals arouses as much concern as sex offenders. The mixture of dread, fascination and revulsion they evoke is reflected in the volume and the quality of press comment when cases come to trial. Popular views about how these offenders should be handled alternate between extremes of punitiveness and proposals that they should all have medical treatment. The public expects protection from the threat of sexual molestation, but opinions about how this should be achieved are as conflicting as they are strongly held.

Although serious enough for the persons directly affected, the size of the problem of sex offences, in comparison with the problem of crime in general, is apt to be exaggerated. Sex offences comprise less than 1 per cent of notifiable crimes recorded by the police (see para 3.3), and of sexual offenders who are convicted only about one in five have done something serious enough to lead to a custodial sentence.

1.2 For those who have the responsibility for dealing with them, sex offenders present awkward problems — in sentencing, in institutional administration, in supervision, and in treatment. They are unwelcome misfits in prison and often unpopular and difficult as clients of the probation and psychiatric services. Many of them have considerable personal and social problems contributing to the risk of re-offending.

Coherent discussion about sex offenders is handicapped by the great variety of types. They range from minor nuisances, to whom the system tends to over-react, to the most dangerous and brutal criminals. They include repetitive exposers, a substantial group of social inadequates, (some of whom are hopelessly locked into an involuntary attraction to children), others who loiter around lavatories for homosexual purposes, and young people whose conduct would be perfectly legal if they or their partners were a year or two older. At the opposite end of the scale, a small minority are seriously violent.

1.3 In view of the current concern to find alternatives to imprisonment whenever possible, and the recent reports on sexual offences produced by the Criminal Law Revision Committee and the Policy Advisory Committee on Sexual Offences, the time seems ripe for a careful reconsideration of policy and practice in this area. This Working Party has tried to take a fresh look at the definitions and forms of control of sexual misconduct and to examine how sex offenders are dealt with at every stage in the criminal justice process, from the decision to prosecute to the decision to release on parole. Our aim has been to formulate practical proposals that will make the system more discriminating, more humane and, above all, more effective in protecting the public.

Our goals are necessarily modest, for it would be foolish to imagine that innovations in law, social or penal treatment could rid us altogether of rapists, child molesters and other sex offenders. Sexual urges are remarkably powerful and persistent, not least in those whose inclinations deviate from acceptable norms, and the law can achieve only a limited degree of deterrence or temporary incapacitation.

1.4 We cannot ignore the fact that abhorrence of other people's sexual habits is often passionate, even if it is not always entirely rational. The condemnation of sexual violence is understandable. Most people regard sexual acts as essentially affectionate, pleasurable and mutual, and rightly condemn the use of sex to express hatred or to inflict humiliation or pain upon an unwilling victim, or to coerce another person for selfish gratification. But even sexual conduct that is loving, pleasurable, mutual and free from violence or exploitation is still condemned by some people, who disapprove of consenting adult homosexuals, or relationships outside marriage. Where children are involved with adults almost everyone strongly condemns the behaviour, whatever the circumstances and regardless of whether there is evidence that such contacts in fact cause harm.

We ourselves have tried to maintain an objective, analytic approach, but the strong feelings engendered by these matters represent an aspect of the problem that must be taken into account before one can make any recommendations.

1.5 In Part I of this Report we have tried to provide some basic information about sex offending, but in doing so we are fully aware that undisputed facts are scarce and that much of the evidence is still controversial. Wherever possible, we have therefore cited our sources of information or opinion, so that readers who want to scrutinise the evidence for themselves can do so through the reference list at the end. In Part II we set out our own opinions and recommendations, referring back, where necessary, to the material provided in Part I.

1.6 As will be seen, we recognise that many of the present laws defining sexual offences were framed in a moral climate different from that existing in Britain today; and accordingly we recommend that certain changes should be introduced so that the law can reflect more rational and responsible attitudes to sexual behaviour. We also advocate improvements and extensions to the facilities for management and treatment of those convicted of sexual offences, and we would like to see attempts made to provide the public with better information on sexual problems.

1.7 We believe that, while the individual should in principle be left free to regulate his or her sexual conduct in private, such freedom should not be exercised at the expense of others. We therefore propose that the law should provide protection for the young, the immature, the psychologically inadequate and all those, who, from one cause or another, are unable to protect themselves from sexual exploitation for the gratification or profit of others. Above all, the law must try to protect people, in this field of conduct as in any other, from violence, wanton cruelty, fraud, exploitation or undue pressure. But, in general, it need not intervene to prevent or punish conduct which mature participants freely choose for themselves, unless that conduct is shown to be harmful.

Accordingly, we have not felt called upon to pass moral judgments on everyone whose activities or attitudes relating to sex may still be found offensive by one section or another within our community. We recognise that this will inevitably occur in a pluralistic society which now embraces a wide range of different ethnic and cultural groupings, and of different or absent religious beliefs. While striving to avoid being influenced by personal prejudice, we have therefore thought it right to recommend a framework for the laws relating to sexual behaviour in which both those living by generally accepted norms, and those whose activities or attitudes differ from them, can find a sense of justice.

1.8 Two official bodies have also been working in this field: the Criminal Law Revision Committee (CLRC), and the Policy Advisory Committee of Sexual Offences, both of which report to the Home Secretary. They have the advantage over us that, as bodies appointed by the Government, they carry more public weight than an unofficial group like our own. But they also have certain disadvantages. In the nature of things, neither of them can be expected to pursue a radical or innovative approach: their official status constrains them to be cautious, even in matters of reform. In addition, the CLRC is composed of seventeen distinguished judges and lawyers (only two of whom are female), whose main concern is with the technical details of the law and with borderline cases, a task which they are eminently well-qualified to perform but which is necessarily narrower than ours.

1.9 Two reports by the Criminal Law Revision Committee (1980, 1984), are closely relevant to our own deliberations. Their *Working Paper on Sexual Offences* was published before our Report was written. The CLRC's Fifteenth Report, which set out their final conclusions, appeared in April 1984, when our Report was nearing completion. In the event, many of our own recommendations for the reform of the substantive law in this field have turned out to be very similar to those now made by the CLRC. In some cases, we have sought to achieve the same objectives by a simpler route, and in others we would go somewhat further than the majority of the CLRC at the present time. The contentiousness of some of the issues concerned is reflected by divisions of opinion within the CLRC itself, but we are glad to report that on all the matters which we have ourselves considered we have been able to come to unanimous conclusions.

PART I

THE FACTS AS WE SEE THEM

CHAPTER 2

What is a sex offence?

2.1 In the criminal law of England and Wales, an 'offence' is an act defined as such by some provision of that law and known technically as an *actus reus*, ie a guilty act. Some such acts – but by no means all of them – are offences only if committed with some particular intention (the *mens rea*, ie guilty intention) specified by the law. For example, trespassing on someone else's property – such as entering his house without his permission – only becomes a criminal offence if the trespasser can be shown to have entered with the intention of committing some separate crime there, such as theft or rape.

2.2 English law defines many thousands of acts as criminal offences (Justice, 1980), but unlike most other legal systems it lacks formal distinctions between different categories. Failing to sign one's driving licence is just as much a criminal offence as armed robbery: both may lead to trial by the criminal courts and the registering of a conviction in their official records. The only differences are the level of court (Magistrates' Court or Crown Court) before which offences can be tried, the maximum penalty (fine, imprisonment, etc) that can be imposed, and whether the suspect may be arrested without a warrant.

2.3 Likewise, the law makes no formal distinction between 'sexual' offences and other offences. How one differentiates is therefore largely a matter of individual choice, and the criteria for classification are open to debate. At one extreme, one might choose to treat as 'sexual' only those criminal acts which actually require the performance of some overt sexual activity – and so, for example, exclude offences such as abducting or detaining a woman against her will even though the intention may have been to coerce her into having sexual intercourse with someone. At the other extreme, one might choose to include every criminal act which has a connection with someone's sexual activities, such as bigamy, procuring abortions, dealing in pornography, or stabbing one's wife's lover.

2.4 In Appendix I, we set out the details of some 43 independent provisions of English law in force in July 1982, all creating offences which either themselves require the performance of overt sexual activities, or have a close and direct connection with such activities. In choosing which offences to include, we have not followed any very precise rules, nor have we been wholly consistent: for instance, we have included offences connected with prostitution, but not with abortion or pornography. We claim no particular merit for our choice, having simply included all the offences listed in the Sexual Offences Act 1956 as well as certain other offences to which the primary label 'sexual' – rather than some other label – can be fairly readily attached. Our list differs only slightly from the offences grouped under the heading of 'sexual' in the Home Office Criminal Statistics.

2.5 For each of the provisions included in that Appendix, we have given its present legal source, in statute or at common law; its legal definition; who may commit it and against whom; any special defences there may be; before which courts it may be tried; and what is the maximum penalty for it. A number of these provisions in fact create more than one offence. For example, under s.4(1) of the Sexual Offences Act 1956, it is an offence for a person to apply *or* administer to, *or* cause to be taken by, a woman, any drug, matter *or* thing with intent to stupefy *or* overpower her so as thereby to enable any man to have unlawful (ie extra-marital) sexual intercourse with her. In law, each of these nine possible acts, committed with either of these two possible intentions, constitutes a separate offence, and the section therefore creates 18 different substantive criminal offences. For each of these, there will also be the associated 'inchoate' offences of attempting to commit it, conspiring to commit it, inciting others to commit it, and aiding, abetting, counselling or procuring its commission. When all these permutations are taken into account, the number of different sexual offences in our law must run to several hundred.

2.6 In considering sexual offenders – and more especially their management and treatment – for the purpose of this report, there is a case for disregarding some of the legal categories of sex offence and confining attention to the persons whose misbehaviour relates to their own sexual impulses. This would exclude prostitutes, procurers, pimps, brothelkeepers, pornographers and others for whom the gratification of (other people's) sexual desires is primarily a source of money. Although we have included them in the Appendix, we shall therefore not consider these offences further.

2.7 As will be seen from the Appendix, the English criminal law of sex is now almost all embodied in statute, principally the Sexual Offences Act 1956, which was largely designed to codify and consolidate the law as it then stood. But it was not always so. At common law, for many centuries, only three specifically sexual offences were known: rape, sodomy and bestiality. All the rest have been added by Parliament, most of them since the accession of Queen Victoria. Even so, the law as it now stands presents some odd features.

2.8 First, the law draws no visible distinction between different kinds of anticipated harm. It deals in exactly the same fashion with the protection of minors from premature erotic experiences, the protection of people in general from violence, fraud or exploitation, and the prohibition of acts which, though they may entail no demonstrable harm, are for religious or other reasons regarded as evil, such as sexual intercourse by humans with animals.

2.9 Second, the maximum penalties provided by the law do not appear to reflect any coherent scale either of anticipated harm or of perceived evil: a 16-year-old boy who fondles his 15-year-old girl friend with her full consent could be sent to prison for two years; a man or woman who has intercourse with an animal could be sent to prison for life; yet it is no offence for a woman to procure a man to have intercourse with her by fraud, or even by drugging him. The fact that some of these maximum penalties are hardly ever invoked nowadays merely adds to the impression that they are no longer appropriate.

2.10 Third, there is a good deal of overlap. If two young people have a few drinks and then go off to make love in the young man's room, the young man could be convicted of any of the following six offences if the young woman was not quite 16 at the time, and the episode did not have her parents' consent:-

(a) unlawful sexual intercourse with a girl under 16;
(b) indecent assault;
(c) taking an unmarried girl under 18 out of the possession of her parents against their will, with intent to have intercourse with her;
(d) taking an unmarried girl under 16 out of the possession of her parents against their will;
(e) suffering a girl under 16 to be on his premises for the purpose of having sexual intercourse with him;
(f) administering a drug to a woman with intent to stupify her in order to have unlawful sexual intercourse with her.

For each of these, the maximum penalty is two years' imprisonment.

2.11 Fourth, the law discriminates strongly in this field – and not always for any very obvious reason – between males and females, both as victims and as offenders. Among the offences in our Appendix (other than 'victimless' crimes) 23 are criminal offences only if the victim is female; 3 only if he is male; and in only 7 cases may the victim be of either sex. Men can commit all but one of these offences: women only around two-thirds of them. If, in the example above, it was the boy who was under 16 and the girl who was over the age, she would be guilty only of the single offence of indecent assault – but the maximum penalty would be 10 years' imprisonment because the victim was a male.

2.12 Among the law's other oddities are these:-

(a) The crime of rape can only be committed *per vaginam*, not *per anum*.
(b) If a man has anal intercourse with a consenting male friend in private, no offence is committed if they are both over 21; but if he has it in private with his consenting wife, both of them commit the crime of buggery at common law and could be sent to prison for life.
(c) Any number of consenting people may take part in heterosexual or lesbian activities – or both – at the same time; but if even one other person (of either sex) is present when two men make love to each other, their conduct thereby becomes criminal, and if it includes anal intercourse both of them could be sent to prison for life.
(d) If two consenting 20-year-olds are found in bed together, that is no offence if they are of opposite sexes, or both female; but it will be criminal if they are both male.

2.13 To make valid comparisons between English sex laws and those of other countries would call for extensive experience of the interpretation and practical application of many different legal systems. We are not qualified to attempt that task. However, even the briefest glance at a selection of modern penal codes shows remarkable agreement on the criminalisation of sexual assaults but extensive disagreement on the control of consensual conduct such as adultery, homosexuality, abortion, pornographic display and juvenile sexual activity.

2.14 For example, the age below which a girl cannot be a legal participant in sexual intercourse varies even within the same nation, being 12 in Oregon, 14 in Missouri, Washington and Georgia and 18 in California, Idaho and Wisconsin. In England it was once 10 (19 Eliz I c7, 1575/6) and was only raised by stages from 12 to 16 during the latter part of the nineteenth century, to discourage parents from selling their children to brothelkeepers (Stafford, 1964). Until the Marriage Act 1929, it remained legally possible for a girl of 12 to marry and have sexual intercourse with her husband, though not with anyone else. Some legal systems, unlike ours, do not criminalise sexual acts where both participants are under age (Honoré, 1978, p. 83), although they may invoke welfare measures.

2.15 Adultery was a criminal offence in Italy until 1978, and in Greece until 1981. In Saudi Arabia flogging and stoning to death are still the prescribed punishments for this offence, and they were stoutly defended at a United Nations conference by the President of the Saudi Court of Appeal. He argued that these were indeed the appropriate punishments 'for such a horrible crime that makes men start to doubt if they are the natural fathers of their children', and causes 'both the family and society to disintegrate' (United Nations, 1980, p. 48). In all these countries the punishments for adultery were directed primarily at the female partner.

2.16 Homosexual behaviour between males remains a serious criminal offence in Moslem countries and in several other parts of the world, including such diverse places as Cyprus, Eire, Mexico, New Zealand and the Soviet Union. The Islamic revolutionary regime in Iran has carried out some well-publicised executions of homosexuals. In the USA, homosexual behaviour is still theoretically criminal in about half the States. In England it was decriminalised for consenting adults over 21 in private by the Sexual Offences Act 1967, but Scotland did not follow suit until 1980, and Northern Ireland not until 1982, following the judgement of the European Court of Human Rights in the *Dudgeon v UK* case in October 1981.

In nearly all European countries, including several in the Eastern bloc, homosexual behaviour *per se* is not a crime, and in many of them it has not been for generations. The only remaining point of controversy in those places is whether the age of consent should be the same as for heterosexual behaviour. A recommendation to that effect by a select committee of the Council of Europe was debated by its Parliamentary Assembly in October 1981 and was later transmitted without comment to member governments by the Council of Ministers. In 1982 France harmonised the age of consent for both heterosexual and homosexual behaviour at 15 (No. 426 Sénat, 25 June 1982). The UK maintains a uniquely large differential of five years. On 13 March 1984 the European Parliament debated and voted by a substantial majority for a resolution urging member states to apply the same age of consent for homosexual and heterosexual acts and calling upon the European Commission to submit proposals to prevent discrimination against homosexuals in access to employment (quoted in *Official Journal of the European Communities*, No. C 104/46, 16 April 1984).

2.17 We shall come back, in Part II of this report, to the anomalies in English law and the contrasting arrangements in other countries, where we shall put forward our suggestions for possible reforms.

CHAPTER 3

How many offences are committed?

3.1 Because sexual acts mostly take place in private, and because a high proportion of the incidents legally defined as crimes concern activities between consenting partners, coming to light only as a result of observation or complaint by a third party, it follows that the statistics of reported sex crimes cannot provide a reliable measure of actual incidence. There can be few individuals who, since the age of ten (when it becomes legally possible to commit a crime) have never at any time during their formative years kissed or performed any sort of sexual gesture, whether playful, serious or merely curious, with another young person under sixteen. Yet all such incidents are technically crimes and, if it were possible to detect and prosecute them all, hardly any males would remain free of the label 'sex criminal'. In days when every homosexual act was illegal the statistics of crimes 'known to the police' could have constituted not even a thousandth of the homosexual incidents taking place in the community. Even serious rapes and violent assaults are often not reported to the police because the victims feel ashamed or compromised, fear publicity, fear the reaction of a fiancée or marriage partner, are scared to denounce the assailant or want to avoid police interrogation, medical investigation and possible cross-examination in open court.

3.2 Changes over time in the numbers of offences recorded by the police are as likely to be due to changed habits of victim reporting and changed methods of statistical record compiling as to real changes in the incidence of the behaviour in question. Surveys based upon self-reported sexual experiences, in spite of the difficulty of obtaining an unbiased sample and the danger of false answers, probably give a better indication of the incidence of sexual misconduct than do official statistics of crimes. Figures from the recent British Crime Survey (Hough and Mayhew, 1983), for example, suggest that only one quarter of the offences of indecent assault upon women of sixteen years or older which took place in 1981 were officially recorded. Data from the National Opinion Research Centre in Canada also suggested that reported rapes amounted to only a quarter of the figure obtained from self-reports (Bowker, 1979).

Very much more dramatic discrepancies between victim reports and crime statistics have been found in some American surveys. In one such inquiry 6 per cent of 2,016 women university students, in response to an anonymous self-report questionnaire, claimed to have experienced a definite rape. Many others claimed to have been coerced into intercourse against their wishes by force or threat, but in circumstances they did not regard as amounting to rape. Of the 1,846 male respondents in the same inquiry, 2.4 per cent admitted to having committed an act of rape (Koss and Oros, 1982). In a survey in San Francisco covering a supposedly random sample of women residents, a staggering 44 per cent reported having been subjected to at least one completed or attempted rape (Russell, 1982).

In spite of all their limitations, however, criminal statistics do provide a useful starting point. At least they reflect the volume of crime the criminal justice system is called upon to deal with and the nature of the incidents that are reported to police. These, after all, are the happenings about which action has to be taken and policies decided.

3.3 Among crimes recorded by the police in England and Wales (strictly 'notifiable offences recorded by the police') only a small fraction, less than 1 per cent, are sex crimes. The following is a summary of the statistics for 1983 (based on Home Office Statistical Bulletin 5/84).

Theft and handling stolen goods	52.5%	(1,705,924)
Burglary	25.1%	(813,386)
Criminal damage	13.7%	(443,316)
Fraud and forgery	3.8%	(121,791)
Violence against the person	3.4%	(111,230)
Robbery	0.7%	(22,119)
Sexual offences	0.6%	(20,410)
Other	0.3%	(8,742)
	100%	(3,246,918)

3.4 The recorded sex offences were made up as follows

Indecent assault on a female	53.1%	(10,833)
Unlawful sexual intercourse with a girl under 16	13.6%	(2,773)
Indecent assault on a male	10.7%	(2,178)
Indecency between males	6.7%	(1,362)
Rape	6.5%	(1,334)
Buggery	2.9%	(588)
Gross indecency with a child	2.5%	(511)
Unlawful sexual intercourse with a girl under 13	1.2%	(254)

Incest	1.2%	(243)
Procuration	0.8%	(161)
Bigamy	0.5%	(92)
Abduction	0.4%	(81)
	100%	(20,410)

3.5 These figures do not include offences of male soliciting and indecent exposure which are not classified as 'notifiable offences'. The number of persons *prosecuted* for these offences in 1982 (the latest year for which statistics are available) was, respectively, 919 and 1818.

3.6 The figures of convictions are of course much lower. The latest figures available are again those for 1982. In that year some 475,000 persons were found guilty of indictable (serious) offences in England and Wales; 6,614 of them (1·4 per cent) were found guilty of sex offences. The figures are as follows

Indecent assault on a female	34.3%	(2,226)
Indecency between males	17.3%	(1,145)
Male soliciting	11.9%	(787)
Indecent assault on a male	9.3%	(616)
Unlawful sexual intercourse with a girl under 16	6.3%	(419)
Rape	6.1%	(402)
Procuration	5.0%	(329)
Gross indecency with a child	3.5%	(231)
Buggery	3.2%	(209)
Incest	1.5%	(100)
Unlawful sexual intercourse with a girl under 13	1.1%	(71)
Bigamy	0.3%	(22)
Abduction	0.3%	(17)
	100%	(6,614)

These figures do not include the generally less serious summary (non-indictable) offences such as indecent exposure, for which 1,568 men were found guilty in 1982.

3.7 These official classifications (which generally include attempting or assisting in the misbehaviour) reveal little of the nature of the incidents, and indeed omit some cases which would be regarded by most people as clearly sexual. For example, sexually motivated homicide (fortunately a very rare event) would appear under crimes of violence against the person, the fetishist's habit of stealing women's underwear from clothes lines would be included under thefts and homosexual indecencies in public places are occasionally prosecuted and recorded as breaches of the peace or dealt with as nuisance offences under local or park bye-laws.

3.8 Within these limitations it is still possible to deduce a good deal about the kinds of incidents commonly dealt with by the courts. Apart from 'offences by prostitutes' (which, like indecent exposure, are not indictable offences), persons convicted of sex offences are nearly always males. Although females are occasionally convicted for sexual molestation of a minor of either sex, or for aiding a rape or assault by a man, such cases are rare. Fewer than 1 per cent of persons found guilty of indictable sex offences are female.

3.9 An important survey by Home Office researchers (Walmsley and White, 1979) included an estimate of the proportion of convictions for sex offences which resulted from behaviour which, although in law indictable and therefore classed as 'serious', in fact was consensual and involved no violence and no intimidation of an unwilling victim. They used as their sample all persons convicted of indictable sexual offences in England and Wales in 1973. They counted incidents as consensual only where the documentary sources gave clear evidence to that effect. Cases in which young victims submitted out of fear or mere obedience were counted as non-consensual. They deliberately left out of account the 18 per cent of the offenders who had been involved with children under ten. This conservative evaluation still left a high proportion of offenders, 43 per cent, who had been convicted for activities with consenting partners.

3.10 The relatively high 'age of consent' for homosexual contacts and the strict enforcement of standards of public decency where homosexual acts between males are at issue, result in many homosexual offences in which the participants are fully consenting. Walmsley and White estimated that among persons convicted of indictable offences with victims or partners aged over ten, 34 per cent of the heterosexual offenders, but as many as 80 per cent of the homosexual offenders, had been convicted for purely consensual acts. Outside the prisons, forcible homosexual attacks on males (other than on young boys) are apparently rare, but recent American studies suggest that more such cases may come to light as readiness to report increases (Forman, 1982; Kaufman *et al*, 1980).

3.11 Another important feature revealed by the Home Office survey was the high proportion of child victims or participants. Unlawful sexual intercourse necessarily involved girls under sixteen, but of the female victims of indecent assault as many as 69.9 per cent were under sixteen, as were 31.8 per cent of the victims of rape and 72.9 per cent of the victims of incest. On the other hand, the commonest of the homosexual offences, indecency between males, hardly ever involved a victim under sixteen, and was necessarily consensual, as it would otherwise have been dealt with as an indecent assault.

The high proportion of victims of tender age is no new phenomenon. A woman police surgeon, reporting on some 2,000 victims of alleged sex crimes examined by her during the years 1927 to 1954, noted that over four-fifths were under sixteen and over half were girls under thirteen (Wells, 1958).

3.12 Offences involving significant physical violence comprise a very small proportion of the sex offences dealt with by the English courts. Even among rape cases, which rank as about the most serious among the sex offences, injurious violence is rather rare. A recent survey of crimes initially recorded as rapes by the police in six English counties over a period of five years (Wright and West, 1981) showed that although some physical force was used in most cases, few victims (about 5 per cent) sustained an injury requiring medical attention.

3.13 Police statistics show considerable variation between different areas in the incidence of sex crimes. Police areas which include large conurbations record more crimes of all kinds, including sex crimes, per head of population, than do predominantly rural areas. This no doubt reflects real differences in the level of crime in the community; but some variations, particularly in the incidence of offences that are predominantly consensual, are more likely to reflect differences in police activity or prosecution policies and practices. The incidence of homosexual offences of indecency between males, which largely depends upon police surveillance of public lavatories, shows quite remarkable variations which are otherwise difficult to understand. In 1982, the police in the West Midlands recorded 96 cases of indecency between males, a figure exceeded only by the Metropolitan Police, who reported 170. Bedfordshire, Cumbria, North Yorkshire, Suffolk and Dyfed Powys *together* reported a total of 12.

3.14 It is a popular misconception that recorded sex crimes are increasing; in fact, the reverse is the case. From 1973 to 1983, the number of offences of violence against the person in England and Wales rose from 61,299 to 111,230, whereas the number of sex offences dropped from 25,736 to 20,410. There have been comparable decreases in recorded sex crimes in other European countries, such as Denmark and Italy.

3.15 Although the totality of recorded offences, – which are mostly non-violent and less alarming than their legal descriptions (such as 'assault') might suggest, – has been decreasing, the most serious category, rape, has shown the opposite trend. From 1973 to 1983 the number of rapes recorded by the police in England and Wales increased by 33.7 per cent, from 998 to 1334. During this period, intense publicity about rapes, and appeals for rape complainants to be awarded more respect and credibility, may have caused a higher proportion of incidents to be reported, and perhaps influenced the police to record a higher proportion of reported incidents as rapes rather than indecent assaults. There was a particularly marked increase of 22 per cent in notified rapes from 1977 to 1978, which the compilers of *Criminal Statistics* suggested may have been contributed to by the operation of the Sexual Offences (Amendment) Act, 1976 (Home Office, 1979, p. 52).

3.16 The belief that most apprehended sex offenders are 'dirty old men' is refuted by the statistics. In 1982, of all persons found guilty of indictable sex offences in England and Wales, 23.8 per cent were under twenty-one and another 23.7 per cent under 30. Walmsley and White (1979) found that 50.2 per cent of those convicted of rape were under twenty-one: only 1.2 per cent were aged fifty or more. Among those convicted of indecent assault on a female, 37.1 per cent were under twenty-one, and only 16.4 per cent over fifty. Older men were more prevalent among those involved with young children. Among 252 offenders convicted for indecent assault on a female under ten, 32.1 per cent were under twenty-one, but 29.4 per cent were aged fifty or over (Walmsley and White, 1980, p. 34 table 13).

Incest is exceptional in the age structure of offenders and victims, – since some three-quarters of convicted offenders are fathers aged 30 or more who have had intercourse with their daughters. Most of the rest are brothers in their teens who have offended with their sisters. Over the period 1972 to 1982, 54 women were convicted for incest, of whom 8 were under 21 and another 8 aged 40 or more. Most cases of father-daughter incest concern incidents repeated over months or years; brother-sister incest much more often consists of isolated incidents. They probably go unreported even more often than father-daughter contacts. Mother-son incest is rare.

3.17 Although sex offenders are often credited with being particularly persistent in their misbehaviour, in fact, it is only a small minority who reappear repeatedly in court on sex charges; the vast majority have only one conviction for a sex offence in the whole of their lives. A survey by a Cambridge University team (Radzinowicz, 1957, table 53) revealed that

84 per cent of the 1,919 offenders studied were not reconvicted of any sex crime during a period of four years following conviction (or following the release of those imprisoned). Homosexual offenders and offenders against children are more likely than others to be reconvicted, but 90 per cent of the aggressors against females aged sixteen or more were not reconvicted of a sex crime during the four year follow-up period. Simiarly low recidivism rates have been reported in other countries. In a large Danish study in which the records of 2,934 sex offenders were traced for periods of twelve to twenty-four years, only about 10 per cent were reconvicted for a sex crime (Christiansen *et al*, 1965, 1983).

3.18 This generally optimistic outlook for an absence of repeat convictions needs some qualification. Once a sex offender has had two convictions, the chances that he will have still further convictions are greatly increased. Moreover, although the risk of reconviction for a sex offence is relatively small, that small risk persists for a long time. Soothill and Gibbens (1978) and Gibbens, Soothill and Way (1981) followed over many years the criminal records of men convicted for rape or for serious offences against young girls. They found that the proportion reconvicted doubled when offenders were followed for twenty-two years compared with estimates made after only five years, although it was still only a minority who were reconvicted at all for any further sex offence.

It must also be remembered that some sex offences have a low reporting rate and a still lower clear-up rate. In one American survey a sample of convicted rapists and child molesters, in response to an anonymous questionnaire, admitted that the sex offences for which they had been apprehended were less than half the number they had actually committed (Groth *et al*, 1982).

3.19 For a fuller appreciation of the varied nature and seriousness of the incidents classed as sex crimes one needs to consider the results of studies of individual offenders and victims. Already, however, the available statistical studies point to some important general conclusions. In absolute numbers, officially recorded sex crimes are relatively few in comparison with other kinds of crimes, but the victims are often young, sometimes very young. In a substantial proportion of sex crimes the activities are consensual. This is particularly true of homosexual crime. Sex crimes involving serious physical violence are rare. Offenders detected in repeated sex crimes are relatively unusual.

CHAPTER 4

What happens to the victims?

INVOLVEMENT OF CHILDREN

4.1 Protection from crime is supposed to be a prime object of social policy. Yet surprisingly little attention is paid to the victims whose interests that policy is supposed to serve. The characteristics of victims, the effects that offences have on them, the ways they might be helped and the reasons for their vulnerability are all topics at least as important as the studies of offenders.

Because the victims in such a high proportion of reported sex crimes are children we shall consider them first.

4.2 The vast majority of offences against children involve no hurtful physical force, but violence is not the only risk. Premature sexual experience, and especially sexual contact with adults, is widely believed to be potentially very damaging. Firm evidence is hard to come by, however, and authorities on child development hold to widely differing views, but clinical reports point to a multiplicity of possible adverse effects. An inappropriate sexual approach may be very shocking to a child who has been solicitously shielded from sexuality (Kirchoff and Thelen, 1976) and it has been credited, in some cases, with setting up inhibitions, guilt feelings and neurotic fears that lead to sexual anxiety or frigidity in later life (Finch, 1973; Burgess *et al*, 1978; De Francis, 1971; Rush, 1980; Constantine, 1981). In other cases it has been held responsible for stimulating sexual appetite and promoting delinquency (Weiss *et al* 1955), prostitution (James and Meyerding, 1978, Silbert and Pines, 1981, 1982) or distortions of personality development (Bender and Grugett, 1952) and even suicide (Goodwin, 1981).

In interpreting these findings from clinical studies allowance has to be made for the fact that they have been largely derived from reports of non-consensual assaults on children from problem families (whose prior emotional disturbance may have been the reason for the offence coming to notice) or recollections by adults whose maladjustments may have no causal connection with their early sexual experiences. The high incidence of early sexual abuse reported by delinquents might be explained as a consequence of the behaviour of the delinquent-prone young which exposed them to greater risk of molestation (Gruber, 1981). Evidence on the effects of non-coercive sexual contacts with adults on normal children who were not distressed or disordered before the event is particularly hard to obtain.

4.3 One reason for supposing that children must necessarily find any sexual approach unpleasant or alarming is the belief that they are naturally innocent – that is, asexual. Historically, this belief is relatively recent (Aries, 1962, De Mause, 1974 Ch. 1). It reached a peak in Victorian times, but was then somewhat undermined by the spread of psychoanalytic ideas about infantile sexuality and it has been further challenged by the more objective observations of modern psychologists (Constantine and Martinson, 1981). Freud's concept of a period of latency between infancy and puberty is not supported by present-day notions of continuous development. It is now known that the capacity to respond reflexively and sensually to the point of orgasm when the genitals are stimulated, autoerotically or otherwise, is present from infancy. Some children are inhibited by their awareness of adult disapproval, but others, long before puberty, are capable of sexual interactions with both adults and other children that go a long way beyond mere curiosity.

4.4 Anthropologists have described societies with customs very different from our own where juvenile sexual learning was positively encouraged. Children were allowed to play sex games openly, parents could pacify children with sexual caresses, and adolescents were given meeting houses where they could practise sexual intercourse (Ford and Beach, 1952; Money *et al*, 1977; Currier, 1981). Such permissiveness appeared to have no discernible ill effects upon subsequent marriages and sexual deviations were seemingly rare. For reasons not fully understood, unwanted pregnancies in girls too young to marry were much less frequent than would be expected if adolescents were to behave in this way in our society today.

An incident cited by the child psychiatrist Hedy Porteus (1972, p. 31) shows how differently children from other cultures may react to sexual things. Missionaries working with the Australian aboriginies were getting along well with the native children until they brought out some European dolls, after which the children wanted no more to do with them. It took time to find out what had gone wrong. Lacking genitals, the dolls appeared to the children to have been mutilated, and they took fright because they thought the missionaries intended to do the same to them.

4.5 Given the frank displays of sexuality which are now seen on television and in magazines, children cannot easily be shielded from sexual information. Some professionals take the view that there is no need to do so, that it is healthy to allow children some overt expression of their sexual interests. The psychiatrist Alayne Yates (1978), for example, suggests that parents should openly acknowledge and positively encourage their children's budding sexual interests and development. It is plausible to suppose that sexually aware, educated and uninhibited children would be less likely to form unsuitable attachments to adults than those more innocent, more easily led and more readily shocked. The need to improve basic education in schools on the topic of sexual feelings and behaviour (as opposed to information on reproductive anatomy and physiology) has been argued by Stevi Jackson (1982), a lecturer in social studies. She contends that a more frank approach would not only allay sexual anxieties but might prevent the development of sexist attitudes and double standards. We return to this issue of sex educations in our recommendations in Part II (see paras 9.1 – 9.7).

4.6 Arguments for the supposed benefits of greater permissiveness towards child sexuality often ignore the fact that the prevailing standards in this field are part of a much wider network of norms and values determining the social, economic and psychological roles and status of children in our culture. Changes in sexual attitudes may be impractical or maladaptive without changes in many other respects. This point has not been lost upon some radical sociological theorists who believe that fundamental changes in sexual attitudes must await a revolution in the political and economic sphere (Foucault, 1979). However that may be, the idea that sexual contacts with adults can be a helpful learning experience for the young, repugnant as it is to most parents, is not without its supporters today. Pronouncements in favour of sexual liberation for children are put forward by such organisations as the North American Man-Boy Love Association, the René Gunyon Society and, in England, the Paedophile Information Exchange (O'Carroll, 1981; Plummer 1981a). This is a tiny minority whose views are suspected of being influenced more by the interests of paedophiles than the needs of children. Man-boy relationships, of a teacher-pupil complexion, on the model of 'Greek Love', feature more prominently in these writings than heterosexual paedophilia (Rossman, 1979; Kramer, 1976). Needless to say, these ideas are strongly opposed by authorities who believe that sexual contacts between adults and children are invariably exploitative of weakness and potentially very damaging (Densen-Gerber and Hutchinson, 1978). On the other hand, there are case histories on record of children who have seemingly benefited from a sexual friendship with an adult without this preventing the development of normal sexual interests in adolescence and a sound marital adjustment in later years (Wilson, 1981). One Dutch psychologist, who examined 25 boys aged between 10 and 16 who were known to have a sexually active relationship with an adult male, found that they were on the whole quite positive about the enjoyment and benefits of their experience and reported no negative effect upon their general sense of well-being (Sandfort, 1982). It would seem that the panic reactions which so often greet the discovery of sexual attachments in childhood are not always justified.

4.7 In practice children vary in their reactions to sexual contacts with adults. Depending on the attitudes and ideas the child has acquired from parents and others, an incident can be frightening, exciting and interesting, or merely unattractive; or it can provoke confusion, embarrassment and guilt. The meaning and significance the child attributes to the behaviour determines its reactions more than the physical acts themselves.

A certain amount of coy seductiveness among small girls tends to be encouraged as natural and charming, provided the sexual element is not too overt, but some girls will actively solicit and seem to enjoy the sexual attentions of adults (Mohr *et al*, 1964). For children who receive little attention or affectionate interest at home, the warmth and security they can obtain through a sexual relationship with an outsider may be a more important inducement than the erotic experience itself (Burton, 1968). In a different context, and at a somewhat later age, boys from problem families who form attachments to older men, and runaways who allow themselves to be picked up at bus or rail terminals by paedophiles willing to provide shelter and pocket money, are also looking for more than just erotic adventure (Ingram, 1979).

The state of knowledge on the difficult issue of the effects of sexual contacts between children and adults is well summed up in a scholarly review by authors from the Institute of Psychiatry, London (Powell and Chalkley, 1981). They conclude that there is little ground for saying that a paedophile experience will necessarily damage a child, but they go on to point out that catastrophic reactions may sometimes occur in special circumstances, for instance if violence is used or if the child has some pre-existing emotional problem.

4.8 One way to try to obtain a balanced view of the effects of child-adult sexual contacts is by retrospective inquiry among adults to see how many recall having had such experiences, and what effects, if any, this appears to have had upon them. This was done with a large sample of white American women by Kinsey (Gagnon, 1965) and with samples of American students by Landis (1956) and Finkelhor (1979). A similar investigation recently completed in England at the Cambridge Institute of Criminology, based on women registered with a particular general medical practice, has yielded results in agreement with the high incidence figures reported in America (Nash and West, 1985).

Whereas the number of sex offences against children recorded in criminal statistics suggests that these are comparatively rare events, questioning of samples of people from the general population shows that a substantial proportion of both males and females have had some sexual experience with a much older person than themselves when they were children or juveniles. Finkelhor found that 19.2 per cent of women students and 8.6 per cent of men students recalled such an incident. In the case of the girls, the great majority of their first experiences had happened before they were thirteen (mean age 10.2). The most common experience for both sexes was some form of genital fondling. In the Landis survey, about a fifth of the women students and about 14 per cent of the men recalled having had some such experiences before reaching the age of fifteen. Among the girls, especially those brought up in cities, the commonest early experiences was that of seeing an exhibitionist. In the Kinsey survey 24 per cent of his total sample of 4,441 women reported some experience with an adult in their pre-pubertal years. A much earlier American research based on an inquiry among married women (Hamilton, 1929, Table, 279) found that 25 per cent of 120 women questioned reported having been 'frightened or disgusted by the sexual aggressions of persons of the opposite sex' when they were under twelve. A more recent survey among women in San Francisco found that 28 per cent reported having had some sexually abusive experience before they were 14 (12 per cent with a person in the family, 20 per cent with a person outside). Only 2 per cent of the family incidents and 6 per cent of the outside incidents had been reported to the police (Russell, 1983).

A survey of a sample of nurses in Sheffield by Gittleson *et al* (1978) asked exclusively about indecent exposures. Of 100 women interviewed, 44 recalled one or more such incidents. Their average age when questioned was 33 years, but half of the incidents they recalled happened before their fifteenth birthday. Only half of the incidents had been mentioned to members of the family. Women who had confided in family or friends often said that the reactions of others were more distressing to them than the incident itself.

4.9 Victim surveys show that, because of difficulties in communication with parents on matters of sex, the majority of sexual approaches experienced by children are not mentioned to anyone at the time. This accounts for a large part of the huge discrepancy in the apparent incidence of offences according to official statistics and according to victims' recollections.

It seems inherently improbable that experiences that are so commonplace should have serious, long-term ill effects. On the whole, the victim surveys confirm that conclusion. In the Kinsey study, only 5 per cent of the women questioned who had experienced some sexual contact with adults when they were children were suffering any severe maladjustment as adults, and only 1 per cent of them attributed current dificulties to their early sex experiences (Gagnon, 1965, p. 189). Among married women, the proportion who reported regularly achieving orgasm during sexual intercourse was unrelated to whether or not they recollected some adult-child sexual incident.

4.10 However, sexual misbehaviour with children can sometimes have very adverse consequences. The majority of the incidents revealed in surveys involve relatively mild intrusion, such as intimate touching in a friendly, non-forceful manner. The victim surveys also show, however, that the minority of forceful or brutal aggressions against girls is very much more liable to produce disturbance both immediate in the form of acute anxiety symptoms, and long-term in the form of sexual frigidity or disturbed relations with the opposite sex (Finkelhor, 1979). In the Kinsey survey the few examples of long-term ill effects attributed to sexual molestation were heavily concentrated among those who had suffered coercive experiences as children. The survey by Nash and West (1985), however, found that non-violent incidents also sometimes led to lasting distress, as girls grew up and began to appreciate the stigma attached to such incidents and to feel guilty about having been involved. A particularly high incidence of aggressive sexual abuse when they were children has been reported by women who later became street prostitutes (Silbert and Pines, 1982).

INCEST VICTIMS

4.11 Incestuous contacts are also apt to be particularly traumatic. A young girl sexually molested by her father or by a man in *loco parentis*, however gentle the approach or whatever justifying rationalisations are used, nearly always feels guilt or anxiety at the time and emotional turmoil later. The incidents typically begin in pre-pubertal years, with the father undressing and fondling the child when they are alone, or stealing into her bed during the night. The secrecy surrounding these occasions, the contrast between father's attitude at these times and his normal adult stance, and the bodily sensations and reactions induced can be confusing and anxiety-provoking to the child. She may feel uncomfortable about what is happening and want to stop, but complies because she is scared to disobey and has been instructed on no account to tell her mother. Gradually the incidents become habitual and the activity progresses to incestuous intercourse, in return for which the girl may receive attentions and favours she enjoys, but which add to her guilt feelings. In relation to her mother, she has now become the 'other woman' in a strange marital triangle. With the passing of time, and a growing realisation that if she denounces her father her mother might disbelieve or punish her, or that the family might be broken up, she accommodates herself as best she can, much as some physically abused children accommodate cruelty for fear of losing their parents altogether.

In incest situations children are often victims in more than a purely sexual sense. Therapists working with these families have noted, for example, that the affected girl's relationship with her mother seems to have largely opted out of normal wifely and maternal functions, leaving the child emotionally deprived and unusually dependent upon intimacy with her father.

4.12 The calm with which some girls appear to accept the incestuous role, and may even exploit the power they acquire over the father, does not necessarily mean that they are contented, or that they would have consented in the first place had they been old enough to realise the implications and to make an informed choice. Tensions may reveal themselves in a falling off in school performance, psychosomatic symptoms or sexual delinquencies. Unlike the girl approached by a stranger, who can usually walk away or does not need to repeat the encounter, the incest victim often feels caught up unwillingly in a progressively worsening family drama. At adolesence, when she wants to have boy-friends, her incestuous father is apt to become jealously possessive and restrictive. A few incest victims react with rebellious sexual precociousness, escape into unsuitable premature marriage, or run away from home into a life of prostitution. Others emerge apparently unscathed by their early experiences. Reactions to incest are certainly varied and complex, but without necessarily agreeing with the paranoid attitudes of the more extreme representatives of 'incest survivors', it is clear that sexual interference by parents can sometimes cause great harm. (Goodwin, 1982; Mrazek and Kempe, 1980; Meiselman, 1978; Courtois, 1979, 1980; Herman, 1981; Young, 1982; Ward, 1982).

4.13 One of the worst features of molestation of girls in their own homes, where they are virtual captives of the situation, is that in a substantial minority of cases, as physical maturity approaches, sexual intimacies progress to repeated acts of intercourse and to risk of becoming pregnant. Relatively few ever become pregnant, but those who do experience, in addition to all the usual problems of unwanted pregnancy in a young girl, the dread of public exposure and of her father's probable imprisonment should the family's desperate attempts to conceal the true paternity fail.

4.14 In incestuous unions, similar recessive genes, each carrying a potential for abnormality, are liable to come together to produce a defective baby. The risk is particularly great in families which are genetically not particularly well endowed in the first place. In some large study (Seemanova, 1971) 161 children produced by incest were compared with 95 children born to the same incestuous mothers but from matings with unrelated partners. Of the children of incest, 14.3 per cent were stillborn or died during the survey. Of the comparison group, all were born alive and only 5.3 per cent died subsequently. Some two-fifths of the surviving children of incest, compared with only one in twenty of the other group, displayed definite physical abnormalities. Many of the abnormalities, such as deaf-mutism, microcephaly and cardiac deformities, were seriously incapacitating. In another survey by Adams and Neel (1967) the children of 18 pregnancies resulting from incest were compared with those from pregnancies in 18 unmarried mothers of similar age, socio-economic status, intelligence, race and stature. Only one from the latter group was born with a major abnormality, compared with 11 of the children of incest, of whom 2 died within 24 hours.

Some authorities, such as Maisch (1973, p. 81–2) argue that researchers tend to exaggerate the purely genetic risks of incest. In the Seemanova study, for example, it was not possible to control for maternal age at the time of the birth, and it is known that the first born of very young mothers are at a raised risk of congenital defects regardless of the consanguinity of their parents. Clearly, however, there is no room for complacency about the genetic risks of incest.

4.15 Genetic risk does not seem to be the main reason for society's condemnation of incest. The majority of the members of the Home Office Policy Advisory Committee considered the genetic risk 'not in itself sufficient ground for retaining the offence in its present form' (Criminal Law Revision Committee, 1980 para. 114). This view was broadly shared by the Criminal Law Revision Committee itself (1984, para 8.11). Even where the risk is much worse than it is in most incest cases, for example where a prospective parent is known to have a fifty per cent chance of being a carrier of Huntingdon's chorea, society pursues a policy of counselling rather than legal coercion. Incest between siblings, which carries as much genetic risk as parent-child incest, does not attract the same horrified condemnation: siblings are generally on a more nearly equal footing, so that neither party is victim of the other's abuse of power and trust.

BOY VICTIMS

4.16 Boys involved sexually with adults present particular problems because the offenders are nearly always male and the incidents therefore homosexual. Heterosexual contacts between boys and older females are rare, or at any rate rarely give rise to complaints. Boys differ from girls in being more often involved with each other in masturbatory games, without this necessarily implying any lasting homosexual tendency (Langfeldt, 1981). Boys are also more likely than girls to be active collaborators rather than unwilling recipients of adult sexual attentions, if only because the reported incidents tend to occur when they are older and in situations in which they could escape (Virkkunen, 1975). Whereas the predominant concern about heterosexual molestation of girls is that they may find the experience off-putting, and thereby become anxious, frigid or even lesbian, the concern for boys involved homosexually with older men is that they may find the experience attractive and be seduced into homosexuality.

4.17 The possibility of homosexual seduction in childhood bringing about an adult homosexual orientation has been greatly exaggerated. Most adult males with an exclusively homosexual orientation who have had such experiences in childhood report that their homosexual interests and fantasies developed before they had any overt contact with an adult (Bell *et al*, 1981). In other words, a homosexual tendency is more likely a cause than an effect of the paedophilic incident. Moreover, heterosexual males very frequently recall having had sex contact with an older male when they were young without this having made any lasting impression upon their sexual preferences (Schofield, 1965, p. 58). Furthermore, studies of young males who have worked as homosexual prostitutes (Freund, 1974), and follow-up studies of boys known to have been at some time involved with older males (Doshay, 1943; Tindall, 1978; Tolsma, 1957) show that these experiences do not suppress a basic heterosexual orientation. On the other hand, imprisoned homosexual paedophiles often claim to have been seduced as boys, but such testimony is suspect of being motivated by a need for self-exculpation.

In October 1969 the Dutch Parliament, acting on the advice of a committee headed by a professor of social psychiatry (Speijer, 1969), abolished the law criminalising consensual behaviour with persons of the same sex aged between sixteen and twenty-one. The committee cited, among others, surveys by Giese (1964) and Gebhard *et al* (1965), showing that up to half of adult homosexuals questioned reported having had their first contacts by the age of fifteen usually initiated by mutual agreement, often after a period of waiting for the opportunity. They concluded that by the sixteenth year 'the sexual propensity is developed to such an extent that a youngster who is heterosexual cannot be diverted by "seduction" into permanent homosexuality' (*op cit* para 7.4 (i)).

4.18 A more realistic concern about homosexual liasions between youths and more privileged older men is that they may be corrupting in a non-sexual way because they often involve financial and social patronage. The effect can be to seduce a young man away from regular work, to stimulate unrealistic material ambitions and to undermine his ability or determination to pursue a disciplined career of work and training. When the liaison comes to an end he may turn to frank prostitution or to crime. Girls who have been temporarily 'kept' by wealthier older men are in a somewhat similar position, but they have the possibility of solving their problem by marriage.

Prostitution, whether heterosexual or homosexual, sometimes leads to crime. In homosexual prostitution the pressures are particularly apparent. Male prostitutes are less in demand and earn less than females. They lack the physiological capacity to satisfy in quick succession a series of clients each wanting them to produce an orgasm. Few achieve a status equivalent to the successful call girl. When youthful attractiveness is fading, or business is slack, the temptation to take advantage of the physical and social vulnerability of their clients by robbery or extortion must be great.

EFFECTS OF INTERVENTION ON CHILD VICTIMS

4.19 Even when they have been the victims of a totally unprovoked sexual assault, women may be reluctant to report the matter for fear of repercussions in their family or the effects of unfavourable notoriety. These considerations are greatly amplified in the case of child victims. Sometimes an investigation, conducted sympathetically, may relieve a child's anxiety, but more often the reverse is true. Emotional over-reaction by parents to a minor incident that might not otherwise have made much impression can arouse a child's guilt and cause more trauma than the offence itself. The child suspected of having encouraged an offender, or made an unjustified allegation, risks critical or punitive reaction from parents and teachers. If the offender is part of the family circle, denials, counter accusations and bitter recriminations may ensue and cause the victim great distress. In cases where the offender was the father, the mother, who may have ignored or connived at what was happening, may choose to blame the victim rather than her husband. Doctors and police who are obliged to investigate the evidence for a crime may find it necessary to interrogate the victim in ways that are frightening, embarrassing and guilt-provoking. Probing physical examinations of the genitalia or anus by police surgeons in the presence of witnesses can be even more stressful to children than to adults subjected to similar procedures, who are presumed to have a greater understanding of the nature of the evidence sought and the need to find it. Not surprisingly, research suggests that cases leading to official legal action, as opposed to cases dealt with informally, produce more severe and lasting ill effects upon victims (Gibbens and Prince, 1963). Walters (1975, p. 113) states categorically that; 'Most of the psychological damage, if any, stems not from the abuse but the interpretation of the abuse and the handling of the situation by parent, medical personnel, law enforcement and school officials, and social workers.' There is much to be said for directing interventions more towards the needs of the child than towards the needs of law enforcement (Wald, 1982).

4.20 Many authorities believe it to be preferable in the interests of the child to deal with cases of sexual abuse in family settings without resort to prosecution. In the Netherlands a 'confidential doctor' service has been developed to which instances of known or suspected physical or sexual abuse can be referred in confidence (Doek, 1978; Besharov, 1981). In some areas of Canada cases of intra-familial sexual abuse are handled exclusively by the child protection services and only referred to the police for prosecution as a last resort when further abuse cannot otherwise be prevented (Cormier and Cooper, 1982). Co-operation between police and social services in El Paso, Colorado has created an Incest Diversion Program for non-violent, first-time incest perpetrators who plead guilty and agree to undergo a treatment program for not less than two years. In this arrangement of conditional non-prosecution, criminal charges are filed and only go forward if the perpetrator fails to complete the rehabilitation program (Topper and Aldridge, 1981). Although no such formal system exists in England, a project in Devon and Cornwall has been initiated in which liaison between police and social services permits the decision to prosecute to be deferred so long as the suspect co-operates in preventive measures. In California a system of co-operation between the courts and treatment agencies, while not by-passing criminal procedures, allows the judge to defer sentence. This permits the offender to participate in a comprehensive scheme of management and treatment for the whole family, which, if successful, avoids a custodial sentence (Giarretto, 1981).

One of the most convincing indicators of the success of these schemes is the increase in the number of incidents brought to notice without a proportionate increase in the number of families that have to be broken up.

4.21 Welfare schemes for incest cases, despite their concern for the best interests of victims and their efforts to rescue families in distress, have a hard time coping with the many agencies with different responsibilities that are involved. Bander *et al*, (1982), describing the setting up of an American Sexual Trauma Treatment Program, remark that even a state agency supported by federal funds has difficulty in liaison with police, prosecutors, courts, authorities dealing with child custody, doctors producing the physical evidence of sexual abuse and lawyers looking after the rights of the defendant. The sharing of information with case workers in a protective service, to say nothing of the sharing of decision-making, does not come easily to these varied authorities.

4.22 Legally enforceable processes for the protection of children at risk of sexual involvements do not necessarily require the prosecution of an offender. The social services have a statutory obligation under the Children and Young Persons Act 1933 s. 44 to concern themselves with the welfare of children and to take steps for the removal of children from 'undesirable surroundings'. One of the steps that can be taken is to apply to a juvenile court for a compulsory 'care order' which, if granted, results in a transfer of responsibility for the child, including parental rights, to the local authority social services department. Proceedings for taking a child into care involuntarily can also be initiated by the police or by the National Society for the Prevention of Cruelty to Children.

The Children and Young Persons Act 1969, s. 2, imposes a duty on the local authority to commence care proceedings where there are grounds for a care order, although it is given discretion not to do so if this would not be in the interests of the child or the public. The grounds relevant to risk of sexual abuse are that the child is 'exposed to moral danger' or that '. . . he is being ill-treated . . .' There is a presumption that the conditions for a care order will probably be satisfied if a person who has committed a sexual offence (or more precisely an offence under Schedule 1 to the Children and Young Persons Act 1933 as amended by the Sexual Offences Act 1956) is, or may become, a member of the same household as the child. This provision comes into operation very frequently when a father, serving a prison sentence for a sex offence, is about to be released and intends to return to the home where his children are living. It also applies if a mother takes into the home a new husband or co-habitee who has at some time been convicted for a sex offence. Similarly, a care order can probably be made if another child who is or was a member of the household has been made the subject of a compulsory care order on grounds of ill-treatment.

4.23 If a parent or household member is being prosecuted for a sex offence against a child the usual procedure is for the social services to apply for an 'interim care order' pending the final decision when a conviction is secured. If a conviction is not secured, a care order may still be sought, because the burden of proof required in civil child care proceedings is different from that of a criminal court. If more urgent action is deemed necessary application may be made for a 'place of safety' order (Children and Young Persons Act 1969 s. 28). This authorises temporary detention, but does not remove parental rights.

Another method of protection, much less often used, is by wardship proceedings in the High Court. Any interested party can institute such proceedings. If wardship is granted the High Court has legal custody of the child and can place him in the care of whoever seems suitable, including the local authority, but it retains the power to change or vary its direction on further application by parents or others so that, in effect, if the social services have care of the child, their jurisdiction is not as absolute as in the case of a care order.

If the social services consider that a care order is not justified, but that still the child may be exposed to some risk, they may leave the child at home but place it on an 'at risk' register, keeping the family under close surveillance and calling periodic conferences attended by representatives of all the authorities who may be involved with the family - such as police, probation officers, family doctor, health visitor, teachers or child guidance clinic staff – but not members of the family themselves.

4.24 The practices and standards operated by social services in relation to children at risk of sexual abuse vary from one area to another. Tragic cases of child deaths from parental violence that might have been avoided by more resolute action (such as the Maria Colwell case in Brighton in 1973, or the Jason Caesar case in Cambridge in 1981) have led to public criticism of the social services and encouraged more cautious policies and greater readiness to remove children from their homes. Risk of sexual abuse is particularly difficult to assess, and harsh decisions are sometimes made. A girl unlucky enough to acquire a stepfather who has had a conviction for a sexual offence at some time in his life may well find herself banished from home, supposedly in her own interests.

A recent inquiry addressed to family doctors, police surgeons, paediatricians and child psychiatrists sought to find out what happens in practice in this country when cases of child sex abuse are reported. The 622 professionals who responded had dealt with 1,072 such cases in one year. Most of the cases were of the more serious type involving actual or attempted sexual intercourse. Girl victims outnumbered boys by six to one. Three-quarters of the perpetrators were known to the child. Reporting led to prosecution of the offender in 43 per cent of cases. In 13 per cent of the cases the child was taken into care (Mrazek, Lynch and Bentovim, 1983). In a somewhat similar American survey of child abuse, far fewer cases of sex abuse, only 5 per cent, led to criminal justice action. However, in this American survey, 17 per cent of the reported sex abuse cases led to a placement of the child in foster care, whereas this happened in only 12 per cent of the cases where the complaint was of non-sexual violence or abuse (Finkelhor, 1983).

4.25 If the incident reaches the stage of prosecution, and the child needs to be interrogated again to check what replies might come out in court, and if the offender pleads not guilty and the child has to be sceptically cross-examined in the course of a trial, the stress increases, both in quality and duration. If the outcome is that the child's father or someone she has been fond of is publicly disgraced and sent to prison, as a direct result of her evidence against him, she cannot but feel remorse. If notwithstanding her evidence the offender is acquitted, she may find herself under suspicion. If the offender is one of the family and is not imprisoned, or if he returns home after imprisonment, the child may be compulsorily removed from the home by a court order on the application of the social services. Children dealt with in this way, including siblings who have not been directly involved with the offences, may rightly feel that to be placed in an institution, as if they were incorrigibly delinquent, and to lose the security of a parental home, is a severe punishment totally undeserved.

4.26 Secondary victimisation by the peer group is a further consequence little discussed in textbooks. If the offender is a family member and sent to prison, even though the child is supposedly not identified publicly, the circumstances often become known to neighbours and schoolfellows, and she may expect to suffer snide remarks, prying overtures, teasing comments or undeserved ostracism because she is no longer considered by some parents fit company for their children. Since the whole family is disgraced by association with a sex offender, the child victim has to suffer the unhappy consequences inside as well as outside the home. In the case of a boy found to have been associating with an adult male, and hence readily assumed to be a 'queer', his treatment by peers who hear about it can be equally cruel.

All these untoward consequences are of course ultimately due to the offender's behaviour, but some, at least, might be mitigated by greater circumspection in the management of cases of child sex abuse.

CHILD WITNESSES

4.27 The necessity for child witnesses in sexual cases to give evidence in court has been a matter of some discussion. The Thompson Committee's report on Criminal Procedure in Scotland (Scottish Home and Health Department, 1975, p. 164–5) considered this issue. The majority of the representations made to the Committee by psychiatrists, social workers and others supported the view that children should continue to participate in the trial, arguing that they were not so seriously affected by giving evidence as was generally supposed. Most of the damage to children was thought to occur before the trial, occasioned by delay and by being subjected to a multiplicity of questions, from parents as well as others, over a protracted period. It was considered that in relation to sexual offences the credibility and reliability of witnesses was particularly at issue and that the child witness should therefore be seen and heard in court to satisfy the interests of justice and to be fair to the accused.

Alternative procedures were considered, such as: 'the provision of hearsay evidence to the court, whereby an adult would narrate to the court the gist of an account of the circumstances given to him spontaneously and informally by the child.' Another suggestion was 'that the child's statement made to the police in the presence of his parents could be lodged with the court and the police and the parents could be examined thereon in court.' The Committee, while recognizing the inevitability of 'a certain amount of distress', ended by making no recommendation for change.

4.28 Many people with experience of children's reactions to interrogation do not share the attitude of the Thompson Committee. Gibbens and Prince (1963) in a careful comparison between sex abuse cases dealt with informally and similar cases necessitating appearance in court, concluded that the latter group showed significantly more psychological disturbance, both immediate and longer term.

Some countries have in fact developed special procedures for the protection of child witnesses in sex cases. Best known is the Israeli system which employs youth interrogators, who are social workers, or others experienced in interviewing children. They are given almost exclusive power to examine children thought to have been victims of sexual abuse, although the police can put questions to the child on the occasion of the initial reporting or discovery of an offence where delay might impede the investigation. A child under 14 cannot be required to give evidence in court unless the youth interrogator permits it. The interrogators also control, in the interests of the protection of the child's mental health, the medical examinations, offender identifications or other investigations which need the child's participation. The interrogator presents the prosecution with statements taken from the child together with a report on the outcome of his own inquiries and evaluations, and these can be utilised at the trial in lieu of a personal appearance by the child witness (Reifen, 1973).

In Denmark and Sweden the task of interrogating child witnesses in sex cases is allocated to women police officers with specialised experience or training who conduct the inquiries in a relaxed manner and in language suited to the child's age. The interviews are tape-recorded, and can be used by the policewoman in support of her testimony before the court (Libai, 1980).

4.29 The main objection to relieving child witnesses of the ordeal of a court appearance is the infringement of the defendant's right to confront and question his accuser. On the other hand, a more careful and relaxed inquiry by an experienced interrogator may provide a better means of detecting false accusations based on childish fantasies. Such incidents are by no means unknown. Following the sensational trial of a politician, which arose out of an alleged homosexual liaison, a schoolmaster was prosecuted for immoral behaviour with his boy pupils. At the last moment one of the witnesses against him confessed that the stories had been made up out of malice, the idea having been conceived after reading about the trial.

The use of video recordings of children's testimony (which might be acceptable to both defence and prosecution in place of the personal appearance of the child witness) has been proposed, but objected to on the grounds that juries need to assure themselves of the validity of testimony by watching the child's reactions in court. These issues are being debated by a CIBA Foundation working group under the chairmanship of a psychiatrist, Professor Sidney Brandon (Porter, 1984).

INVOLVEMENT OF ADOLESCENTS

4.30 Adolescent girls under sixteen involved in offences of unlawful sexual intercourse with youths of much the same age as themselves, or even with older men, are technically victims of the male's offending behaviour. In actuality, they can be socially and physically quite mature, more so sometimes than their youthful sex partners and, on a common sense evaluation, at least equally responsible for the occurrence. Prosecution of the male in such cases is often against the wishes of the girl concerned, who may suffer as a result many of the unfortunate consequences already mentioned. The girl may identify her young partner as her lover, and suffer indirectly from any penalty imposed on him, especially if she has revealed his identity under parental pressure against his wishes. Sometimes it is not the girl herself who tells, but social workers in whom she has confided. They can be subpoenaed for the purpose. If she has had relations with a number of males, or persists in relationships considered unsuitable, again she risks being dealt with as a child 'in moral danger' and placed compulsorily in a residential home on the recommendation of local authority social workers. A prime reason for many girls being taken into the care of the local authority, especially girls who have run away from home, is their sexual behaviour (Byles, 1980). Traditionally, boys' sexual promiscuity causes less concern.

4.31 Consensual sexual relations between a girl approaching sixteen and a youth or young man are relatively rarely prosecuted. It has been estimated that 12 per cent of English girls have sexual intercourse before reaching sixteen (Farrell and Kellaher, 1978, p. 21) and American survey have found even higher incidences of sexually experienced minors (Schultz, 1980, p. 365). The number of pregnancies in girls under sixteen greatly exceed prosecutions of males for unlawful sexual intercourse. Even when it is known that sexual intercourse has taken place, in the absence of any coercion or a large age gap between the participants the police are inclined not to prosecute.

4.32 From the standpoint of both offender and technical victim it is a relief that the police exercise such restraints, but that only makes it seem harder and unfairer when a prosecution does occur, especially if the reasons for it appear unconnected with the sexual behaviour itself. In the course of a report on the policing of such cases, one investigator commented on the variability of practice in different areas and on the fact that the police are sometimes aware that parents try to manipulate authorities into a prosecution when they discover their child is pregnant, although up to that point they may have known all about her sexual relationships and never thought of complaining (Mawby, 1979).

4.33 The situation of the pregnant child and her family is difficult enough without the added complications of police intervention. The moral dilemma of what to do about the pregnancy is a prime concern. Sometimes girls of 13, 14 or 15, who have little idea of the harsh realities of child care in a one-parent setting, are persuaded by over-optimistic advice to go through with a pregnancy and retain the baby, to the long-term detriment of both mother and child.

Where a child is retained the possible financial implications of proof of paternity can sometimes outweigh humanitarian considerations, with the boy's parents trying to dissuade him from an admission while the girl's parents are trying to persuade her to give evidence against him.

Police enquiries, decisions to prosecute, and finally court proceedings can all take a considerable time, during which the pregnant girl may have to break off a potentially beneficial attachment and lose a chance of eventually marrying her baby's father. There have been cases, however, in which a marriage has taken place in spite of the father having first had to serve a custodial sentence for unlawful intercourse with his future wife (National Council for One Parent Families, 1979, para 306).

4.34 Apart from issues of morality, the use of the criminal law to control the sexual conduct of young persons is usually justified by reference to the need to discourage couples from having babies when their age and social circumstances are such that they could not be expected to undertake parental responsibilities. To be weighed against this however, is the argument that so long as under-age sexual contacts remain criminal, sex education in schools and the supply of information and practical aids to contraception to young girls is discouraged. It is known that schoolgirls who become pregnant are more likely than most to be under-informed or misinformed about contraception and to have difficulties in obtaining access to contraceptive aids (Shaffer *et al* 1978; Phipps-Yonas, 1980). The professionals who have to counsel youngsters – teachers, psychologists, social workers and doctors – are conscious that by advising on contraception they could be accused of abetting the crime of unlawful sexual intercourse. The Home Office Policy Advisory Committee (1979, para 27) disposes of this suggestion by citing a Department of Health circular advising that a professional person who gives a young girl help with contraception does not act unlawfully. This view was challenged in July 1983 when a Roman Catholic mother of ten children applied to the High Court to declare that circular itself unlawful. Her counsel argued that doctors who do this facilitate a crime and, in strict law, commit an offence (*Guardian*, 20 July 1983). In the event the judgment went against the applicant. Mr Justice Woolf is reported to have said (*The Times* 26th July 1983) that giving juveniles under sixteen 'advice or assistance with regard to contraceptive measures with the intention thereby of encouraging them to have sexual intercourse' was a criminal act. However, 'in the majority of situations the probability was that a doctor would be able to follow the advice (in the DHSS circular) without rendering himself liable to criminal proceedings'. The provision of contraceptives to avoid a generalised risk of pregnancy did not directly assist in the commission of a particular act of unlawful sexual intercourse. The finding stimulated a doctor to write to the *Guardian* (2nd August 1983) pointing out that to give a girl under sixteen a medical examination without her parents' knowledge or consent might be an assault. This view was echoed in a judgement of the Appeal Court (20 Dec 1984), which reversed the previous decision of the High Court, and pronounced confidential treatment for girls under 16 illegal.

Regardless of the final legal outcome, the issue will remain sufficiently emotive and controversial to give health workers reason to doubt their immunity from legal action if they follow the dictates of a concience that leads them to help sexually active young persons. An acrimonious debate on the educational activities of the Brook family planning clinics (see Ronald Butt in *The Times*, 16 July 1981) shows that the objections, legal and otherwise, are not limited just to doctors' prescriptions. Organisations such as The Responsible Society want the law to prevent adults in any way facilitating juvenile sexual activity.

4.35 Another consideration affecting the control of juvenile sexual activity is the risk of venereal infections, which naturally increases with any increase in sexual promiscuity. Some contraceptive devices provide a degree of protection from some of the commoner infections, but the best protection, apart from the avoidance of promiscuity, is diagnosis and effective treatment. Recent increases in less treatable conditions, such as genital herpes, hepatitis B and the rapidly emerging and deadly acquired immune deficiency syndrome (AIDS) give a new impetus to the arguments for moderation in sexual habits, especially male homosexual activities which are more closely linked with hepatitis and AIDS than are heterosexual ones (Fluker, 1981; Cahill, 1984; Green and Miller, 1983).

4.36 The present high 'age of consent' for male homosexual contacts effectively criminalises the love life of large numbers of young men who feel that they are being unfairly stigmatised for following a natural bent. Although prosecutions for private behaviour between young men over eighteen are rare, the state of the law does have effects upon individual attitudes and cause distress in a number of ways that are little appreciated except by those involved, as a recent London questionnaire survey of young homosexuals, nearly all aged 16 to 20, revealed (Trenchard and Warren, 1984). Because an open admission of sexual activity is effectively an admission of crime, this inhibits youths from confiding in parents or seeking information or counselling elsewhere, encourages youth organisations to ignore the needs of young homosexuals, or to pretend that they do not exist, and prevents 'gay' bars and clubs from welcoming the young who may be seen as 'jail bait'. The result is that many feel unhappy, socially isolated, guilt-ridden and perhaps tempted to look for sex contacts in lavatories or other unsuitable venues. In the London survey 19 per cent said they had attempted suicide because they were gay (*op cit* p. 145). Among young people seeking advice in 1982 from *Parents' Enquiry* (an organisation set up by Rose Robertson to help young homosexuals and their families) 55 per cent had already made more or less serious suicidal attempts (cited in Galloway, 1983, p. 6). The situation of young male homosexuals would be eased by implementation of a recommendation of the Criminal Law Revision Committee (1984, para 6.18) which would effectively lower the 'age of consent' from 21 to 18, but not to 16, as urged by the European Parliament (see para 2.16).

MATURE VICTIMS

4.37 As the figures quoted earlier (para 3.11) showed, sexual offences involving physical violence are more often directed against mature females than against small girls. This has also been found to be the case in America. Hursch and Selkin in Denver (1974) noted that a quarter of all sex offences, but only 13 per cent of forcible rapes, were committed against children. Offenders inclined to violence are not the sort of men to select child victims out of timidity if their true preference is for a sexually mature girl or woman. The fact that adults are likely to be less compliant than children in the face of an offender's demands, and more likely to struggle against him, may add to the risk of violence.

The belief that a grown woman cannot be overpowered against her will by a lone offender is certainly false. It takes no account of the paralysing effect of fear in the face of threats or the sight of weapons, no allowance for inexperience of physical combat, no appreciation of the swift exhaustion of a victim struggling with a much stronger assailant, and no understanding of the reactions of someone subjected to increasingly severe beatings until she submits. Many rapes occur in circumstances in which there is no possibility of summoning help, so that the victim can see no end to the situation. In addition, the nature of the offender's sexual demands, which may include oral or anal sex, genital manipulations or penetration with objects, can inspire revulsion and overpowering fear of pain or injury.

4.38 Women can derive little comfort from the contradictory advice put out on how to protect themselves from sexual assault. Some womens' organisations, especially in America, advocate the carrying of protective devices, such as cartons of pepper, or training in physical combat. Passive resistance and attempts to appeal to or reason with the assailant are probably safer and as effective as counter-attacks which may provoke further violence (Bart, 1981).

4.39 Even when the physical brutality incurred is minimal the experience of sexual assault can be terrifying, especially if the victim is taken by surprise, or if she is particularly young, inexperienced or a virgin. The immediate reaction in many instances is one of shock, soon compounded by mixed emotions of anger, humiliation, self-blame and anxiety about the reactions of others to what has happened (Burgess and Holstrom, 1974). Realistic concern about the possibility of pregnancy or venereal infection following a rape, and irrational feelings of being somehow defiled or degraded can be aggravated by the suspicious or rejecting attitudes of husbands or boyfriends.

4.40 The work of rape crisis centres, and the experience of the Criminal Injuries Compensation Board, show that sexual assaults can sometimes produce severe and lasting adverse consequences. Victims who appear calm and rational at the time of the crisis are not necessarily immune from delayed reactions. Common sequelae include chronic anxiety, recurrent nightmares, obsessive preoccupation with what has happened, depression, loss of confidence, fear of going out and, most noticeably, disturbance in sexual relationships. The more violent and stressful the assault the more likely it is to be followed by severe and lasting consequences. Individuals who were anxious or neurotic before the incident are particularly prone to react badly. The potentially serious effects of rape are now well documented by researchers (Peters, 1975; Katz and Mazur, 1979; Becker *et al* 1979, 1982; Ellis, 1983; Kilpatrick *et al* 1981). In one such investigation, 41 women, free from previous mental or emotional disturbance, who had been seen in a hospital emergency room following rape, were interviewed 1–2½ years later (Nadelson *et al* 1982). Over half reported continuing sexual problems which they attributed to the rape, notably loss of interest, avoidance or complete frigidity. Half were still fearful of being alone, three-quarters had become unduly suspicious of others and many felt that their lives were being restricted.

4.41 As mentioned in Chapter 3, the victims of heterosexual attacks are often adolescent girls. Nearly half of the convicted rapists in the Home Office survey had been involved with victims in the age range 13 to 17 inclusive (Walmsley and White, 1979, p. 62). This probably reflects the ages of maximum attractiveness and availability to the offenders, many of whom are only a year or two older than their victims. But no age group is entirely immune from sexual assault and even aged women are occasionally attacked. It has also been noted that victims can be of singularly plain and unprovocative appearance. This might be particularly understandable where the motive is not primarily sexual. Moreover, it may be that some rapists, especially those with sexual inhibitions, are put off by girls who look too aggressively sexual.

4.42 In the fantasies of rapists, in some questionable cinematographic portrayals, and in the private salacious thoughts of many ordinary males, women forced to submit to intercourse become highly aroused and achieve an exciting orgasm. This comforting myth ignores the fact that most victims are thoroughly frightened or revolted, that the normal preparatory excitation and lubrication will not have occurred, and that the sensations usually described are of acute discomfort rather than pleasure.

4.43 The reactions of other people to the adult female who falls victim to a sex offender are often less than sympathetic and have been dubbed the 'second assault' (Williams and Holmes, 1981). A prevalent stereotype of the rape victim is of a woman who behaves and dresses provocatively and contributes to the offence (Mazelan, 1980). Awareness of these negative reactions and fear of loss of reputation doubtless contribute to the rape victim's reluctance to report the offence to the police. Another important factor is the secondary distress caused by the processes of criminal justice which can affect adults almost as cruelly as children. In order to prove that a sexual crime has been committed against a female who is over sixteen evidence corroborating some non-consensual molestation must be forthcoming, otherwise even if the complainant is believed her unsubstantiated word alone cannot convict the suspect.

Incidents in public places where independent witnesses are available are the easiest to substantiate, but these are generally not the most serious cases. For instance, there may be witnesses to such minor annoyances as bottom pinching or the encroaching leg from an adjacent cinema seat, all of which count as assaults. One adolescent youth, convicted of multiple sexual assaults, had been in the habit of cycling close to the pavement and stretching out a hand as he rode by to touch fleetingly the breasts of female pedestrians while in full view of passers-by.

4.44 In the more serious cases, offenders often strive to protect themselves by the easiest means, which is to accuse the victim of lying. Independent witnesses being usually unavailable, and the evidence necessarily circumstantial, trying to substantiate a complaint can be difficult and embarrassing. In the absence of signs of struggle, and particularly if the victim and offender were known to each other, the police may be reluctant to prosecute because the case rests on one person's word against another and if brought to trial a conviction would probably not be obtained.

4.45 Many victims of rape have been upset or angered by sceptical police interrogation, not appreciating, perhaps the desirability of testing the strength of the case before serious charges are brought against a suspect. Feeling challenged, some victims may be tempted to exaggerate. Nobody really knows the true incidence of completely false accusations of rape, but some undoubtedly occur. The motives are sometimes understandable, such as to disclaim responsibility for a situation, or perhaps a pregnancy, for which the girl would otherwise incur blame. Sometimes accusations are made out of spite or jealousy (see para 6.13).

4.46 The erotic thoughts of normal men and women often include images of raping or being raped (Masters and Johnson, 1979; Wilson, 1978; Malamuth, 1981). This has led to suggestions that some rape complaints are merely exciting, wishful fantasies. In one survey in America, in which 285 married women were interviewed, up to a fifth of them reported erotic fantasies with masochistic themes such as being raped, tied up, humiliated or forced to expose the genitals (Fisher, 1973). It cannot be assumed from such evidence, however, that the women would either want their fantasies translated into brute reality or that they would be likely to claim that such imagined events had actually happened.

VICTIM SUPPORT

4.47 Many rape victims need support and counselling in coming to terms with their own feelings and in coping with the sometimes unsympathetic, unduly suspicious or morally judgemental attitudes of friends, family or interrogators. The criminal justice system, being geared primarily to securing evidence for conviction, tends to neglect these victim needs, and this can cause grievance, particularly to victims who have suffered rape. Having subjected themselves to unpleasantly intimate interrogations and medical examinations, they may then be left for a long time with no information as to what action is being taken, what charges, if any, are to be preferred, whether the suspect is at large, or when she may be required to appear as a trial witness. Victims who have to make a court appearance are liable to find themselves anxiously awaiting the frightening experience, sometimes in close proximity to the offender's relatives, with less guidance about what to expect in the courtroom than the offender may receive from legal advisers provided by the state. Most victims are uninformed about the complexities of the judicial process and liable to be upset when, for reasons not understood or not explained, cases are dropped, charges are brought for lesser offences than rape, or a guilty offender is acquitted for lack of corroborative evidence. The prosecution, preoccupied with technological efficiency, neglects the victims' need for at least reassurance, if not some recompense, in return for their time and trouble.

The need to develop more helping services for the victims of crime in general, and crimes of personal violence in particular, is rapidly gaining recognition. A number of voluntary organizations now undertake counselling and befriending services for victims. The National Association of Victims Support Schemes (34 Electric Lane, London SW9 9JT) is a resource for developing and co-ordinating these efforts.

pe crisis centres run by voluntary enterprise have sprung up to ed. They are more fully developed in the United States, where sometimes located within the hospital facility that provides the l examinations of rape victims and where the police collaborate gly because they recognise the victims' need for support while they are co-operating in the effort to bring offenders to justice (King and Webb, 1981, Osborne, 1982).

The women's movement has had an undoubted influence for good in alerting police to the dangers of unwarranted scepticism or injudicious comments when dealing with rape complainants. Harry O'Reilly, formerly supervising sergeant of the New York City Sex Crime Investigation Unit, has been particularly influential in persuading American police authorities to adopt a more sympathetic stance and to co-operate with victim support groups. He points out that policemen are quite capable of doing this in other contexts, for example when they have to break the news of the death of a relative in a road accident. He recognizes that some women victims might be shy of talking about intimate sexual details to a man, but argues that the officer's attitude is more important than the officer's sex (O'Reilly, 1982; Keefe and O'Reilly, 1976).

Relations between the police and the rape crisis centres in England have tended to be rather fraught, the police believing that the existence of a service for victims could divert complainants from initial contact with them and thus delay reporting and lessen the chances of detection and conviction. Representatives of the English centres continue to complain of the alleged 'contempt, disbelief and insinuations or direct accusations that they have provoked the rapist' which women experience at the hands of the police (London Rape Crisis Centre, 1982, p. 13). They also resent the fact that the complainant's wishes do not seem to count in the police decision whether or not to prosecute and what charge to bring.

Rape crisis centres are unpopular in some quarters – and hence possibly less effective than they might otherwise be – because so many of them have a deep commitment to radical feminist ideology (Amir and Amir, 1979). This has given rise to suspicions that the individual needs of victims in distress may take second place to the promotion of political causes.

4.49 The Sexual Offences (Amendment) Act 1976, goes some way towards meeting the complaint that the victim of rape is liable to be confronted during the trial by questions intended to suggest that she is of loose morals and so to cast doubt upon her credibility. The Act provides that 'except with the leave of the judge, no evidence shall be adduced or asked at the trial, by or on behalf of any defendant at the trial, about sexual experience of a complainant with a person other than the defendant'. In addition, s. 4 of the Act prohibits the publication of any 'matter likely to lead members of the public to identify' the woman complainant. The defendant's anonymity is likewise preserved unless and until he is convicted. According to Barbara Toner (1982), questions about the complainant's sexual history, which one might have expected to be allowed only exceptionally since the passing of this Act, have in fact been frequently requested by defence counsel and allowed by judges.

4.50 Married women who are subjected by their husbands to unreasonable sexual demands or to physical abuse can lay complaints of assault or cruelty, but unless they are legally separated they cannot charge their husbands of rape. In its *Working Paper on Sexual Offences*, the Criminal Law Revision Committee (1980) acknowledged that a husband's immunity to charges of rape 'does not rest on any sound basis of principle and is in some quarters much resented' (para 37). They recommended abolition of the immunity with the proviso that prosecutions for rape within marriage should be brought only with the consent of the Director of Public Prosecutions. In their final report, however, the Criminal Law Revision Committee (1984, para 2.85) were divided over whether the crime of rape should include non-consensual sexual intercourse within marriage, but they were agreed that it should do so if the couple were not cohabiting.

PRISON VICTIMS

4.51 In the sub-culture of prisons the more criminally experienced inmates tend to dominate and set the tone, and sex offenders can themselves become victims of persecution. An unwritten code develops which individuals break at their peril. Anything beyond forced or minimal co-operation with persons in authority is disapproved, and anyone who 'squeals' about rule-breaking or crimes by fellow prisoners is harshly condemned. The most hardened and aggressively antisocial types are awarded respect: the timid, weak and criminally unsophisticated earn contempt. The typically meek and mild child molester exists at the very bottom of the heap, despised by everyone, the butt of ridicule, ostracism and bullying.

4.52 Much has been written by American sociologists about the dynamics of the inmate sub-culture, particularly as it relates to matters of sex in men's prisons (Lockwood, 1980; Scacco, 1975; Sykes, 1971; Weiss and Friar, 1975).

One of the ways in which a pecking order is established in American prisons is by hints and taunts about being 'queer'. If these are not responded to with a sufficient show of courage the prisoner loses status and risks further bullying that may, given the opportunity, lead to actual sexual attacks and anal rape, regardless of whether the victim is in fact homosexually inclined. It is as if men deprived of their own status in the outside world need to find others still lower than themselves to look down upon.

4.53 Child molesters, the most despised variety of sexual deviant, provide the easiest scapegoats. The moral values of the inmate culture enable men guilty of disgraceful crimes to distance themselves from what they consider to be offences far worse than anything they themselves have done. The remarkable extent to which sex deviants attract the hatred of other prisoners has been shown over and over again in the course of prison riots in North America, when prisoners temporarily in control of an institution have seized the chance to massacre them. In 1971, during a riot in a Canadian penitentiary in Kingston, rampaging prisoners dragged men from protective segregation cells (most of whom were sex offenders) tied them to chairs arranged in a circle, draped them in sheets, and after a mad kangaroo court trial, danced around the victims, screaming derisively and beating them into insensibility with iron bars. The bodies were left piled on one another for hours. Those who successfully feigned death survived. One child molester who did not was murdered, another sustained severe brain damage resulting in disinhibition and worsening of his sexual misconduct (Scott, 1982; Desroches, 1974).

Even worse atrocities took place during a riot at a prison in New Mexico in 1980. The more fortunate were burned to death by gasoline or paint thinner thrown into their cells followed by lighted matches. Less fortunate, James Perrin, a 'baby raper', was dragged from his cell, tied to the bars, and slowly scorched to death with an acetylene torch, starting at the genitals, progressing to the face, the agony being prolonged by periodic revivals before recommencement of the torture (Stone, 1982).

4.54 Nothing quite so dramatic has been reported from British prisons, although ex-prisoners' accounts often mention the harrassments and attacks, with such things as razor blades and boiling water, to which sex offenders are subjected, and to which some prison officers are said to turn a blind eye (Wright, 1982, p. 61; Coggan and Walker, 1982, p. 219). Official sources are reticent about the problem, but the need to protect certain sex offenders from the hostility of their fellow prisoners is officially recognised, and is occasionally mentioned in official publications. For example, the Gibson inquiry into disturbances at

Wormwood Scrubs Prison on 31st of August 1979 (Home Office, February 1982, para 14) referred to the development of conflicting groups or fractions among the inmates. One of these was made up of 'the weaker elements, including some sex offenders, who seem to have banded together in the face of intimidation and exploitation by other prisoners . . .'

A system of official protection is institutionalised in the shape of Prison Rule 43, which states that: 'Where it appears desirable, for the maintenance of good order and discipline or in his own interests, that a prisoner should not associate with other prisoners, either generally or for particular purposes, the governor may arrange for the prisoner's removal from association accordingly'.

The phrase 'in his own interests' is intended to provide protection from threats, abuse and violence, and among those to whom it applies sex offenders predominate, although other categories, notably informers, are by no means negligible. Prisoners are placed on Rule 43 either on their own application or on the initiative of the prison authorities. Those placed on Rule 43 as a disciplinary measure 'for the preservation of good order' are in a minority.

4.55 The vast majority of sex offenders protectively segregated under Rule 43 are so placed at the outset of their sentence when they arrive in a local prison, but many of them remain no more than two or three months in this situation, although some spend their entire sentence under protection in the local prisons. Inevitably this means that they cannot enjoy the same facilities or privileges as are given to other prisoners. Some protected prisoners share accommodation, but for those who do not it has sometimes been claimed that their situation amounts to near solitary confinement. Such depressing and spartan conditions have been described by H.M. Inspector of Prisons as 'unacceptable' (Home Office, 1981, para 6.11).

The number who apply for and are granted the protection of Rule 43 is greatly affected by the nature of the admission procedures and whether these draw attention to the character of the man's offences. There is, however, an irreducible hard core of notorious individuals whose need for protection is unavoidable, either for a substantial period or for the whole of their sentence. Accordingly the authorities have set up in Gloucester, Wakefield and Maidstone prisons, large-sized units or wings housing some 400 former Rule 43 men. They enjoy freedom of movement within their own section of the prison, but these units sometimes have more applicants for protection than there are vacancies (Home Office, 1981, para 6.15). Even where a Rule 43 unit has been set up, continued vigilance by officers is needed to prevent abuses. We have heard, for example, that at one prison it was found essential to issue the food trolleys to different wings in a random way to ensure that prisoners working in the kitchen would not know which trolley was destined for the Rule 43 unit, and so could not adulterate the food with broken glass or excrement.

4.56 The prison authorities have tried to reduce the numbers of men seeking protection. The procedure on reception and the handling during the first few days of imprisonment are particularly important as it is then that most applications for Rule 43 are made. Transfer schemes have been developed in some regions to move men from the local prison where they are initially received to a more distant establishment before they apply for Rule 43. Transfers at a larger stage enable some men in training prisons to rejoin the general population at some other establishment. Cases are regularly reviewed to ensure that there is a genuine and continuing need for protection. This is necessary in order to see that those who have a special need are admitted to the main protection units, since local prisons cannot be expected to provide facilities suited to long-term stay in such circumstances. Local prisons, must however, provide for minimum requirements and it is an advantage to have a named senior person, such as a Deputy Governor, responsible for overseeing the system.

4.57 The attitude of the staff and the organisation and morale of the institution have an important bearing upon the incidence of bullying or violence among inmates. Prisoners sometimes complain that prison officers facilitate the persecution of sex offenders, for instance by deliberately letting it be known during reception procedures when a sex offender is being admitted (Home Office, 1981, para 6.6). Officers may appear by their attitude to encourage, if not actually to participate in, the expressions of contempt for these offenders. It would hardly be surprising if some officers, in common with so many others in the wider community, failed to disguise a perfectly understandable hostility. Nevertheless, they have a duty to set an example. In Grendon Underwood psychiatric prison, where open and sympathetic discussion of personal problems with staff and inmates together is an integral part of the regime (and where violence results in immediate transfer to another prison, often with a more restrictive regime), sex offenders, of whom there are many, do not need to call for special protection.

CHAPTER 5

Who are the offenders?

GENERAL CONSIDERATIONS

5.1 A rough but useful distinction can be made between sexually deviant offenders whose motivation appears to be to gratify unusual inclinations (such as sexual contact with children or with young persons of the same gender, or indulgence in odd rituals such as genital exposure to strangers in public places) and offenders whose sexual behaviour and inclinations would be regarded as normal under different circumstances. Both sexually deviant and sexually non-deviant offenders are sometimes violent or aggressive, but the non-deviant offenders are more likely to be so as they are also more likely to choose as victims mature females capable of resistance. Deviant offenders who commit indecencies with children are rarely, and exhibitionists, almost never, violent.

5.2 Whether their sexual predilections are ordinary or unusual, few sex offenders fit the stereotype of the ruthless brute, driven by uncontrollable cravings, who deserves the label 'psychopath'. Many of them appear to be rather conventional and unremarkable personalities, and to feel considerable guilt whenever they have acted thoughtlessly or selfishly to satisfy a sexual impulse.

5.3 Sex offenders have a relatively high incidence of convictions for non-sexual crime. The overlap between sexual and non-sexual criminality has long been known to criminologists, but the explanations are not immediately obvious. One theory suggests that the link is more apparent than real. Sexual misconduct has an increased likelihood of detection and reporting when it occurs in delinquent groups or families who are already under surveillance by authorities. For example, incest in problem families whose members are well known to police and social services is much more likely to be reported than consensual incest in middle class, non-criminal families. But common sense suggests that such factors as social deprivation, drunkenness, parental incompetence and large families living in overcrowded, substandard conditions, which are all noticeably frequent among incest cases coming to court; do make some contribution to the problem and are not just a reflection of the way families are picked out for prosecution. Moreover, the criminal antecedents of men who commit brutal sex assaults on women are unlikely to be the product of selective reporting, since the victims in all such cases have good reason to lay a complaint.

VIOLENT OFFENDERS

5.4 Aggressive sex offenders are much more likely than non-violent deviant offenders to have criminal convictions for both sexual and non-sexual crimes. They share characteristics in common with the generality of delinquents, being predominantly youthful, working class, poorly socialised and often unemployed. This was true of the offenders in a survey based upon police records in six English counties concerning all incidents indentified as rapes or attempted rapes over a five year period (Wright, 1980). The great majority, 87 per cent, were attacks by a single assailant, 55 per cent of whom were under twenty-one. Some 60 per cent of assailants were known to and named by their victims. Of rapes by strangers, a significant proportion occur in the course of housebreaking, and whether the initial motive is sex or theft is uncertain.

The characteristics of aggressive heterosexual offenders were aptly summed up by researchers who conducted an extensive survey for the Indiana University Institute of Sex Research (founded by Alfred Kinsey). They described such men as 'criminally inclined . . . who take what they want, whether money, material or women, and their sex offences are by-products of their general criminality.' (Gebhard *et al*, 1965, p. 205).

5.5 Because so many rapists are young and crime-prone it does not follow that their assaults are peculiarly brutal or that they constitute a risk to every woman in the street. Wright's survey showed that most attacks by lone assailants occurred after the victim had agreed to accompany the offender, sometimes in his car, sometimes to a secluded spot, and 36 per cent of the crimes took place at the home of either the offender or the victim. The violence or threat involved was usually no more than necessary to ensure compliance. Injuries were more frequent among those victims who had put up some physical resistance.

The commonest sequence of events in these rape cases was of a young couple meeting and drinking together in a bar or disco, then going off somewhere together, thereby giving the male the opportunity to insist on intercourse, by forcing if necessary.

5.6 Gang rapes, in which a girl is lured or captured by a group of young males, each of whom has forcible sexual intercourse with her are particularly likely to be committed by youthful offenders. Initial contact frequently occurs in the street, often with an intoxicated victim. Group rapes, more often than lone offences, occur out of doors or in a car, the offenders more often succeed in obtaining the sexual acts demand (doubtless due to the ease with which a victim can be overpowered by several males), the process is more often accompanied by gratuitous brutality and the self-proving bravado common to adolescent gangs, and the victim more often sustains at least minor injuries (Wright and West, 1981).

5.7 The behaviour of young rapists is, to a certain extent, the product of their environment, the prevalent outlook towards women as sex objects rather than individuals and the conception of violence as an acceptable means of obtaining what one wants. Where violence is commoner than in England, in New York City for example, reported rapes are more frequent and more often involve significant injury to the victim (Chappell and Singer, 1977). The observation that rapes tend to occur at specific times, notably in the late evening and at week-ends, and that incidence varies so much according to the ethnic and social class of both offenders and victims, all point to the influence of social habits and attitudes in bringing about these offences (Dietz, 1978). Among the undeveloped cultures studied by anthropologists it has been observed that societies tend to have many rapes where the general level of violence is high, where women have low status, and where pre-marital sex is not tolerated (Sanday, 1981; Otterbein, 1979).

5.8 Most rapists are not seen by themselves or by others as psychologically abnormal, at least not any more so than the average thief or burglar. People feel they understand these young men's motives only too well. In fact, according to surveys by an American psychologist, a substantial proportion of males harboured rape fantasies or thought that they might commit rape if they found themselves in a situation in which they would not be punished for it (Malamuth, 1981; Malamuth and Check, 1983). But the assumption of psychological normality does not hold true for the minority of rapists whose crimes are particularly brutal or repetitive, or who take complete strangers by surprise. Clinicians regularly detect abnormal sexual attitudes and emotions among these offenders (Groth, 1979). Several varieties of disturbance have been described.

5.9 Some violent sex offenders are undoubted sexual deviants, sadists who become fully aroused only when they can subjugate a victim and inflict pain and humiliation. Offenders with this perversion combined with an impulsive, ruthless personality can be particularly dangerous and persistent in their crime and account for some sexual homicides.

The American psychologist Gene Abel developed a technique for distinguishing, for purposes of treatment, rapists with a sadistic drive from others whose aggressive behaviour was intended to do no more than make intercourse possible. He used a penile plethysmograph, an instrument for registering the involuntary changes in volume of the penis during sexual excitement. Whereas many sexual aggressors, like most men, were maximally aroused by pictures or taped descriptions of consensual intercourse the sadist's fantasies and maximal arousals were triggered by scenes or stories of sexual violence (Abel *et al*, 1978). In a recent comprehensive survey of the available evidence on this point, a psychologist from the Mental Health Centre at Penetanguishene (where many of Canada's most violent sex offenders have been treated) concluded that aggressive rapists' sexual arousal patterns are indeed different from those of the average man. They are not at all put off, as most men are, by sex stories or pictures in which the woman is subjected to violence, pain or distress. Sadistic rapists represent a small group at the end of a continuum characterised by greater sexual arousal to sexual violence than to consenting sex. A few are aroused only if the sex activity includes considerable violence. (Quinsey and Chaplin, 1982; Quinsey, 1984).

5.10 Feelings of sexual inadequacy, real or imagined, and doubts about their masculinity are frequently found among the more serious and repetitive of aggressive offenders (Halleck, 1971). They resent their inability to captivate or dominate women, they become oversensitive to rejection, unreasonably demanding and jealous because of their own insecurity, and liable to develop an irrational hatred of women. Given their suspicious and hostile attitudes their sexual relationships are often fraught and emotionally unsatisfying (Cohen *et al*, 1971). The more disappointments they feel the greater the risk of relieving their frustrations in vengeful attacks upon innocent strangers, attacks which are as much to express aggression as to satisfy lust (West *et al*, 1978). The distinction between the emotional release which some socially inadequate men obtain by being cruel to women and asserting dominance by brutality is not always easy to disentangle from true sexual sadism, that is the deriving of erotic gratification from the infliction of pain. Autobiographical material from men under treatment suggests that both elements may be present in varying combinations (Levine and Koenig, 1982).

5.11 Insights into the twisted motives of some of the more abnormal and violent offenders may assist in attempts at treatment, but they cannot provide a complete explanation. Many men experience similar problems, but it requires in addition a character liable to vent his feelings in violence for emotional frustrations to be translated into aggressive sexual crime. Many of these sexually violent men, besides having particular conflicts in the sexual sphere, have also experienced the same kinds of chaotic or cruel upbringings that are commonly associated with violent criminality in general.

5.12 On occasion, violent sexual crimes are inspired by guilt rather than lust. Prostitutes are at risk of ill-treatment by clients who turn sour after intercourse because they blame the woman for having tempted them into shameful acts. For the same reason, homosexual males who have taken a willing young stranger home to bed are sometimes beaten up afterwards. Sex-related murders of children are not necessarily committed out of lust, as happened in the unforgettably appalling crimes of Ian Brady and Myra Hindley the 'Moors murderers' (Sparrow, 1966; Williams, 1967), but because the offender experiences a frenzy of guilty panic at the thought that the child might give him away. In sex-related murders by psychotics, acting under the influence of delusions or at the command of hallucinatory voices, themes of sexual guilt and sinfulness are more prominent than lust. The 'Yorkshire Ripper', for example, apparently believed he was out to fulfil a divine mission to rid the world of loose women, not to commit rape. The jury did not accept this explanation, but the psychiatric evidence that the man really was deluded became overwhelming after he was sentenced to imprisonment and needed to be transferred to Broadmoor.

PAEDOPHILES

5.13 Deviant offenders attracted to young children cause the greatest concern. The characteristics of convicted paedophiles are well known from many published surveys (Cook and Howells, 1981; Groth and Birnham, 1978; Panton, 1978; Swanson, 1968; Taylor, 1981). They are typically non-violent in their offences and often unassertive or socially inhibited in everyday life. Some of them adopt a protective pseudo-parental stance towards the children with whom they have 'affairs'. Like other kinds of sex deviant many of them report having had poor relationships with their parents (the domineering mother and weak or absent father being the typical constellation) and having been brought up in a very restrictive and prudish way in regard to sex matters. A recent survey conducted through members of the Paedophile Information Exchange confirmed that these characteristics apply to paedophiles in the community as well as to those coming under clinical scrutiny following a conviction (Wilson and Cox, 1983). Relatively few paedophiles have convictions for non-sexual crimes. On average they are considerably older than rapists, their offences often continuing into middle age. Many are unhappy about their sexuality, and would accept help to control or to change their impulses, but others either do not want, or do not believe it possible, to change their ways.

5.14 Some paedophiles are gentle and loving towards the objects of their desire and may have intense emotional attachments with a minimum of overt physical expression. The empathy with children that they develop would be admirable in other contexts. By engaging in games, or offering presents and treats, they become skilled at making themselves interesting companions and persuading children to co-operate. Their sexual requirements are often limited to looking and touching, activities not unknown to children in their play with each other. Even when they fondle children in a crudely sexual way they are able to convince themselves that they are doing no harm. Aside from their sexual quirk they can be highly moral and much respected citizens. The popular image of the cleric and the choirboy is not without some foundation.

5.15 Persistent paedophiles who engineer themselves into situations in which they have legitimate excuse for contacts with children sometimes gather around them small groups of children willing to participate in sexual games. Burgess *et al* (1981) studied a number of what they called 'sex initiation rings', that is small groups of children recruited by an offender, sometimes with the aid of one or more similarly inclined accomplice(s). The children know each other and are aware of each other's involvement, sometimes witnessing each other's participation. They are generally initiated into sexual practices gradually, with aid of pornography, undressing games and suitable rewards. Burgess considered that a key factor in maintaining the children's co-operation was peer pressure – competing with each other to secure the adult's attention and interest and wanting to be seen to be daring enough to do whatever others were willing to do. Awareness of the disapproval of parents if they found out about their secret games, and fear of retaliation from others if they revealed what had been going on, effectively prevented or delayed the detection of offences. In hostels and residential schools, where a paedophile is on the staff, all of the children may know about him, and think they know which among them is willing to participate in sex acts, and who is his 'favourite', but still they keep the information to themselves. In all-male establishments paedophile incidents are far from rare, but adolescent boys have good reason to be wary of revealing contacts for which they might themselves incur blame or lose masculine status.

5.16 The majority of paedophiles are attracted only to girls, a minority like only boys, and some will make contact with chidren of either sex. Many molesters of girls are not true paedophiles, in the sense of having a strong or exclusive preference for children. They resort to children because their physical, mental or social inadequacies prevent them from securing an adult partner (Freund *et al*, 1972). Many of them have had extensive but unsatisfactory experiences in adult relationships and failed marriages. In contrast, men who seduce small boys are nearly always true paedophiles. In spite of the common belief that all homosexual males are prone to molest boys, regression from adult homosexual relationships to sex with children is rare (Groth and Birnbaum, 1978; Newton, 1978).

5.17 Men who approach small girls are usually relatives, lodgers or friends of the family, persons who in the ordinary course of events have the opportunity for a more or less intimate relationship with the intended victim. Encounters between adult strangers and small girls are mostly limited to sexual exhibitionism. Because homosexual paedophiles are less numerous, boys are less likely to meet one in their immediate family circle. Offences against boys, when not committed by male youth workers, teachers and others with privileged access, are much more often committed by strangers making contact in cinemas, amusement arcades and other public places where children congregate. Homosexual offences against boys usually involve some bodily touching; homosexual exhibitionism, except as an invitation to closer contact, is relatively unusual. Possibly because successful contact with a stranger in a public setting can hardly occur if the boy is totally unresponsive, and also because the men involved are true paedophiles, initial contacts are often followed by repeated meetings. Sexual contacts between girls and adults who are familiar to them often stop after a first attempt, when the offender finds his actions unwelcome.

5.18 Many adults who consider their inclinations normal are aware of a mild attraction to certain children – a fact confirmed by plethysmographic surveys (Freund, 1981) – but they would not act upon such impulses, and have not need to do so because they have access to adult relationships. Frustrated men who use children as substitute sex objects are more problematic than the true child lovers. They are often gross social inadequates and their approaches to children can be selfishly inept, often drunken and sometimes violent. In the Indiana Institute survey it was said of prisoners who had been sexually violent with chidren that they 'combined dullness, alcoholism and an asocial attitude into a lifestyle that brought them the distinction of being the most criminal and recidivisitic of all the groups . . .' (Gerbhard *et al* 1965, p. 154). Like some of the more violent rapists of mature females they came from conflict-ridden or broken parental homes, had turbulent heterosexual affairs with adult females, and adhered to Victorian sexual attitudes: 'the double standard, the division of females into good and bad girls, the strong desire for a virgin bride, minimal foreplay in coitus, and a reliance on prostitutes.' (*op cit*, p. 153). This is the type of character responsible for most of the fortunately rare offences of forced vaginal or anal intercourse, acts which can cause severe pain and genital injuries to a child victim to say nothing of the psychological damage.

INCESTUOUS FATHERS

5.19 Incestuous fathers most often start their molestations before their daughters reach puberty. Because they have had a sexually active marriage, and because they are rarely convicted for interfering with children other than their own, they are not generally considered to be true paedophiles. However, this view has been questioned by an American psychologist (Abel *et al*, 1981). Using a plethysmogrpah to register penile erection, he found that some incest offenders were readily aroused by viewing pictures of children. Some men have been known to marry widows or divorcees with the specific intention of obtaining access to step-daughters. Be that as it may, the typical incest offender limits his misbehaviour to his own household. Often he appears a devoted family-centred man. Dull, frigid, depressed, sick or uncaring wives are often blamed, sometimes unfairly, for tacit connivance, but it is likely that natural reluctance to face an exceedingly hurtful truth accounts for the seemingly wilful blindness of some of the wives of incestuous fathers. Others deliberately ignore what is happening for the sake of keeping the family together or avoiding scandal.

5.20 Like other sex offenders incestuous fathers are a decidedly heterogenous group. Many are good providers and conscientious fathers and in no way deviant apart from their sexual misconduct. Some become sexual bullies only when drunk. While some are psychological tyrants who treat wives and daughters like slaves, more usually the incestuous father is effectively 'in love' with his child and liable to become overpoweringly possessive. While not the monsters of popular belief, these men manage, by rationalisations and defensive denials, to ignore the harm they may be doing. When matters come to light many are eager to confess, express relief from their burden of guilt, and welcome counselling to prevent relapse. Experience suggests, however, that some of them are liable to drift away from treatment after a time unless under some obligation to see it through.

EXHIBITIONISTS

5.21 The compulsion to 'flash' the penis from a safe distance is a very common form of deviant sexual behaviour. In practice, as well as by legal definition ('indecent exposure . . . with intent to insult a female') this form of annoyance is directed towards women, often young women or schoolgirls, and sometimes specifically towards pre-pubertal children (Bluglass, 1980).

Although indisputably heterosexual, exhibitionists tend to be inhibited in their sexual relationships and, if married, they are liable to be dominated by their wives. They are particularly liable to embark on sprees of exposing when marital or other forms of stress reach a peak (Hackett *et al*, 1980). A wife's pregnancy sometimes appears to act as a precipitating event. The exposing ritual seems to afford an excitement of a different quality from their ordinary sexual relations. The offenders do not always exhibit an erection or masturbate, some do so later to the accompaniment of fantasies of shocking women or impressing them. When this is the underlying motivation, a reaction of contemptuous indifference on the woman's part, which is probably becoming a commoner response, provides no encouragement to further offending.

5.22 Of course not all exposers are true, repetitive exhibitionists. For many it may be a transient or 'one-off' occurrence in adolescence or during intoxication. The incidence of reconviction for first offenders is so low that referral for psychiatric examination and treatment is often thought unnecessary. Most exposers attempt no closer contact, but for a few it can be prelude to sexual molestation, especially if the subject of attention is a child. Mentally impaired men, for example, may try exposing as a crude form of invitation to further sexual acts. Occasionally, offenders who were really initiating an actual sexual assault are charged with indecent exposure, either because they were interrupted at an early stage, or because sufficient evidence to support a more serious charge was not forthcoming.

HOMOSEXUALS

5.23 A large proportion, probably a majority, of men convicted for homosexual offences are guilty of nothing more than soliciting another adult, or behaving improperly with another man in a public place. The venue is most often a public lavatory, but sometimes it is a parked car or behind a bush, places that would not normally excite the attention of the police if the behaviour was heterosexual.

After the passing of the Sex Offences Act 1967, by which private, consenting sex between adult men ceased to be a criminal offence in England, convictions of men for indecency in lavatories greatly increased (Walmsley, 1978). The most likely explanation is not that the behaviour in question has become more prevalent, but rather that s.9(2) of the Act introduced summary trial for the offence. This made it much easier for the police to bring prosecutions, since men would readily plead guilty and receive a fine (doubtless wanting to get the matter over quickly and hoping to avoid publicity) and the necessity to produce corroborative witnesses to the alleged offence could be avoided. A substantial proportion of the men convicted for this form of misconduct are married, living an ostensibly heterosexual life style, and not part of the homosexual sub-culture (Humphreys, 1970). For them, public exposure is dreaded far more than the penalty imposed by the court. The reasons why many homosexual men are prepared to risk the consequences of arrest in such circumstances are rather puzzling, but certainly some do so because they find other ways of making contact more problematic (see para 6.10).

5.24 The offence of soliciting by men, defined as 'to solicit or importune in a public place for immoral purposes' (s.32, Sexual Offences Act 1956) was introduced by the Vagrancy Act 1898, apparently with the intention of controlling men touting the services of female prostitutes, but it has been used exclusively against men seeking sex partners of the same sex. The solicitation does not have to be for purposes of prostitution to constitute an offence, as it does if a woman solicits, since 'immoral purposes' refers to any homosexual act, whether criminal or not (*R v Graham Ford* [1978] 1 A11 ER 1129). Imprisonment of women who solicit has recently been abolished (s.71, Criminal Justice Act 1982), but imprisonment remains a penalty for soliciting by males. The Criminal Law Revision Committee (1982, para 3.35) in their *Working Paper on Offences Relating to Prostitution*, recommend that 'the law should in future penalise homosexual soliciting only where it is done for purposes of prostitution'. The Law Society (1983, para 3.3) go further and suggest that the punishment should be the same for both sexes and that soliciting by males should also cease to be an imprisonable offence.

5.25 According to the Sexual Offences Act 1967, sexual acts between males are not counted as being in private if one or more other persons are present. Prosecutions for group sex in a private house must be rare, if they occur at all, but the law is used to prosecute acts of indecency in male saunas, gay clubs and other places where homosexuals congregate. The Criminal Law Revision Committee (1984, Part X) favours abolition of the 'more than two persons' rule, while making it an offence for two or more persons to have sexual intercourse or to perform an act of gross indecency (including buggery) in a public place, or in a place visible from a public place or from other premises. This new offence would apply equally to the control of heterosexual clubs, both being regarded as open to the public.

5.26 Men who involve themselves with young boys cause more serious concern. Among homosexual offenders prosecuted for indecent acts with the young, a smaller proportion is actually involved with prepubertal children than is the case among men prosecuted for indecent assault on girls. This cannot be taken as evidence of a real difference in the age preferences of homosexuals and heterosexuals. More likely, the difference arises from society's greater condemnation of men who have sex with teenage youths than of men who go to bed with girls in the same age range. The likelihood of prosecution is greater when the misconduct is homosexual. The higher 'age of consent' for male homosexual activity gives some statutory recognition to this discrimination.

5.27 As many of the under-age males involved with homosexual offenders are adolescents rather than children, it is not surprising that many of them are willing collaborators, either for sexual pleasure or for financial gain or perhaps both.

Except in closed, all-male institutions such as youth prisons, where intimidation is feasible, aggressive homosexual attacks upon adults are unusual, apart of course from attacks occasioned by jealousy (which are in principle no different from crimes of heterosexual jealousy) or violence following homosexual encounters by men who do not fully acknowledge their own deviant propensities. Men are better able than women to deter a would-be assailant, but there may be deeper psychological reasons why homosexual males rarely commit spontaneous, violent sex assaults.

Actual violence against young boys is also rare, but as with offences against small girls, a young victim may be induced to comply out of fear of disobeying an adult, or because he does not comprehend the full significance of the acts required.

5.28 Offenders who have anal intercourse with boys are charged with buggery and liable to particularly severe punishment. However, unless the act is forced, in which case the behaviour is analogous to rape of a young girl, it often occurs in the course of an intimate, continuing relationship. Such offenders are not necessarily obnoxious or uncaring, and it is questionable whether the precise details of their sexual contacts should in itself be an important factor in assessing the seriousness of their offence, although it can provide clues to the nature of the relationship. At present consensual buggery with a boy under 16 carries a maximum sentence of life imprisonment. The Criminal Law Revision Committee (1984, para 6.15) proposes that this should apply only if the boy is under 13, and that it should be 5 years for buggery with a youth under 18.

5.29 Homicidal attackers of boys have much the same characteristics and motives as were described in connection with attackers of girls, except that their violent inclinations are directed towards males. Murders of boys by sadists, although extremely rare, are well known to the public from the attention given to such matters by the press. One of the worst instances took place in Houston, Texas, when a sadistic deviant, together with some younger accomplices, tortured, butchered and buried the bodies of dozens of youngsters over a period of years. The victims were for the most part socially alienated youths from poor backgrounds whose disappearance provoked minimal official concern until the scandal broke (Olsen, 1974). The same was true of some of the estranged young homosexuals adrift in London who were the victims of the more recent mass murderer Dennis Nilsen (Lisners, 1983, p. 113).

5.30 It used to be assumed by some psychiatrists that all men with deviant sexual inclinations were necessarily inferior in moral standards and peculiar or neurotic in personality. Since the Kinsey surveys demonstrated that persons with a pronounced or exclusive homosexual orientation were numbered in millions, and since the gay liberation movement has drawn public attention to the many socially effective homosexuals in the community, belief in the malignant nature of the homosexual condition has become more difficult to sustain. Indeed, some sociologists would suggest that homosexual behaviour is essentially situational, or at any rate conditioned by life circumstances and cultural attitudes, rather than an expression of some innate peculiarity of the individual (Plummer, 1981). The search for personal attributes peculiar to the homosexual is believed by some authorities to be a misguided and wasted effort as would be an analogous search for the characteristics of heterosexuals. Recent surveys of persons engaging in other forms of unconventional sex, such as sado-masochism and fetishism, lend support to the contention that there is no invariable connection between sexual deviations and abnormalities of personality (Gosselin and Wilson, 1980), although, as explained in the pages that follow, there are trends observable in particular cases.

5.31 Homosexuals who are apprehended for an offence may well tend to have characteristics that are not typical of homosexuals in general. Those who commit aggressive homosexual assaults, or homosexual murders, or who molest small boys probably have more in common with offenders who commit analogous heterosexual crimes. Homosexual males who are not integrated into the gay sub-culture – perhaps because they are married, or in sensitive employment, or are too shy, fearful or guilt-ridden to come out into the open – often lack experience in finding sexual partners in safe or acceptable ways. Hence they are particularly liable to make clumsy approaches or unwise contacts that lead to arrest for importuning or to robbery, blackmail or assault (Miller and Humphreys, 1980).

ORIGINS OF SEXUAL DEVIATIONS

5.32 Theories about the causes of sexual deviations are mentioned later, in the discussion on treatment, where they have greater relevance. However, one factor which is very frequently cited, namely fear of normal heterosexual relations, is worth mentioning now because it has implications for the kinds of character one expects to find among sexual deviants. The fear may arise through a sexually repressive, guilt and anxiety-provoking upbringing, or through concern, realistic or otherwise, about sexual competence, acceptability and chances of painful rejection. The deviant activity supposedly represents a substitute sexual outlet that is felt to be easier or less frightening than intercourse with adult women. In ordinary sexual relationships men are conventionally supposed to be the initiators and to take the lead. Since high anxiety can render men impotent and unable to fulfil their expected role, this could be a reason why men are more prone to escape into alternative forms of sexual expression than are women, for whom a passive role in sexual relationships is more socially acceptable.

5.33 The theory that anxieties and inhibitions play an important part in inducing sexual deviations fits in well with the observation that many exhibitionists, molesters of girls, and even some rapists are socially inhibited and often conspicuously ineffectual, unskilled or totally inexperienced in acceptable heterosexual relationships, in spite of having heterosexual desires. The theory also fits the known characteristics of many homosexual paedophiles, but it is less obviously applicable to the generality of persons with a predominantly homosexual orientation, many of whom are at ease with their sexual inclinations and resentful of any suggestion of psychological malaise. The theory clearly has no application to the very uninhibited, criminally inclined, young sexual aggressives. There is more than one road to the development of sexually deviant behaviour.

5.34 Sexual offenders are evidently a very heterogeneous population. No single theory could be expected to explain all these different kinds of deviant behaviour, although each one may be usefully applied to certain sections of the sex offender population. Many sex offenders have no particular distinguishing features beyond the fact that they have been caught breaking a social rule, but others can be seen to belong to identifiable sub-groups with contrasting characteristics. Recognition of this is important in the assessment of offenders' dangerousness, likelihood of persistence, or prospects of response to punishment or treatment.

CHAPTER 6

How are the offenders brought to justice?

PUBLIC PERCEPTION OF CRIME

6.1 In a democracy governed by consent, the activities of the police, the laws they uphold, and the punishments meted out by the courts are all subject ultimately to the will of the people. Without a considerable measure of public support the justice system would be unworkable, for it depends largely on the majority obeying the rules, disapproving of the minority who do not, and co-operating in their detection and punishment. This means that the actions taken by the criminal justice system must be in general conformity with public opinion. If policing is inadequate or too officious, if punishments get out of line with what people deem reasonable, if the law no longer reflects the standards of ordinary life, dissatisfaction will make itself felt and changes will be demanded.

There is little risk of the public taking sexual offenders too lightly, since the belief is widespread that sex offenders are persons of exceptional depravity and that permissiveness towards sexual licence or sexual deviation encourages crime. In his 1983 Darwin Lecture, the Lord Chief Justice appeared to support this view, arguing that 'so long as permissiveness or immorality increases, so will crime, both in quantity and nastiness'. He deplored, for example, the use of the innocuous sounding jargon word 'gay' for men who are homosexual and/or buggers, which 'corrupts the language and gives tacit approval to the situation which is being so mis-described'. He found it small wonder, in view of the proliferation of pornographic magazines and videos, that 'violent crime becomes more violent and sexual crime more horrible and perverted.'

6.2 Public opinion about the commoner forms of law-breaking such as traffic infractions, shoplifting, or burglary is reliably informed by life experience. Only a minority, fortunately, are ever directly affected by sex offences. Consequently attitudes to these matters are more likely to be influenced by traditions, rumours and personal prejudices. One factor that can strongly influence public attitudes to sex offences and offenders is how they are dealt with in the hands of the media of publicity. On the whole, coverage by T.V. and national radio does not seem to be either disproportionate or distorted; major police hunts and trials are reported no less fairly in this field than in any other field of crime. But the same cannot, in general, be said for the press. A recent survey of Scottish newspapers showed that, as a proportion of crimes mentioned, offences involving sex were over-represented numerically fourteen times (and by area of print seventeen times) in comparison with the actual incidence of these offences among officially recorded crimes (Ditton and Duffy, 1983). Newspaper editors seem to be convinced that the public wants to read as much as it can about sex, and that sex offences will therefore always be news and will always sell copies. We are in no position to judge whether that conviction is always well-founded, but it undoubtedly results in sex offences receiving far greater coverage in the public prints than their frequency alone – as a proportion of crime in general, or even of serious crime – would warrant.

6.3 There are of course differences in the manner of that coverage as between local and national papers, and as between the 'popular' and the 'quality' press. Local papers appear to vary widely in their editorial policy, some giving great prominence to every trial with any sexual element, and others not. The popular nationals have adopted a standard set of clichés which they apply uniformly to all violent sex offenders, ringing the changes without any apparent discrimination between 'beast', 'fiend', 'monster', and 'maniac', thereby encouraging their readers to think about all sex offending in such terms, regardless of whether these labels are either correct or comprehensive. The use of such epithets, implying that sex offenders are animals who need not be treated with humanity, promotes highly punitive attitudes. These are further reinforced by frequent references to the need for 'tougher' sentences (Jones, 1980). In January 1982, after a rapist received a fine, a furious outcry followed, reflecting the press assumption (asserted also to be public opinion) that rapists ought always to be sent to prison. For weeks afterwards the press, including the quality press, found space to report a noticeably larger number of rape cases than usual.

Besides fostering questionable generalisations about the nature of sex offences and the proper response to sex offenders, selective press reporting also gives the impression that sex offences are more prevalent than they are in fact. Probably a minority of people realise that sex crimes constitute less than 1 per cent of notifiable offences.

6.4 The tendency to use more items of a similar kind once a particularly sensational case has captured headlines is a noticeable feature of press reporting. This 'amplification spiral', as it has been dubbed by sociologists, is partly caused by the system of lineage payments for news supply. The effect is to encourage an atmosphere of 'moral panic' in which public horror and disgust is artifically stimulated, and the understandable destestation of sex offenders is unnecessarily reinforced.

To give just one example, in July 1983 the popular press reported the case of an irate father tried for a serious assault against a sex offender who had been convicted for an offence against his child. On July 13, the *Express* ran the headline 'Campaign to Free Father Who Beat Up Sex Beast' while the *Sun* had a headline 'Father in Two Attacks on Fiend'. In the event, the Appeal Court reduced the gaol sentence on the father referred to (*Guardian* 30 July 1983), but in the meantime the popular papers had featured a contrasting case at Nottingham Crown Court when a child molester had been imprisoned. That offender had also been assaulted by the child's father, who had not been prosecuted. The case, which was headed 'Dad Who Beat Pervert Goes Free' in *The Sun* (15 July) also had headlines in the *Daily Express, Daily Mail, Daily Mirror* and *Daily Star*.

One danger of this kind of sensational reporting is that it could provoke citizens into unlawful acts of retaliation against an offender who has been reported to have been let off lightly. For example, under the headline 'Fury as a Beast is Freed', the *Star* (13 October 1983) described how a child molester, given three years' probation, had locked himself in his flat. The victim's mother had declared that he should be castrated.

REPORTING TO THE POLICE

6.5 The press may make assumptions or promulgate views which influence opinion, but in the last resort it is the ordinary citizen who decides how seriously to treat sexual misconduct. Before any official action is taken on an offence the incident has to come to notice. This may occur by the spontaneous complaint of a victim, by the report of a third party, or by direct observation by the police. Before the incident can be reported it must be perceived as a crime. This is a more important consideration than it seems at first, because the dividing line between permissible and offensive styles of sexual approach is difficult to define. Standards vary with age, sex and social class, and with individual upbringing, sensitivity and experience. What one person considers acceptable another may call a sexual assault, and what one regards as vigorous love-making another may call rape. This allows great scope for misunderstandings between the sexes, especially where there is a gap in age or socio-cultural background.

Children often have only the vaguest conception of the connections between sex and crime. Young victims of sexual molestation by adults often think that as they have been involved in the disapproved behaviour they must not tell their parents. Children are apt to think of sexual teasing or bullying by schoolfellows, either heterosexual or homosexual, as belonging to that part of life that must never be revealed to adults. When such sexual incidents take place within the family, even if unwelcome, they are often deliberately concealed from outsiders through shame and fear of the inevitable repercussions.

6.6 Offences are not necessarily reported when they come to the notice of third parties. Parents whose young children have had contact with a molester may decide not to report it because they wish to avoid the additional trauma of police interrogation. They may connive at the sexual liaisons of their older children either because they do not support the legal condemnation of such conduct, or because they feel that these matters are out of their control. Medical practitioners who come across under-age love affairs through the treatment of venereal infection, or the provision of contraception, do not generally report them to the police. Even when they know or suspect that a child has been the subject of sexual abuse by a parent, they may on occasion prefer to deal with the matter privately, without reporting it to the social services. Since the offence of 'compounding a felony' was abolished in 1967, citizens do not in fact commit a crime by such a failure to report.

Third parties are more likely to bring suspicions to notice if they happen to be in contact with the police for other reasons. This is how fully consensual offences sometimes come to light. In one case, for example, when premises were being searched by the police for stolen property, the landlady told them that one of her tenants frequently entertained youths in his room overnight. Enquiries began and the man was eventually convicted of buggery. In another instance, police looking into a complaint about a barking dog were informed that the complaining neighbour had made his young daughter pregnant. The allegation was eventually proved to be true.

THE PROSECUTION PROCESS

6.7 There are some legal processes for the protection of children from sexual approaches that do not necessarily involve the prosecution of an offender. The power to take children considered to be 'in moral danger' into the care of the local authority has already been mentioned (see para 4.21). Another example is the procedure by which known offenders are kept from working with children. The Department of Education maintains a list of former employees who have been involved in sex offences and who are forbidden to accept any other teaching post. The ban is not always permanent. If representations are made that the offence took place away from work, did not involve a young person, and did not imply any risk to pupils, the individual may be allowed to teach again. Private organisations dealing with young people do not have access to this list and do not have the right to search criminal records (as do employers in government departments), so they sometimes unwittingly recruit persons who already have convictions for offences with children.

When sex offences come to light employers are very ready to order dismissal, and in this they are generally supported by industrial tribunals. For instance, in the case of *Wiseman v Salford City Council* [1981], IRLR 205, concerning a teacher in a college of further education, the Employment Appeal Tribunal upheld the decision to dismiss a lecturer in drama following a conviction for homosexual indecency. It was not suggested that he had shown sexual interest in this students or in other young persons, but the Tribunal concluded that in this controversial area risk could not be excluded and the dismissal was justified.

Some protection from known offenders is achieved by the staff of prison establishments alerting the local authority social services to the impending or possible release to their area of any prisoner guilty of sexual offences against a child. Home Office Circular Instruction No. 45/1978 gives precise directions how and when this is to be done in the case of offences against children and young persons in the home. In practice warnings are often given also about men who have offended with children outside the home.

6.8 The recorded incidence of offences such as indecent exposure is governed by the readiness of members of the public to report them. The recorded incidence of offences such as soliciting by prostitutes, soliciting by homosexual males, and indecent behaviour in public lavatories, is largely determined by local police policy, since witnesses at the scene rarely complain and it is therefore only by taking the initiative themselves that the police are able to observe and prosecute these offences. That is one reason for the extreme local variations in the regional statistics of such cases, which reflects their differing importance in the eyes of different Chief Constables and the differing amounts of time allocated to pursuing them. Some police forces, such as Greater Manchester, have been criticised for wasting resources over these comparative trivia. On the other hand, if the local police become too apathetic, members of the public concerned about scandalous conduct in the vicinity of their homes and children may come to accuse them of neglecting their responsibilities. Comments in the press also provide a stimulus to police action.

6.9 The operation of police discretion does not prevent a substantial number of juveniles under seventeen from being convicted for sex offences, both heterosexual and homosexual. In 1982 in England and Wales, some 600 offenders under 17 were found guilty of indictable sexual offences (Home Office Criminal Statistics, 1982, Table 5.2). In the survey by Walmsley and White (1979, Appendix B), juveniles constituted 19.8 per cent of offenders convicted of indecent assault upon a female, 9.3 per cent of those convicted of incest (presumably betwen siblings), and 10 per cent of those convicted of the homosexual offence of indecent assault on a male. The likelihood of a youngster's sexual conduct leading to prosecution varies from one locality to another, according to police policy and to the extent of consultation between the police and the social services (Mawby, 1979). Some prosecutions arise because sexual irregularities come to the notice of the police in the course of their inquiries into runaways, thefts and misuse of drugs. Those young persons who are selected for prosecution exceptionally, or for apparently arbitrary reasons, may well feel a grievance, but of course some prosecutions, especially of violent juveniles, are absolutely necessary.

6.10 The methods sometimes used by the police for detecting consensual homosexual acts in public places have excited adverse comment. Common techniques include the use of spy holes in public lavatories, the use of plain clothes policemen to attract solicitation, and the trailing of male couples to secluded spots that still count as public places for prosecution purposes (Meldrum and West, 1983). Offenders in these cases often complain of exaggeration in the evidence produced against them by the police. The raiding of men's saunas and occasional raids on private parties by a posse of police looking for evidence of men engaging in sexual acts are particularly calculated to arouse the wrath of gay groups and civil libertarians (*Gay News* No. 259, March 1983, pp. 4, 35).

The use of police decoys in plain clothes to trap homosexuals was criticised in the course of a House of Commons debate on the Police and Criminal Evidence Bill on 14 May 1984. An amendment was proposed, but defeated, to prevent a policeman making an arrest for homosexual indecency in the absence of corroborative evidence from a third party. A Home Office minister explained that in some circumstances only an officer out of uniform can see precisely what is going on. However, he told the House that the Metropolitan police would be given clear advice that officers on plain clothes duty should never act as agents provocateurs.

6.11 On the Continent of Europe some public lavatories have unisex arrangements and women attendants, effectively avoiding both nuisance and the need for police involvement. The individual, closed off cubicles that have been constructed in some London Boroughs are also effective and probably no more costly than frequent resort to the criminal justice system. It could be that some reduction in lavatory nuisances might be achieved if the police here, as in many cities in Europe and America, were prepared to tolerate private membership saunas catering to homosexuals seeking sexual contacts. It has to be realised that homosexuals cannot easily find others similarly inclined in ordinary heterosexual resorts, and that social pressures work against male cohabitation. One reason given by homosexuals for clandestinely frequenting lavatories is that this is the only place where they can find a sexual partner, either because there are no 'gay' bars in their area or because they are too young or too poor or too afraid of local gossip to make use of them.

6.12 It has been rightly said that the police are the gatekeepers of the criminal justice system. They not only decide what crimes are worth looking out for, they also decide when information brought to them warrants the assumption that a crime worth investigating has occurred. At a later stage, the police, guided by their legal advisors in prosecuting solicitors' departments, decide whether to prosecute and on what charges, whether connected offences are charged separately or allowed to be 'taken into consideration', and what selection of evidence (including information on the offender's antecedents and character provided before sentencing) to put before the court. In most other countries (including Scotland), some or all of these functions are performed by independent officials, such as investigating magistrates or Procurators Fiscal. Some time ago the all-party lawyers' group *Justice* (1970), and more recently the Royal Commission on Criminal Procedure (1981), put forward proposals for a modification of the considerable powers of discretion as to prosecution presently exercised by the police in England and the government has now accepted these proposals, issued a White Paper and promised legislation (Home Office Law Officers' Dept 1983). As regards sex offences however, it could be that allowing the investigating police officers considerable discretion about which cases should be taken seriously actually results in fewer prosecutions than would otherwise be the case. It remains to be seen what effect the introduction into England of the proposed new independent prosecution agency will have.

6.13 A crime complaint brought to the police should be logged in a 'crime book', but if the allegations are frivolous or patently false this may not be done. Complaints recorded by the police initially are not necessarily counted as crimes in the end. Police are often thought to be unduly suspicious of women's complaints of sexual assault. In the rape survey conducted by Wright (1980), about one in four of the recorded complaints to the police were finally classed as 'no crime'. This seems a large proportion, but some women and girls may well lay false charges out of malice, fear of pregnancy or to preserve their reputation in the face of a suspicious parent, husband or fiancée. One police surgeon (Stewart, 1981) claimed that sixteen out of eighteen rape complainants he examined for the Royal Ulster Constabulary had made false allegations. In Scotland, another police surgeon (MacLean, 1979) conducted a more careful prospective study of all cases of alleged rape investigated over a five year period. He concluded that 29 per cent of cases were definitely false accusations, and a further 18 per cent probably false. Common reasons for false allegations were teenagers making excuses for coming home late, women trying to cover up extra-marital relations, and prostitutes angered by a client's failure to pay. On the other hand, complainants quite often withdrew their evidence not because their allegations were unwarranted, but because they began to feel anxious at the prospect of appearing in court and answering embarrassing or searching questions. The police have a more difficult task than is commonly realised in trying to sort out these complications.

6.14 In the face of criticism about the treatment of alleged victims of sex offences, police procedures are coming under scrutiny and some forces are reforming their practices, for instance by having female complainants seen by a woman officer or allowing a relative or friend to be present during questioning.

The police task is made even more difficult if the witness becomes reluctant or evasive as the interrogator probes for corroborative evidence and tries to explore the events leading up to the incident. Inevitably the temptation arises to treat the witness like a suspect. The task calls for officers of special experience, but especially in remote areas there may be none available.

6.15 Doctors also have problems in examining and assessing victims of sexual assault. A questionnaire distributed to an annual conference of British police surgeons in 1977 revealed that of the 1,379 women complaining of rape whom the respondents said they had examined during the past year, 31 per cent were thought to have been laying false complaints. The most interesting finding, however, was that the most experienced physicians, the ones who had seen the most cases, were less sceptical. They thought that the proportion of false complaints was significantly lower, only 24 per cent (Geis *et al*, 1978). This suggests that, given more information and education on the topic of sexual assault, doctors as well as police officers might become more circumspect and more discerning in their judgements.

6.16 The police have an important discretionary power to issue a formal caution to an offender instead of taking him before the court. According to evidence put to the Royal Commission on Criminal Procedure (1979) police often caution the offender where the victim has in some way collaborated in the offence, the commonest example being unlawful intercourse or indecent assault involving a willing but under-age girl. 'Other examples of 'willing victims' are chidren who encourage minor sexual assaults by adults, perhaps for sweets or small financial gain, and in doing so come to no serious harm . . .' (*op cit*, para 49).

Other factors taken into account in deciding to caution an offender include the agreement of the victim or aggrieved party, the absence of any record of similar previous offences, the general good character of the offender, his age (very young or very old), and any special circumstances (such as mental disturbance) that might make prosecution particularly distressing.

6.17 Cases of alleged or suspected sexual contacts between children and parents or other adults in the immediate family circle present the police with particular problems. They are nowadays frequently asked to participate in case conferences called by social workers to assess reports about families and to decide whether one or more of the chidren should be placed on the official register of children 'at risk' of abuse, or whether some other action needs to be taken. The police involvement in these considerations can be fraught with difficulties, for it is they who have the final responsibility for assessing the evidence with a view to prosecution, whereas some of the other participants may be anxious to avoid that outcome, and hence reluctant to reveal the full reasons for their suspicions. In some areas, however, collaboration between police and other agencies has developed to the satisfaction of most agencies involved.

The processes of confidential consultation between police and other agencies in Devon and Cornwall are well developed and have been described by Detective Chief Superintendent Bissett (1982). His force has produced a multi-disciplinary handbook which sets out 'the police guidelines issued by the nine main agencies to the thirty departments likely to be involved' with cases of intra-familial child sex abuse. He emphasises that case conferences which include a police representative do not necessarily result in prosecution. He quotes examples showing that offenders whose behaviour and circumstances have been brought under effective control can sometimes be dealt with by caution rather than prosecution. In his experience it is possible, in the interests of the child and the family as a whole, for the agencies concerned to share freely and fully the information they possess in order to arrive at the best course of action. However, research in other areas suggests that this degree of trust between social workers, general practitioners, teachers and police is difficult to achieve (Cooper, 1984).

6.18 Although not precluded by the law, cautions are rarely, if ever, given for grave offences. Even so, in England and Wales in 1982 over a quarter of the males suspected of indictable sexual offences were dealt with by way of a caution. Over half of those cautioned (1353 out of 2634) were juveniles, and only 542 were over twenty-one. Apart from unlawful sexual intercourse with a girl under sixteen and 'indecent assault on a female' (the latter probably largely consisting of consensual acts with girls under sixteen) most of the cautions of adult males (232) were for homosexual offences of buggery, indecent assault on a male, indecency between males and male soliciting. A relatively small extension by the police of their cautioning practice could effect a significant reduction in the number sentenced for sex offences.

6.19 Certain offences can only be prosecuted with the consent of the Director of Public Prosecutions. This applies to incest (Sexual Offences Act, 1956, s.37(2)) and also to the homosexual offences of buggery or indecency between males where one of the participants is under twenty-one (Sexual Offences Act, 1967, s. 8). These provisions give some statutory recognition to the desirability, at least sometimes, of shielding young persons involved in illicit sex from the rigours of the criminal justice system. Referring to homosexual offences in his written evidence to the Royal Commission on Criminal Procedure (1978, para 147) the Director of Public Prosecutions commented that the consideration of these cases occupied a sizeable part of his Department's work. 'In 1977 nearly 650 cases involving these two offences were referred to me. In that year the total number of applications for my consent under all statutory provisions was 1,671.'

The policy of the Director of Public Prosecutions about specific situations is not open to public debate. In regard to homosexual offences, according to a citation by Crane (1982, p. 66), the Director of Public Prosecutions, in unpublished evidence to the Royal Commission on Criminal Procedure, explained that he would take into account the relative age of both offender and victim. For instance, he would not normally prosecute a man of twenty-two for a homosexual offence with another of nineteen if there was full consent and no element of corruption. In certain circumstances, however, if, for example, the younger man was a male prostitute and the elder had gone to a public lavatory looking for sex, he might decide to prosecute them both.

6.20 The Attorney General has issued guidelines for the police about appropriate considerations in their decisions to prosecute (*The Times*,

15 February, 1983). These are similar to those which govern the Director of Public Prosecution's decisions. In addition to the key considerations of gravity of the offence and sufficiency of evidence to convict, they include factors such as staleness of the offence, mental or physical infirmity of the offender, and the attitude of the complainant. In addition, the likelihood of a very trivial penalty or the probability of an unusually long and expensive trial for a not very grave offence are mentioned as factors favouring non-prosecution. With young offenders, the damage to their future prospects through the stigma of a conviction favours a caution rather than a prosecution. In the case of sex offences where the girl or youth has been a willing party, the relative ages of the parties and whether there was an element of seduction or corruption are taken into account.

6.21 In incest cases, where the accusation is made by a child who could be suspected of malice, corroboration might be thought essential but is very difficult to secure. In practice a high proportion of defendants plead guilty – almost nine out of ten (Manchester, 1978). The considerations of 'public interest' which guide the Director of Public Prosecutions in prosecuting incest cases are confidential, but presumably, as in other offences, he takes into account such matters as the age of the victim, the staleness of the case, whether the acts were fully consensual and the likely consequences of prosecution upon the victim. The decisions sometimes seem harsh. Manchester (*op cit*) quotes an example of a prosecution for brother-sister incest where the participants were fifty-six and forty-five respectively. Because the number of incest offences known (or cleared up) in the criminal statistics greatly exceeds the number of persons prosecuted, some writers (eg Bailey and McCabe, 1979; Hall-Williams, 1974) have assumed that many known offenders are not prosecuted. In reality the numerical discrepancy is largely due to some offenders being prosecuted for more than one offence. On Home Office figures over four-fifths of known male incest offenders are prosecuted and about 90 per cent are either prosecuted or cautioned. This estimate cannot take into account discretion exercised at a lower level, for instance when police decide that the evidence is insufficient to establish that the offence has occurred, or where they interpret the reported incidents as indecent assaults rather than incest.

6.22 Sometimes it is easier to establish or to secure a confession that an indecent assault by a father upon his daughter has occurred than to prove the crime of incest, which requires an act of intercourse or attempted intercourse. Cases charged as indecent assault on a young female do not have to be referred to the Director of Public Prosecutions. Evidently technical considerations not directly relevant to the seriousness of the crime govern to a great extent the cases seen by the courts, but those who are prosecuted and convicted are liable to be punished severely. Of 92 males sentenced for incest at the Crown Court in England and Wales in 1982, as many as 70 received immediate imprisonment. Only 9 were put on probabion. This was a higher rate of imprisonment than was imposed that year on men sentenced for 'wounding or other acts endangering life' (Home Office, 1983, Table S 2.1 (A)). Where the offender's co-operation in some form of treatment seems indicated, this can be made a requirement of probation, but that seems to happen infrequently in incest cases (see para 6.40).

THE TRIAL PROCESS

6.23 Discussion of personal sexual matters can be particularly painful when it has to take place in the public arena of the courtroom. The evidence and argumentation necessary to establish the details of alleged acts and motivations touch upon what many people regard as their most private concerns. The public exposure of sexual preferences, inclinations and fantasies can produce extremely emotional reactions of guilt, humiliation and embarrassment to the person under scrutiny, and arouse strongly prejudicial responses of disgust or anxiety among some of those compelled to listen, including victims, investigators, lawyers, witnesses, jurors and judges. The resulting tensions enhance all the worries and fears associated with trials for crime.

6.24 Defendants in sex trials are often without the support of a family, either because they were already isolated, or because relatives feel contaminated by the great disgust which sex offending arouses and so wish to distance themselves from the situation. Sometimes they have good reason to do so, for the families of exposed sex offenders can find themselves the victims of hostile anonymous letters and telephone calls and cut off from neighbours who had previously been their friends.

6.25 Since the Bail Act 1976 came into force police have less often taken the initiative in considering whether and on what grounds to make objections to the granting of bail. In sex cases, however, more than in other types of crime that carry similar maximum penalties, police do still frequently use various provisions of the Act to oppose bail. The popular presumption that sexual misbehaviour results from uncontrollable drives and desires leads to concern about the likelihood of further offences and thus to objections under Paragraph 2(b) of Schedule 1. Because the ordeal of a sex trial is so great, and because many sex offenders have no family support and no accommodation, the risk of absconding also justifies objections under Paragraph 2(a) of Schedule 1.

Bail may also be refused under Paragraph 3, that is for the defendant's own protection, on the grounds that if he were not in custody he would be liable to become the victim of assaults.

6.26 A surprisingly high proportion of defendants in sex trials plead guilty. The wish to get the dreadful business over as quickly as possible with the least publicity is a powerful factor both in promoting guilty pleas and in influencing consent to a summary rather than a jury trial. It is commonly believed that a lesser sentence is likely if the offender pleads guilty in order to relieve the victim of the embarrassment of giving evidence in court. This puts considerable pressure not only upon the defendant but also upon the lawyers representing him. For this reason, and also because of a natural disinclination to have to challenge alleged victims about nauseating details, lawyers may be less than enthusiastic about pursuing even a strong defence.

6.27 Like everyone else, prosecutors may find if difficult to maintain impartiality in the face of conduct that seems peculiarly revolting. Understandably, they sometimes fail to avoid the use of what Archbold (41st edn, para 4.177) refers to as 'unnecessarily emotive language which on any view can only excite sympathy for the victim or prejudice against the accused or both (eg where sexual offences . . . are alleged to have been committed in highly aggravated circumstances)'. Even judges are not immune. For example in a rape and buggery trial of three juveniles aged 14, 15 and 16, who had been involved with a 14-year-old girl, the prosecuting counsel referred to the alleged conduct in such terms as 'beneath that of animals'. The judge said he was so upset he would adjourn for an hour to regain his equilibrium before passing sentence. In imposing sentences of 6, 8 and 10 years' detention respectively, the judge attributed the whole incident to the availability of pornography. A copy of a mildly pornographic 'girlie' magazine had been found in the bedroom of the 16-year-old offender. What made these events particularly horrific was that 3 adults came upon the scene and a further act of intercourse occurred. When, later, two of these adults were arrested and charged they could not be persuaded to plead guilty and spare the young girl the necessity to give oral evidence. As a result they were punished less severely than the boys who had pleaded guilty. They were allowed to plead guilty to the lesser charge of indecent assault for which the maximum sentence is two years.

6.28 Many more actual instances of the unfortunate consequences of the pressures experienced at sex trials might be given, but two must suffice. A middle-aged, lonely man of good character, who had been in the same job as a night watchman for 20 years, was accused by some schoolboys (one of whom had been buggered by his elder brother) of buggery and indecent assault. He was proceeded against for the latter offence and virtually insisted on consent to summary trial, because he felt such unbearable embarrassment and humiliation. His solicitor finally persuaded him against this course. At the committal stage one set of allegations was dismissed and at the jury trial the schooboys' evidence was not accepted and he was acquitted. Had he been left to follow his first impulse – one shared by many similarly placed defendants – he might well have been convicted.

In another case a young man of previous good character who was in regular employment was accused of an act of indecency in a public lavatory and of assaulting the two police officers who arrested him. He maintained his innocence throughout. The police officers had minimal injuries, but there was medical evidence of a violent assault upon the defendant. He gave a clear account of what took place and denied indecency or that any persons other than the police were present. The prosecution brought no witnesses other than the arresting officers. The prosecuting counsel offered to accept a plea of guilty to assault and not guilty to indecency. Terrified of the prospect of a sex trial, and against the advice of his counsel, he accepted the 'bargain' and was duly convicted of an offence that would otherwise have been very difficult to prove.

SENTENCING STATISTICS

6.29 It is a matter of opinion whether the courts deal too harshly or too leniently with sex offenders, but certainly they are discriminating. Despite the considerable and wholly understandable public concern about sex crime, the courts recognise that many sex offenders are guilty of no more than comparitively minor offences. Sentencing practice reflects this reality. The courts readily award long sentences when this seems merited, but in fact most sex cases are not of this order at all. On the odd few occasions when seemingly serious offences have not attracted a substantial sentence, a great deal of unfavourable publicity has followed. Nevertheless, sex offences tend to attract more severe sentences than do most other identifiable offences. For example, in 1982 little more than a third of the persons sentenced at Crown Courts for offences of violence against the person were given immediate imprisonment, compared with over a half of those sentenced for sex offences (Home Office, 1983, Table s 2.1 (a)). Then again, although sex offenders constitute less than 2 per cent of persons found guilty of indictable crimes (other than traffic offences) they comprise 4 per cent of men serving sentences of imprisonment and a substantially higher proportion of men serving life sentences. A Home Office survey of men under life imprisonment revealed that one in six were serving their sentence for an offence committed against a woman or child under sexual circumstances. Among those who had been detained for periods of more than fifteen years more than half had committed such offences (Smith, 1979, Tables 15,23).

6.30 In 1982, just over 6,600 persons were sentenced after being convicted of an indictable sexual offence. Half of them were dealt with by means of a fine or a conditional or absolute discharge and almost one-sixth by means of a probation or supervision order. By contrast only 22 per cent considered to have committed a serious enough offence to require a sentence which involved their immediate custodial detention. Table 6.30 gives the full figures.

Table 6.30

PERSONS SENTENCED IN 1982 FOR INDICTABLE SEXUAL OFFENCES – BY SENTENCE

Sentence	*No sentenced*	*% age*	
FINE	2578	39.0	
DISCHARGE	740	11.2	
PROBATION (Including supervision)	1023	15.5	
ATTENDANCE CENTRE	61	0.9	
COMMUNITY SERVICE	61	0.9	
CARE	51	0.8	
HOSPITAL ORDER (S. 60 of Mental Health Act 1959)	21	0.3	
RESTRICTION ORDER (S. 65 of Mental Health Act 1959)	9	0.1	22.0 Custodial Sentences
DETENTION UNDER SECTION 53(2) of Children and Young Persons Act 1933	15	0.2	
DETENTION CENTRE	63	1.0	
BORSTAL TRAINING (Including recall)	80	1.2	
IMPRISONMENT	1282	19.4	
SUSPENDED SENTENCE (Including partially suspended sentences)	603	9.1	
Otherwise dealt with	28	0.4	
	6615	100	

6.31 Indecent exposure, as a summary offence, has not been included in Table 6.30 but of the 1,573 persons who were sentenced in 1982 after being found guilty of this offence only 3 per cent received custodial sentences and 4 per cent suspended sentences. Two-thirds of them (65 per cent) were fined or discharged, and just under a quarter (24 per cent) were placed on probation. The maximum penalty is six months' imprisonment, but only one of the 52 persons imprisoned received a sentence in excess of three months.

6.32 To summarise, just over one in five indictable sexual offenders received a custodial sentence in 1982. This is the overall figure for offences ranging from the trivial to the serious; for a clearer picture, the sentences passed for each of the main offence categories must be considered in turn.

Indecent assault on a female

6.33 One-third of those sentenced in 1982 (2,261) had been found guilty of an indecent assault on a female. Most such offences are comparatively trivial, and 61 per cent of offenders were fined, discharged or placed on probation or supervision; but 21 per cent of those sentenced were adjudged to have done something serious enough to require an immediate custodial sentence and a further 12 per cent were given suspended sentences. The maximum penalty available to the courts is 2 years' imprisonment, but 5 years if the female concerned is under 13. Of the 411 persons sent to prison for this offence in 1982, 38 received sentences in excess of 2 years. The Home Office study of sexual offences (Walmsley and White, 1979 and 1980) found that custodial sentences were more often imposed where the victim was a girl aged under 13 or where the offender was aged 30 to 49. Offences committed on girls under 13 had a custodial rate of 15 per cent in the year studied (1973), and offences by men aged 30 to 49 a rate of 20 per cent; where the two factors were combined and a man aged 30 to 49 assaulted a girl under 13 the custodial rate was 24 per cent. But if the victim was 13 or over or the offender was a young man aged 17 to 29 or a man over 50, no more than 10 per cent of the convictions resulted in a custodial sentence; and where a man of 50 or over assaulted a girl of 13 or over the custodial rate was only 3 per cent.

Indecency between males and importuning (soliciting)

6.34 Almost three in ten of those sentenced in 1982 (1,930) were men who had either committed an indecency offence (usually in a public lavatory) or else had been soliciting for homosexual purposes. Less than two per cent of these men received an immediate custodial sentence; 96 per cent were fined, discharged or placed on probation; under 2 per cent were given suspended sentences. Although the maximum penalty available to the courts is 2 years' imprisonment, and 5 years if the offence of indecency is committed by a male over 21 with a male under 21, in practice it is rare for a sentence of over 6 months to be imposed in the former case, or one over 3 years in the latter. Eleven sentences in excess of 6 months were imposed in 1982, but none in excess of 3 years.

Indecent assault on a male

6.35 In 1982, some 620 persons were sentenced for the offence of indecent assault on a male. These cases nearly all concerned activities, consensual or otherwise, with boys under 16. Again, most (62 per cent) were dealt with by fine, discharge or probation, but 20 per cent led to an immediate custodial sentence, and 14 per cent were given suspended sentences. The maximum penalty is 10 years' imprisonment, but of the 116 persons sent to prison in 1982 only 24 received sentences in excess of 2 years. The Home Office study found a similar sentencing pattern for assaults on males as for assaults on females. Offenders of 30 to 49 involved with males under 14 had a custodial rate of 30 per cent; at the other extreme, offenders of 50 or over involved with males of 14 or over had a custodial rate of only 5 per cent.

Unlawful sexual intercourse with a girl under 16

6.36 Just over 400 offenders were sentenced in 1982 for unlawful sexual intercourse with a girl under 16. This offence involves consensual intercourse with a girl of 13, 14 or 15 (there is a separate offence of intercourse with a girl under 13). 61 per cent were fined, discharged or placed on probation, 20 per cent received an immediate custodial sentence and 12 per cent were given a suspended sentence. The maximum penalty for this offence is 2 years' imprisonment; in 1982 of the 75 sent to prison only 27 received sentences in excess of six months. The Home Office study indicated that the older the offender and the younger the girl, the greater the chance of a custodial sentence being imposed. Young men of 17 to 29 whose offence was with a girl of 15 had a 10 per cent custodial rate, whereas males aged 30 or over whose offence was with a girl aged 13 has a custodial rate of 47 per cent.

Rape

6.37 Just over 400 persons were sentenced in 1982 for an offence of rape or attempted rape; that is less than 5 per cent of all persons sentenced following an indictable sexual offence. Sentencing practice reveals this to be regarded as about the most serious sexual offence of all (equal only to incest with a daughter under 13 or buggery with a boy under 14). Although these figures include a small number convicted of the much less serious offence of unlawful intercourse with a mental defective or a mental patient, 94 per cent of those sentenced received an immediate custodial penalty. 3 per cent received a suspended sentence and only 2 per cent were fined or placed on probation. Of the 309 men sent to prison all but 47 received sentences in excess of 2 years and 80 received sentences of longer than 5 years. The Home Office Research Study indicated that the custodial rate for rape and attempted rape is about the same, but that the average length of sentence for the full offence (maximum penalty: life imprisonment) is some 2 years longer than for the attempt (maximum penalty: 7 years).

Gross indecency with a child

6.38 Some 230 persons were sentenced for offences of gross indecency with a child under the age of 14. The behaviour typically involves the encouragement of a child to behave indecently towards the offender, for example by touching him in such a way as would have constituted an indecent assault if the older person had behaved in such a way to the child. 62 per cent were fined, discharged or placed on probation, 18 per cent received an immediate custodial sentence, and 16 per cent were given a suspended sentence. The maximum penalty for this offence is 2 years' imprisonment; in 1982, of the 39 sentenced to imprisonment, 13 received over six months.

Buggery (including bestiality)

6.39 In 1982 just over 200 persons were sentenced for offences of buggery or attempted buggery. The offence carries various maximum penalties according to circumstances. Consensual buggery between males over 21, but not in private, carries a maximum of two years' imprisonment, consensual buggery with a young man under 21 carries a maximum of five years, non-consensual buggery with a male over 16 a maximum of 10 years, and buggery (whether consensual or not) with a boy under the age of 16, or with any woman (including one's consenting wife), carries a maximum of life imprisonment, as does bestiality. The varying levels of seriousness indicated by the variety of maxima are reflected in normal sentencing practice. In 1973, the year studied by Walmsley and White (1979) only four men were convicted of bestiality and none were sent to prison. Neither did consensual buggery between adult males result in a custodial penalty. Consensual buggery with under-age males of 14 to 20 led to a custodial sentence in just over half the cases; buggery with a boy under 14 and a non-consensual buggery with an adult (akin to rape) led to custodial sentence for at least four out of every five convicted offenders. Twenty-two males were convicted of buggery with a female; twelve of them received custodial sentences, mainly those whose behaviour had been non-consensual or with young girls. In all, of the 209 persons sentenced in 1982 for offences of buggery 59 per cent received an immediate custodial sentence and only 21 per cent were fined, discharged or placed on probation; 17 per cent received suspended sentences. Of the 121 sent to prison, 69 received sentences in excess of 2 years, of which 15 were in excess of 5 years.

Incest

6.40 The maximum penalty is the same for all forms of incest: 7 years (or life imprisonment if with a girl under 13). One hundred persons were sentenced for this offence in 1982, mostly for incest by a father with a young daughter, a crime regarded very seriously by the courts. Of all incest offenders sentenced in 1982, 9 per cent were given a suspended custodial sentence and only one sixth (17 per cent) were fined, discharged or placed on probation. Almost three quarters (73 per cent) received an immediate custodial sentence. Of the 71 sent to prison, 28 received a sentence in excess of 2 years, but only one received more than 5 years. In practice the courts treat more leniently the small number of cases of incest between siblings that come before them, even though the young offenders concerned are more likely to have a criminal record than are the older men who have been involved with their daughters. The Home Office study (Walmsley and White, 1979) revealed that in the year under survey, 1973, three-quarters of the fathers found guilty of incest with their daughters were given custodial sentences compared with only one-fifth of the brothers (aged over 17 and sentenced in adult courts) who were found guilty of incest with their sisters.

Unlawful sexual intercourse with a girl under 13

6.41 Some 70 persons were sentenced for offences of unlawful sexual intercourse with a girl under 13. The charge implies that the girl may have consented, but naturally enough the courts are sceptical about the consent of a girl of such tender years being fully valid. On occasion incidents amounting to rape are dealt with as unlawful intercourse to avoid the need to prove non-consent. These offences are therefore regarded as serious and 42 per cent of persons convicted received an immediate custodial sentence; a further 18 per cent were given a suspended sentence. Only 32 per cent were fined, discharged or placed on probation. The maximum penalty is life imprisonment. Of the 27 sent to prison, 16 received a sentence in excess of 2 years, of whom 2 received sentences of over 5 years.

The Home Office study again showed that the sentences depended on the age of the victim and offender. Offences by adult males under 25 had a custodial rate of 36 per cent, but offences by males over 25 or over with girl under 12 had a custodial rate of 80 per cent.

Procuration, abduction and bigamy

6.42 The other three offences, shown in the Criminal Statistics as sexual offences but not specifically covered by this report, are procuration, abduction and bigamy. In 1982, the numbers sentenced for these offences were 330, 17 and 22 respectively. Almost a quarter (24 per cent) of those sentenced for procuration received a custodial penalty and 11 of the 77 who were sent to prison received more than 2 years. Five offenders were sent to prison for abduction offences and three for bigamy; two of the former received more than 2 years but no bigamist received more than 6 months.

6.43 The statistics so far cited include a few female offenders. Of the 6,615 (indictable) sexual offenders sentenced in 1982, 61 (under 1 per cent) were females. Of these, 24 were sentenced for offences of procuration or bigamy, which we are not considering; five of these received custodial penalties (none of them exceeding 2 years). Of the 37 others, 15 were sentenced for indecent assault on a male, and 10 for indecent assault on a female; five of these received custodial sentences, one of them for more than 2 years. Only one of the remaining 12 female offenders received a custodial sentence: for aiding and abetting an offence of buggery a woman received over 6 months but not more than 1 year. (The Criminal Statistics do not show the terms of imprisonment more precisely).

Conclusion

6.44 Tables summarising the preceding information on sentences appear in Appendix II, but before concluding this section, some brief comments seem appropriate. It will become clear that the percentage of convicted persons given custodial sentences is a useful measure of the perceived seriousness of an offence. The 1982 figures are mostly typical of recent years, although there was a spectacular rise in the custodial rate for indecent assault on a female (from 19 per cent to 25 per cent). Indeed, since the beginning of the 1970s, there has been little systematic change in the custodial rates for the various sexual offences, although there have been fluctuations from year to year in some categories. The custodial rates for the indecent assault offences have been increasing slightly, as the numbers of such offences recorded have diminished, perhaps because of some of the most trivial offences are no longer reported. There has also been an increase in the custodial rate for rape, which has coincided with the greater publicity for the offence since the mid 70s. In 1978, something of a peak year for the imposition of custodial penalties for almost all sexual offences, 95 per cent of adults (persons of 17 or over) convicted of rape received an immediate custodial sentence. The figure in 1982 was over 94 per cent.

SENTENCING POLICY

6.45 Considered simply as a tariff of punishment, the range and severity of sentences, and the differing scales applied to different crimes, are largely matters of tradition. The quantum of punishment considered to be 'deserved' by a particular crime is a subjective value judgement. Some readers, having looked at the figures given in the preceding paragraphs, will think the current tariff too harsh, too lenient, or too biased in favour of or against particular offences; but there are no objective criteria against which one can decide who is right.

6.46 A less fashionable theory of sentencing looks at the process from a utilitarian point of view rather than simply as retributive justice. It regards the court decision as an opportunity for intervening to help the offender to avoid re-offending. How far this is practicable depends on the evaluation of various ways of 'treating' offenders, which is the topic of the next chapter. Suffice it to note at this point that probation orders, or without requriements as to residence or for submission to some nal scheme of treatment, offer an alternative to a straightforward iff punishment. The offender is brought into contact with a supervisor ıd counsellor, and sometimes with more specialised helping services, which has the chance to make use of in an effort to change his ways. If the procedure could be made into an effective instrument for reducing offences, it could be argued on both practical and humanitarian grounds that it should be used as often as possible in place of imprisonment, especially for non-violent offenders.

6.47 However, the more extensive use of probation for sex offenders, might not meet with public approval. In June 1983 a man with many convictions for sex offences with boys was placed on probation so that he could receive voluntary hormone treatment which, according to medical evidence, would reduce his sexual urges and bring his behaviour back under control. One Member of Parliament was reported to have called the decision unbelievable, the kind which would encourage a lynch law. The outcry in the press was such that the judge felt impelled to take the unusual step of making a public explanation. The man the newspapers called a 'sex monster' was, according to reports to the court, a pathetically inadequate immature personality with a history of epilepsy and suicidal tendencies. The only alternative would have been imprisonment for many years under the restrictive conditions necessary for his protection from other prisoners (*The Times*, 22nd June, 1983). Later in the year, while the *Express* was running headlines reporting protests against a judge who had just given a man convicted of rape a suspended sentence of imprisonment, *The Times* (3rd Dec 1983) was reporting the decision of a judge in South Carolina who gave three men convicted of rape a choice between castration and 5 years on probation, or 30 years in jail.

6.48 An offender whose persistent misbehaviour is sufficiently prolonged and serious (assessed by the number and recency of convictions and the amount of imprisonment previously imposed) may be given an extended sentence. Such sentences may exceed the normal tariff or the statutory maximum for the current offence, but may not exceed ten years if the maximum is less than ten years, or exceed five years if the maximum is less than that. The extended sentence provision may be applied when 'the court is satisfied, by reason of his previous conduct and the likelihood of his committing further offences, that it is expedient to protect the public from him for a substantial time' (Powers of the Criminal Courts Act 1973, s. 28). Prisoners given extended sentences, if released on parole, are subject to the conditions of their parole licence for the full length of the sentence instead of only to the two-thirds point, as is ordinarily the case. The sentence thus provides both longer incarceration and longer supervision on release.

The extended sentence provision is not needed for the most serious offenders of all, who can be given life sentences, but it can be used to protect the public from less serious but more often repeated offences of, for example, child molestation.

6.49 One of the purposes for which life sentences are not uncommonly imposed is to protect the public from dangerous offenders who will probably commit grave offences in the future unless their attitude or mental state changes. Responsibility for deciding the moment of release is thereby transferred to the Parole Board and the Home Office, who have the benefit of contemporary reports on the prisoner's condition (Thomas, 1979, p. 302). The Court of Appeal has held that a life sentence was correctly imposed on evidence that an offender was subject to abnormal sexual drives or fantasies (*Chaplin*, 1976, *Criminal*

Law Review 320). Life sentences also provide some protection when signs of impending relapse occur. Release is on a licence of indefinite duration, which means that the offender can be recalled to prison at any time.

In so far as the supposed dangerousness of an offender reflects some mental abnormality, it might be thought more appropriate to commit him to a special (ie high security) hospital, than to impose indeterminate custody in an ordinary prison. However, as mentioned later (see para 7.56) there are serious impediments to the use of the hospital order system for sex offenders. The abnormality may not amount to a mental disorder within the meaning of the Mental Health Acts, and even if it does it may not be possible to find a hospital able and willing to accept the offender patient. The Mental Health Act 1983 makes treatability a criterion for the suffering from psychopathic disorder, and the treatability of sex offenders diagnosed as psychopaths is often open to dispute. For all these reasons many of the abnormal sex offenders who quality by virtue of the nature of their crime to receive a life sentence will continue to be thus dealt with. Moreover, dangerous sex offending is not necessarily indicative of mental abnormality, still less of treatability, so life sentences will continue to be required for the purposes of tariff justice.

6.50 The present system of life sentences and extended sentences – the latter being in practice used very rarely – is not adequate, in the opinion of some authorities, to protect the public from potentially dangerous offenders. Moreover, the present system, with its considerable and unexplained variations in punishments, allows a semi-covert and poorly controlled element of protective sentencing to be incorporated into judges' decisions. For these and other reasons, a Howard League Working Party on *Dangerous and Criminal Justice* (Floud and Young, 1981), came to the conclusion that the need for protection from identifiably dangerous offenders should be recognised in law and brought under proper statutory control. Rather than have to resort to discretionary life sentences, judges should have the power to pronounce a 'protective' sentence on grounds of dangerousness, relying on evidence given in open court in specifying the types of 'dangerous' conduct that might render an offender eligible for a protective sentence, but serious sexual assaults were singled out as an important category. The offender's rights were to be guarded by means of a review at regular intervals by a quasi-judicial tribunal who could recommend release if protective custody seemed no longer necessary.

6.51 The protective sentences for dangerous offenders envisaged by the Floud Committee proposals concern offenders sent to prison rather than to psychiatric institutions, although pyschiatric evidence would be called to validate the assessment of dangerousness in the case of sex offenders. In North America, statutes specifically directed towards the control of dangerous sex offenders used to operate in most states for the purpose of securing commitment for an indefinite period to a closed state mental hospital on grounds of 'psychopathy' – on the assumption that serious or persistent sexual misconduct was itself evidence of abnormality. In Canada, however the 'dangerous sex offender' label resulted in indefinite detention in a penitentiary (Greenland, 1977; 1984). In either event, decision to release was long delayed and was made particularly difficult for parole boards or for psychiatrists by the need to make out a case that the sex offender was no longer a danger to the public. Such a proposition is difficult to sustain when a man who is dangerous only to women or children has been segregated from them for years and there is no way to predict how he will react on coming into contact with them again.

6.52 Most of the American sexual psychopath laws have been repealed under pressure from the civil rights movement. Libertarians condemn indefinite incarceration beyond the point required by tariff justice and are critical of the validity of the notion of 'sexual psychopathy' and of the efficacy or even the existence of treatments for the condition in state mental hospitals. The passing of laws, in the absence of resources to implement them properly, was perhaps the basic fault. The American experience suggests that if long incarceration is necessary for the protection of the community, it is probably better to face the fact squarely and make open legal provision for it, as proposed by the Floud Report, than to introduce it under the guise of a pseudo-treatment scheme that has little function other than to delay release and that may unfairly discredit more active and useful psychiatric programmes.

6.53 In England, the parole system has a considerable influence on the length of time sentenced prisoners remain in custody. The influence has become more important as the percentage of eligible prisoners granted parole has increased. All prisoners on fixed sentences are now eligible to be released on licence after 6 months, or after serving a third of their sentence, if they have been given more than 18 months. The local review committees attached to each prison screen all prisoners as they become eligible and are empowered (subject to the Home Secretary's veto) to recommend parole for prisoners sentenced to less than four years, provided they have not been sentenced for certain specified offences. Recommendations for the release of persons for offences involving sex, drugs, personal violence or arson, have to be referred for the consideration of the national Parole Board, along with the long sentence cases.

The local review committees recommend for release about half of the cases, but it is not possible to determine from the figures published in the annual reports of the Parole Board whether the percentage of sex offenders receiving a favourable recommendation by the review committees is smaller than for other types of offender. It is clear, however, that serious sex offenders serving long sentences are rarely recommended for release as soon as they become eligible, that is at their first review.

Among cases referred to the Board, sex offenders are less likely than others to be released at first review. Of the 551 heterosexual offenders who were referred to the Board in 1983 for a first review, 50.6 per cent were recommended for release by the Board, compared with 56.2 per cent of positive recommendations for all first review prisoners, whatever their offence. Of the 111 homosexual offenders referred for first review, only 47.7 per cent were recommended for release. Under the new procedures instituted by the Home Secretary in 1984, parole will be granted less often than previously to those serving long sentences for sex offences.

6.54 Risk to the public is the most important criterion that militates against release on parole. Sex offences against children under thirteen are considered particularly serious as well as being liable to repetition. If medical treatment is recommended (especially treatment for the problems of out-of-control drinking that feature in the histories of many sex offenders) this favours release so that the programme of treatment will have the backing of the supervision that is a condition of the parole licence. In general, however, the parole system adopts a protectionist policy with sex offenders which, combined with the protectionist element in sentencing, accounts for the high proportion of sex offences among men who spend very long periods in prison on either determinate or life sentences. It has long been argued that the refusal of parole to men who have already been given long sentences because of the nature of their offence amounts to a kind of second sentence. Furthermore, the longer a determinate sentence prisoner is kept in prison the shorter the period of compulsory supervision on parole. The release of sex offenders with a minimal period of supervision, or none at all if parole is never granted, is an inevitable consequence of a conservative discharge policy.

The Parole Board would like to release sex offenders as early as possible, but they are hampered by lack of treatment facilities for these cases, which are needed both for their intrinsic worth and to assure the public that something positive is being done. They are also restricted by present Home Office policy. Their function is that of an advisory body to the Home Secretary, and the new restrictive discharge policies for more serious offenders are not necessarily their responsibility, since their recommendations can be overturned and have been more often of late. Our recommendations for improving the situation are set out in Part II (see para 9.28).

6.55 It is sometimes said that the prisoner's worst punishment comes after he has served his sentence and been released into a world of rejecting relatives, former friends and employers. This may not be true for the conventional villain who has plenty of cronies of similar persuasion, but it is true of many sex offenders. Many have no home to return to, yet many hostels run by voluntary agencies have rules to exclude them. If their previous employment has been in any way connected with young people – as teachers or social workers for instance – or if they have belonged to a self-policing profession – such as law, medicine or the church – their chance of getting back are poor. The Rehabilitation of Offenders Act 1974 allows long past or 'spent' convictions, which did not carry a sentence of more than 30 months' imprisonment, to be effectively erased. After 5 years (or 7 years if the sentence was more than 6 but not more than 30 month's imprisonment) convictions need not be disclosed to a prospective employer, unless it is a public employer, such as a social service department or a school, who is empowered to demand to know even about spent convictions.

These niceties are of little help to sex offenders; they come into effect too late to be of much help. Many employers are too antagonistic to sex offenders even to consider engaging them. Employers are inclined to say, with good reason, that the presence of a sex offender would not be tolerated by existing staff. A survey sponsored by the Apex Trust (Box – Grainger, 1983) noted that of 54 employers questioned none had taken on a sex offender and that 'all employers said that they were least likely to consider former sex offenders'.

Another disability that sex offenders suffer is inevitable questioning by the police when a sex offence occurs in his neighbourhood and the movements of likely suspects have to checked. Men who have obtained a job concealing their history risk not only discovery and dismissal when police visit them at work but also possible blackmail from work-mates or unscrupulous employers.

CHAPTER 7

How are they treated after conviction?

THE RANGE OF APPROACHES

7.1 The term treatment has been used in a number of ways. At its widest, it has been used to embrace everything that could affect the life of an offender, including for example fines, deprivations of liberty and prison discipline. At its narrowest, the term has been used for strictly medical procedures, such as the administration of drugs. In what follows the term is used for all kinds of interventions with individual offenders that are intended, either as a primary or secondary goal, to help them to modify their behaviour so as to avoid or reduce re-offending. This could include, in addition to drugs, psychotherapy and conditioning techniques, behaviour modification by social skills training and educative discussion groups. Such efforts may be undertaken by voluntary organisations, doctors and social workers as well as by persons working within the criminal justice system, such as probation officers and prison staff.

Some approaches used with offenders, such as environmental manipulation, directive advice or the imposition of conditions of liberty are better described as management, since the word treatment still retains overtones of a medical model and seems to imply an expectation of fundamental change in attitude or personality. We therefore use freely words like supervision, control and counselling in the contexts where these seem more fitting than treatment. Management techniques are at least as important in dealing with offenders as traditional treatment approaches.

7.2 Not all sex offenders have special treatment needs or are likely to want or to respond to treatment. For example, the teenage lover of a girl of fifteen, in trouble because her parents have complained, but who probably behaved no differently from many of his peers, is unlikely to see any need for treatment. He may well think that he acted neither reprehensibly nor abnormally, and that nothing in his attitudes or habits need changing. If the offender in this case were middle-aged, he might still hold the same opinion, and still resist advice or treatment, although others would be less likely to agree. A variety of pressures or forms of duress can be brought to bear, but most treatment methods are unlikely to work and scarcely worth attempting if the offender does not want to co-operate.

7.3 As indicated in the earlier discussion on the heterogeneous characteristics of sex offenders, their treatment needs are varied (Brodsky, 1980), and need to be considered under separate headings. For a minority whose sexual conduct is persistent, seriously antisocial and otherwise unmodifiable, the only feasible approach may be by so-called 'chemical castration', that is artificial manipulation of hormone levels in order to produce a diminution of sexual desire and responsiveness. For some whose primary problem is the deviant nature of their sexual inclinations, it may be possible to reduce or modify their unwanted impulses by means of conditioning techniques. Many offenders act deviantly because they lack the social skills to obtain a suitable sexual partner in an approved manner: for them, compensatory instruction and supervised practice may overcome the difficulty. Offenders with irrational anxieties about sexual intimacy, or with particularly ambivalent, suspicious or aggressive attitudes to sexual partners, whose problems are as much in the realm of interpersonal relationships as in the specifically sexual sphere, may respond to approaches on the psychotherapeutic model. Exploration and discussion of their feelings and patterns of behaviour, either individually or in groups, can bring about lasting changes of outlook and open up possibilities for more satisfying sexual relationships and so relieve the tensions that might otherwise lead to re-offending. This may sometimes work even with self-centred, aggressive, criminally inclined 'pschopathic' offenders, if they can be confronted with the reality of their misconduct and its consequences for themselves. Finally, for those whose socially disapproved impulses appear too chronically ingrained to change, some benefit may be derived from guidance in the avoidance of situations of temptation and the development of compensatory, non-sexual interests.

7.4 Each form of treatment has its own experts and enthusiasts. Behavioural retraining methods are favoured by most psychologists (Hawton, 1983), but many offenders have multiple problems and for them an eclectic combination of different methods may be the best solution (Crawford, 1981). A period of preliminary assessment to identify the chief problem areas and to set up the targets to be achieved is highly desirable, although not often possible within the constraints of the criminal justice system and the relatively brief periods of remand for examination. The successful enlistment of the offender's active commitment to the attainment of goals shared between himself and the therapist is of crucial importance. Negotiation between the offender and the therapist allows the former's aspirations to be tempered by the latter's experience. As new information about the offender's problems comes to light the therapeutic goals can be amended and updated, always with a view to further progress in the offender's task of ultimately achieving full control of his own behaviour.

A comprehensive treatment programme will often have many facets, but sometimes, where one key factor, such as deviant sexual interest or poor social life, is the prime focus of attention, changes achieved in that one respect can result in a kind of domino effect, with benefits following in many other aspects of the offender's life.

ASSESSING AND MODIFYING DEVIANT IMPULSES

7.5 The degree and nature of deviant sexual interest can be assessed to some extent by questioning an offender about his sexual habits, inclinations and fantasies, by observations or reports of his overt behaviour, or by measurement of his physiological reactions. This last technique involves the use of the penile plethysmograph, a device that consists essentially of a ring or glove that fits over the penis and registers the expansion that occurs during sexual arousal. By presenting pictures or verbal accounts of different sexual situations and noting physiological responses, a man's sexual preference and his degree of arousal to, for example, sadistic scenes or child pornography can be assessed. Some individuals are able deliberately to disguise or modify their reactions in order to mislead the therapist, for instance by not paying attention to the stimulus (Laws and Holmen, 1978). Such cheating is often detectable, however, and some reactions, such as slight changes accompanying incipient arousal, of which the man is unaware, are not easy to control. All in all, assessments with the plethysmograph are likely to be more accurate than reliance on self-reports, and they have the advantage of being readily quantifiable, which facilitates monitoring of changes following treatment (Freund, 1981).

7.6 One approach to the modification of sexual interest is aversion therapy. Deviant material which the subject finds attractive is presented in conjunction with something unpleasant such as a mild electric shock. Given enough repetition, the subject develops an aversion to stimuli which he previously found arousing. In one Canadian study child molesters received coloured light signals when the plethysmograph registered the start of a penile reaction. When reactions occurred in response to pictures of children a mild shock followed. Aversion coupled with such feedback proved more effective than aversion alone (Quinsey *et al*, 1980).

The aversive or 'punishing' stimulus need not be physical. A man can be encouraged to develop his own aversive fantasies, for example by being induced to dwell upon the unpleasant consequences of becoming inappropriately aroused and arrested for an offence (Callahan and

Leitenberg, 1973). Exposers have been made to perform their ritual under aversive conditions, with female nurses watching and making discouraging comments (Jones and Frei, 1977; Serber, 1970).

Satiation is another variant of aversion that makes use of the effect of boredom in reducing sexual interest. The man is isolated in a quiet room and required to masturbate continually while thinking and verbalising about his deviant sexual fantasies (Marshall and Barbaree, 1978).

The aversive technique is particularly useful for men who have a normal sex life apart from some bothersome quirk, such as an inconvenient fetish or an impulse to expose. With persons who lack any acceptable sexual outlet, the suppression of deviant interest, even if successful, provides at best an incomplete solution to their problem, and one unlikely to prove lasting. For this reason, and because they appear punitive, aversive techniques are less often used today. Positive reinforcement of desirable behaviour is thought preferable to the punishment of undesirable responses.

7.7 Orgasmic reconditioning technique depends upon the reinforcing effect of masturbating to a particular sexual fantasy. Subjects are instructed to bring themselves to a climax while deliberately turning their thoughts away from deviant fantasies and towards the sort of approved sexual performance which they would like to acquire (Marshall *et al*, 1977). They can be assisted in the process by the presentation of sexually explicit materials corresponding to the fantasies they are trying to build up. Some workers have tried to improve on the procedure by first projecting slides of deviant material to excite the subject, then 'fading' into non-deviant matter before sexual climax is reached (Barlow and Wincze, 1980).

7.8 Some men are unable to acquire normal responses because they are too anxious and inhibited in heterosexual situations. For them, individualised schemes of what is called 'systematic desensitisation' are sometimes helpful. In these programmes the person under treatment is introduced, for short periods and in easy stages, to situations that come gradually nearer and nearer to those he has found impossibly anxiety provoking, until eventually he can remain calm and effective where previously he was fearful and inhibited. An obvious extension of the method is to employ a suitably trained woman surrogate partner to encourage and guide a man who is impotent through anxiety until he can achieve and enjoy sexual intercourse. The social, ethical and practical problems of arranging for this approach in the case of sex offenders are, of course, formidable.

INDIRECT APPROACHES

7.9 The social skills training approach takes various forms, based on the idea that the prime problem is not the sexual act but the acquisition of a suitable partner (Brodsky and West, 1981; Crawford and Allen, 1979). The subject rehearses his performance in role-playing in situations set up by the therapist. Inept or inappropriate talk, gestures, or responses during social interactions with the opposite sex are monitored so that the subject can receive the coaching and feedback he needs to adjust his behaviour.

7.10 Psychotherapy, utilising methods based on or derived from psychoanalysis such as group therapy, social casework and therapeutic community techniques have been used extensively with sex offenders, although many psychologists have become sceptical of the relevance of such methods to the modification of sexual preferences or the improvement of heterosexual performance. The approach operates on the assumption that behaviour can be changed through self-revelatory discussion of intimate feelings and personal problems. The aim is to bring about beneficial insights into how aberrant habits develop, the motivations which they serve and the undesirable consequences of continuing with them. This in turn promotes desire for change, aids the development of more acceptable social attitudes and lifestyles and helps to break down the inhibitions that stand in the way of obtaining sexual satisfaction in conventional ways. In some of these methods the relationship that develops between client and therapist is considered at least as important as the intellectual content of the discussion. Even those therapists who, as a matter of theoretical principle, eschew the psychoanalytic models, do not hesitate to make use of personal contact and discussion to inspire motivation and confidence in their clients.

7.11 Psychotherapeutic methods are particularly relevant when sex offences arise in the context of personal problems that are not specifically sexual but liable to manifest themselves in, for example, sexual assaults motivated by aggression and a desire to harm or degrade a woman (Cohen *et al*, 1971). An apparently successful programme of intensive group psychotherapy in a small unit or 'therapeutic community', where inmates are meant to be wholly dedicated to the ideal of mutual self-revelation and critical self-scrutiny, and all grades of staff participate in observation and discussion, has been operating for some years within the Canadian Penitentiary Service (West *et al*, 1978). Many murderers and repetitive rapists have spent a period of years in the unit, and some have been freed, so far without any reported disaster. Psychotherapy is especially applicable also in cases of sex offending that arise in the context of marital or family conflict. The partner's participation in therapy is often very desirable. Although in a less intensive and organised fashion, some attempts at psychotherapy with sex offenders are carried out in prisons in England, in particular at Grendon Underwood and with some life sentence groups.

7.12 Not everyone has the facility for the self-questioning introspection required in most forms of psychotherapy, and in any case gaining insight into the possible origins of a problem does not necessarily help to solve it. But the therapeutic relationship between client and counsellor can be utilised for other purposes, such as to give emotional support, encouragement and firm guidance, without necessarily delving into interpretation of behaviour. By inducing offenders to act upon advice on their life-style and how to avoid situations likely to lead to offending, a social worker or probation officer can exert what amounts to a measure of control that would be unattainable in the absence of a previously acquired relationship of trust. Whether this supervisory and controlling influence can be expected to outlast the period of contact with the client is an open question.

MEDICATION

7.13 Sex suppressant medication is often effective in relieving men of obsessive preoccupation with sexual thoughts and temptations to commit offences. It produces physical impotence and reduces sexual interests and psychological arousability. The method is inapplicable to men with a prospect of resolving their difficulties through the development of a normal sex life, or to those who need to preserve a marital relationship. It is usually thought to be appropriate only to men whose chances of re-offending are high, the likely consequences grave and for whom no other form of treatment can be recommended. It has replaced surgical castration, which used to be used quite frequently in Denmark for serious sex offenders, and was said to be a highly successful form of treatment (Ortmann, 1980; Sturup, 1972).

The usual methods are by the administration of oestrogens (female sex hormones) or cyproterone acetate, a synthetic drug which counteracts the activity of androgens (the male sex hormones). Oestrogens can be given in the form of an implant beneath the skin which releases the hormone slowly over a period of months and obviates the need for daily dosing or for checks on whether the patient is taking the drug regularly. Cyproterone acetate is taken orally in tablet form, but in Germany an anti-androgen that can be implanted for slow release has been made.

7.14 Oestrogens have some undesirable side-effects upon men, the most troublesome being swelling of breasts (gynaecomastia), which can be both ugly and painful. More dangerous hazards include a tendency to form blood clots and a slight risk of cancer. The side-effects of anti-androgen are less severe, but still considerable, with a fifteen to twenty per cent incidence of gynaecomastia after prolonged usage and also some increased liability to thrombosis. At the beginning of treatment fatigue and lassitude are common complaints; later on there may be increased weight from fat deposits and loss of body hair. A heavy alcohol intake reduces or abolishes the action of the drug. By the inhibition of spermatogenesis sterility is induced, which is usually slowly reversible after intake ceases, but whether recovery is possible after prolonged dosage remains uncertain. It is conceivable that anti-androgen administration could result in the formation of abnormal sperms and the production of malformed embryos.

The effectiveness of these treatments is greatly dependent upon patient co-operation. Where sexual deviation is combined with anti-social personality traits a substantial proportion of drop-outs can be expected. Reported results have been promising, but varied (Berlin and Meinicke, 1981).

7.15 Psychosurgery, that is the excision or destruction of brain tissue in parts of the temporal lobes or hypothalamus that are believed to be concerned with the regulation of sexual responses, has been used to treat sex offenders in West Germany (Reiber and Sigusch, 1979). Because of the drastic and irreversible nature of these interventions, the primitive state of knowledge of the neural mechanisms involved, and the uncertainty of outcome, these methods have encountered considerable ethical objections. They have rarely, if ever, been used on sex offenders in England.

DIFFICULTIES IN APPLICATION AND EVALUATION

7.16 Society as well as the offender stands to gain from the provision of whatever help or treatment offers a reasonable chance of success. Unfortunately, since treatments, and specialized treatments in particular, are both scarce and expensive, cost effectiveness is extremely important. Rehabilitative schemes for ordinary, non-sexual offenders that have been subject to critical evaluation have mostly been found to have no detectable effect upon likelihood of reconviction (Brody, 1976; Sechrest *et al*, 1979). Assuming the efficacy of attempts to help offenders, it would seem not to be a propitious time to try to promote treatment schemes. Sex offenders, however, constitute a special case since, unlike most thieves and burglars, many of them are aware of having problems that the average man does not have to face, and many would like to receive help if it were available. Moreover, unlike acquisitive offenders, some sex offenders have deviant arousal patterns clearly connected with their misbehaviour, and these can be measurably altered by treatment.

7.17 Reported examples of apparently beneficial changes following treatment are not hard to find, but conclusive, scientific proof of effectiveness in terms the public can understand – namely a demonstrated reduction in likelihood of reconviction – is much more difficult to obtain. As explained already (see para 3.17) reconviction rates for most varieties of sex offender are already quite small without treatment. This means that, unless the treatment is dramatically successful, a large sample is needed to demonstrate a significant reduction. Since some risk of reconviction tends to persist over many years, a very long period of follow-up is needed to assess the full effect of treatment. The worst problem is the virtual impossibility of obtaining a satisfactorily matched comparison group of offenders who have not had treatment. Random allocation of an unselected series of offenders to either treatment or non-treatment would solve the difficulty, but this is rarely possible in the face of legal, administrative and ethical problems. The alternative method of comparing treated cases in one place with apparently similar untreated cases from elsewhere is rarely satisfactory. Those who run treatment programmes for sex offenders – as indeed for anyone else – are necessarily selective in the kinds of offender they are prepared to include. After every effort has been made to find similar cases for comparison, some suspicion must always remain that an effect apparently attributable to treatment might have been due to the therapist's ability to choose cases likely to do well even if they had been given no help.

7.18 In spite of the difficulties, some examples of apparently significant reductions in reconviction rates following treatment have been reported. Peters and Roether (1968) compared 92 sex offenders who were given group psychotherapy while on probation with a control group of 75 similar but untreated probationers. In a two-year period of follow-up 8 per cent of the untreated and only 1 per cent of the treated men were reconvicted for sex offences. Wickramasekera (1976) described an aversive procedure applied to 16 chronic, repetitive sexual exposers. Their offences had been continuing for periods of 4 to 25 years at rates of 1 to 20 incidents monthly. The men were followed up after the treatment for periods varying from 3 months to 7 years, with checks made in police records and inquiries from relatives in addition to the patient's own reports. No relapses were recorded. Even without a control group, this 'before and after' change was clearly significant.

7.19 Changes that might reasonably be expected to result in reduced offending, such as improvement in social skills or diminution of deviant arousal, are relatively easy to demonstrate (Bancroft, 1974; Feldman and MacCulloch, 1980; Gelder, 1979), but whether the changes oberved within the artificial confines of the pschological laboratory or the penal institution transfer successfully to real life situations is another matter. The division of responsibility between penal and civil treatment services means that institutional therapists lose contact with their clients on discharge and therapy ceases just when the offender stands in greatest need of help, namely when the stresses and temptations of freedom have to be faced once again. Often the desire of the ex-prisoner to escape further surveillance is to blame, but even those who would be willing to maintain contact cannot normally continue to see prison-based therapists. Furthermore, hostel placements, which could provide a safe haven for the socially alienated and homeless, as well as facilitating continued counselling, are rarely available to sex offenders because of the refusal of many voluntary organizations to provide for them.

7.20 Attempts to manipulate the sexual responsiveness or the emotional attitudes of offenders are inevitably somewhat artificial when carried out in the confines of an institution which permits no contact with actual or potential sexual partners. Moreover, when therapists have to operate with minimal knowledge of or access to the offender's natural environment, the task of adjusting programmes to provide the best chance of generalizing effects to life outside becomes singularly difficult.

The evaluation of changes seen during treatment in a penal institution is complicated by the limitations of the environment. Prisoners' answers to questions about their feelings are likely to be coloured by a desire to make it appear that treatment is having more effect than is in fact the case, because, rightly or wrongly, they believe that this impression would improve their chances of release on parole. In any case, attitudes and behaviour while under strict observation may correspond little with what is likely to occur in conditions of freedom. On the other hand some offenders who have been previously reluctant to admit the extent of their difficulties (perhaps because of conflict between the pleasures of a deviant way of life and the desire to conform) are prepared to do so once they find themselves in prison and in a situation where continued denials seem pointless.

7.21 Perhaps the worst impediment to treatment of the sex offender in prison is the attitude of fellow inmates (see paras 4.51–4.57). Men who might otherwise like to co-operate fear to do so because to reveal the exact nature of their offences might attract reprisals, including blackmail, at the hands of other prisoners. The pervasive demands of security in prison pose serious obstacles to treatment schemes that require group meetings, free discussion, easy communication between officers and inmates and if possible the involvement of contacts from outside. Security within an institution housing desperate and hostile men requires more than a physically secure perimeter and restrictions on visits if those who work within the walls are to have reasonable safety. Unrestricted contacts between officers and prisoners would increase intolerably the risk of hostage taking, an activity that has always been more common in prisons than in the outside world (Davies, 1982, pp. 136–143). All these difficulties are greatly reduced when sex offenders are placed in a special treatment institution, as at Grendon Underwood psychiatric prison, rather than in a place where traditional criminal attitudes predominate.

7.22 Another difficulty is the matter of timing. Prison sentences are on a different and more rigid time-scale than treatment requirements, which are ideally of variable duration depending upon the methods employed and upon individual needs and responses. A man may have to be released before treatment is considered complete or, more likely, detained long after maximum benefit has been attained, and there is a danger of deterioration if newly acquired skills or attitudes cannot be exercised in a more normal community setting. As McCaldon, a psychiatrist in charge of a Canadian prison treatment scheme, has pointed out, it is wasteful of scarce resources and possibly counter-productive to continue treatment indefinitely, yet likely to be detrimental to have to return the offender to an institution where 'the attitudes of the officers may be very repressive' and where 'other inmates are exceedingly hostile' (Levine and Koenig, 1982, p. 150).

7.23 Finally, what often seems like an insuperable barrier to the setting up of treatment schemes in prison is the inescapable dilemma that resources of all kinds are so limited that the Prison Department has great difficulty in providing even the most basic amenities for inmates and staff. The official view of prison managers and the prison medical service is that such treatment facilities as exist are available equally to all, including sex offenders. That view neglects the particular difficulties sex offenders have in declaring themselves in prison. However, individual initiatives by staff prepared to offer treatment specifically directed towards sex offenders are not discouraged and some examples are cited later.

7.24 As was noted earlier (see para 4.54) there is a small number of prisons, notably at Gloucester and Maidstone, which have special units for housing those still under protective segregation under Rule 43 at the time of their transfer from a local prison. While also housing informers, baby batterers and other unpopular characters, the majority of inmates of these units are sex offenders. The units therefore represent a naturally occurring pool of prospective clients for projects of treatment and research with sex offenders. At present, however, the prisoners admitted to these units are not selected for treatment suitability and the units have not been designed to meet the requirements of therapeutic programmes aimed as behavioural change. Such limited projects as have been attempted so far have had to be carried out on an individual or small group basis with selected prisoners who have opted to participate.

The problem of instituting projects in prison must not be underestimated. A critical article by Richard Henderson, a former Assistant Governor at Maidstone Prison (*Guardian* 2 and 7 March, 1984), deplores the lost opportunities for treatment in Rule 43 Units, and argues that 'the effect of official policy is to put these prisoners "on ice" for the duration of their sentences [and] do virtually nothing to help or even identify their problems.' He argues that the excessively macho stance and hostile attitudes of prison officers serves only to reinforce the sex offenders' inadequacies, brand them as sex beasts and release them worse rather than better 'with the cynical assumption that most of them will be back again . . .' Henderson's views were sharply challenged by the present Governor of the prison (*Guardian*, 13 March 1984).

SOME BRITISH PROJECTS

7.25 A few small-scale experiments have been carried out in England which show that with appropriate organisation and initiative it is not impossible to overcome the difficulties of mounting a treatment programme attached to a prison. Of course, given the present situation of prison overcrowding, and the severe limits on resources, such projects are unlikely to develop further for some time.

A feasibility study into the psychological treatment of sex offenders began in Birmingham in 1974 (Perkins, 1982, 1983). Offenders willing to be assessed who passed through the prison in 1974–6 were interviewed, and 46 out of a total of 72 were considered suitable for treatment on the grounds that they expressed a wish to change their behaviour and were prepared to work with the psychologist to achieve such goals as a reduction in deviant sexual activities and an improvement in social skills. Men imprisoned for the more serious offences (predominantly rape, buggery and incest) were less often willing to volunteer and less often considered treatable than those with less grave offences (such as indecent assault and indecent exposure). The latter group were often recidivistic and perhaps more likely to see something abnormal in their sexual behaviour than were the former, whose offence motivation were more mixed and less exclusively sexual.

7.26 Initially the Birmingham treatment programme was confined to volunteers within the prison who were referred to the psychologist mainly by prison medical officers and probation officers. Later, a collaborative arrangement with the Midland Centre for Forensic Psychiatry allowed treatment to be extended beyond the prison to men referred by probation officers and forensic psychiatrists, and this became the main source of candidates for treatment. Experience showed that treatment was more likely to be taken up by and to be effective with, men in the community. Furthermore, a ban on assessments in prison hospitals using the penile plethysmograph was imposed in 1980.

The treatment methods have been broadly behavioural, attempting to modify factors antecedent to offending, (such as excessive drinking, marital conflicts and lack of opportunity for approved sexual outlets) and factors following offending (such as sexual gratification and relief of hostility towards women). The latter might be helped by aversive conditioning to reduce deviant sex drive, and social skills training to facilitate better relationships with women.

Of 139 offenders seen during the course of the project 108 did not want treatment or opted out or were forced out of treatment for reasons beyond their control, 9 were still continuing and only 10 reached the stage of completion, with both offender and psychologist agreeing that all relevant problems had been dealt with. The remaining 12 were a 'control' group, consisting of men considered suitable who, for various reasons, did not receive treatment. In a follow-up period in excess of four years the fully treated group were re-convicted less often than the control group. The evidence therefore pointed to some positive effect of the treatment, even though it applied to a minority of offenders and was not as powerful as might have been hoped.

7.27 Another example of a prison-based programme was the small therapeutic group for 'Rule 43' sex offenders initiated in 1978 at Maidstone prison by the probation officer Hugh Hawkins. This became the subject of a BBC television documentary entitled 'Jail within a Jail'. Volunteer prisoners joined a discussion group to which outside visitors were invited and experienced volunteers participated and had individual interviews with some of the men. Female victims of rape were among those who came and talked with men guilty of violent sexual assaults. The experience was thought beneficial to men who were socially isolated by reason of their offence and who needed to gain confidence in preparation for their future social relationships. Reactions of anger and frustration in interaction with females were explored and men were encouraged to cope with their feelings in quieter, more constructive ways. A much needed sex education programme was introduced simultaneously. A secondary benefit was the improved knowledge and understanding of the inmates by the officers making reports for the parole authorities, thereby avoiding misrepresentation from lack of information, ensuring that any adverse comments were tested and supported by clear evidence, and where possible enabling reports to include constructive suggestions for the future following release.

A group whose problems were particularly difficult to deal with were the homosexual paedophiles. However, through arrangements handled by the prison officers, a number of these were befriended and counselled by members of a local homosexual organisation. In this way some who would otherwise have had poor prospects were found accommodation and jobs, and some were encouraged and given confidence to seek contacts in the adult gay world instead of among young boys.

Unfortunately, limited resources and staffing problems rarely allow such promising and innovative projects to continue for long, much less to expand and embrace a more substantial proportion of the offenders who could benefit.

7.28 For the reasons already given, therapeutic programmes are far easier to arrange and probably have more chance of success if considerations of safety permit the offender to remain in the community. A small-scale programme was begun by the Avon Probation Service in 1977. Referrals came from local probation officers and from a consultant psychiatrist. This was a discussion group for non-violent sex offenders with more than one previous conviction for sex offence. It was designed to help the men to share what has previously been private and isolating experiences, to ease tensions, to raise self-esteem, to relieve loneliness and to provide social learning opportunities. From a total of 38 past and present members (with an average of 4 previous convictions per man) 8 have been reconvicted for a sex offence – according to a follow-up in mid-1983, which included a record check in central criminal records. Although no systematic comparison was possible, experience suggests that this outcome is better than could be expected of untreated, recidivist offenders (Fox, 1980). Seven of the 8 reconvicted men had been first admitted to the group following an offence of indecent exposure. Of the 22 men who came following other kinds of offences, 17 of whom had been involved with a child, only one was reconvicted.

7.29 One of the conditions for successful counselling and control of sexual misconduct by offenders at liberty in the community could be continuity of therapeutic contact. The late Peter Scott, a much respected pioneer of forensic psychiatry, used to insist on the value to potential re-offenders of a lifeline in the shape of a continuing link with a therapist who could be called upon when tensions mounted or circumstances favouring relapse developed. Professor Bluglass (1982, p. 71) makes a similar point when he remarks upon the value of long-term contact with sex offenders, whether by a psychiatrist, probation officer or social worker. Some sex offenders he had followed for as much as ten years without any recurrence were swiftly in trouble again as soon as he ceased seeing them.

7.30 Many medical and social workers feel concern for the sexual offenders who occasionally come under their care, but they are frustrated by lack of knowledge about how to deal with such problems, by the lack of developed programmes of rehabilitation or treatment to which individuals might be referred, and by the difficulties of co-ordinating their own efforts with those of the other diverse authorities who may be involved. Many probation officers are at a loss for what to do with their sex offender clients, and some of them may limit their discussions to tangential social problems, deliberately avoiding questions about sexuality.

The East Midlands seminar on sexual behaviour is an exercise started by the local probation service to draw together with probation officers people from other services concerned with clients with sexual problems – such as psychiatry, psychology, marriage guidance, family planning, nursing, hostels, police, social services and the National Society for the Prevention of Cruelty to Children. The aim is to learn more about clients with convictions for sex offences with a view to initiating appropriate interventions. The group holds seminars with invited speakers on particular problems (including, for example, child victims, scapegoating of sex offenders in prison, sexually transmitted diseases), occasional case discussions and sex education courses. The programme is a response to a widely felt need that is not being met at all in most parts of the country. The organisation may be influential in affecting the attitudes and methods of individual practitioners, but it has neither the finance nor the official recognition required to implement major policy changes.

7.31 Another small-scale endeavour by the probation service, unhappily discontinued after the officer concerned moved to another area, was begun in Essex (Shaw, 1978). It was used for persistent sexual offenders who would otherwise be in prison, who were willing under the terms of their probation order to take regular but relatively small doses of cyproterone acetate (to reduce libido) and to attend without fail two group sessions each week. One of these weekly meetings was led by the probation officer, the other included trained voluntary workers, predominantly female. The scheme was intended to take advantage of the period of 'sexual calm' produced by the libido suppressant to improve social interaction and encourage the men to discuss their difficulties openly in the security of a confidential and sympathetic group.

It was made clear that failure to attend regularly would result in the man being reported at once for a breach of probation. In these circumstances, the courts proved willing to consider this alternative to custody even with cases that had aroused high public indignation. The scheme required close co-operation with local doctors, and in particular with one who was also a local magistrate, but although it worked out in practice it was attacked by some critics for involving the probation service in coercive medical control.

PROBLEMS OF THE PROBATION SERVICE

7.32 Since the Probation Service is the main agency involved in the management and treatment of sex offenders in the community, and has pioneered a number of promising schemes, the Working Party approached the Association of Chief Probation Officers with some specific questions about the current attitudes, practices and problems of the Service in this connection. Letters and comments were received from 15 Chief Officers.

There was a general appreciation of the need for greater understanding of the sex offender and how to deal with him. Many felt that there was a lack of basic information, or perhaps a tendency to expect all sex offenders to be the same. In some counties the numbers were very few, which ruled out group work and meant that the problem did not arouse much interest. There was a difference between rural and urban areas in the availability of support systems, such as specialised counselling and psychiatric services.

Divergent views were expressed on the matter of collaboration with psychiatrists when the court had added a treatment requirement to a probation order. Lack of rapport was a common complaint, with probation officers not knowing who was seeing the client or whether he was co-operating as required or when the treatment was terminated. Clients sometimes exploit this lack of liaison to deceive the probation officer into believing that treatment is continuing when it is not. If a further offence takes place under these circumstances the system is liable to get bad publicity.

7.33 Probation work with families, although considered desirable, was often found impossible, as for instance when a child or father had been statutorily separated by order of a Director of Social Services. There was some concern about the lack of controls over sex offenders released from prison with no compulsory after-care and sometimes no place to live. The need for improving liaison between prison, probation and social services, especially, in dealing with known paedophiles, was also mentioned. One problem service felt that sex offences within families might be better dealt with through the civil courts. Certainly there was some dissatisfaction with the 'blunt instrument' of criminal justice, which appears to ignore the treatment or welfare requirements of both offenders and victims. An example was quoted in which a teenage girl had mentioned to a probation officer that her father had been sleeping with her each week-end for some years. Alternative accommodation was found for the girl and her sister and the father was provided with a place in a bail hostel. In a sense the problem had already been solved, but when the matter came to court several months later, the probation officer having reported the girl's complaint to the police, the father was eventually sentenced to seven years' imprisonment. This outcome, although perhaps satisfactory as a mark of public disapproval and a deterrent, imposed a considerable burden of guilt on the girl, who had retained a lot of affection for her father and may not have anticipated the consequences of her revelations.

SOME AMERICAN PROJECTS

7.34 The value of treatment programmes for sex offenders is more readily accepted in America than in Britain (Delin, 1978). A survey published by the U.S. Department of Justice reviewed 23 different schemes operating in various places (Brecher, 1978). Problems of evaluation were analysed in some detail. It cannot be said that any programme had produced irrefutable evidence of effectiveness, but at least they demonstrated feasibility and promise. A few examples must suffice.

One well-established programme is the treatment unit set up by Dr Geraldine Boozer in South Florida State Hospital, which aims to rehabilitate incarcerated rapists and other serious sex offenders, largely by means of group discussions and self-help enterprises. Wives and girl friends are drawn into the system and special attention is given to after-care following a gradual transition to the free community. For instance, ex-offenders are given pocket telephones which they can use to dial another ex-offender volunteer for support whenever he feels the urge to re-offend creeping up on him. There is also a private group of sex offenders and ex-offenders meeting voluntarily, independent of the institution. Men who have passed through the programme but still feel the need for help can enrol in this. A prominent feature of the system is the proselytising role of members of the group still under treatment who are prepared to talk to visiting dignitaries, representatives of womens' groups and so forth, arguing for more enlightened approaches to sex problems and putting their members forward as examples of what can be done. Group loyalty and fear of betraying the 'cause' is a powerful factor in keeping misconduct under control.

7.35 Another well known American programme operates in Washington State under the powers conferred by a Sexual Psychopath statute which enables the courts to commit sex offenders to hospital for a thorough assessment, which can last up to 90 days. If the therapists find them suitable for the regime, the court can then commit them for treatment. Initially they are confined to the hospital wards, but usually for somewhat less time than they would be likely to spend in prison under sentence, after which they are allowed gradually increasing periods at liberty under supervision until they are finally released into the community with a requirement to report back at stated intervals. The phased release begins only after the sentencing court has received favourable reports from the therapists and given its consent. If reassuring reports are not forthcoming, the court can substitute a punitive sentence for the treatment order. This formal and public procedure helps to motivate co-operation and is a safeguard against abuse by either the offender or the authorities.

7.36 The Washington regime runs on a 'guided self-help' principle. The chief therapeutic activity is participation in intensive discussion groups at which the offender is required to present before his peers and the therapist a very frank and truthful autobiography, including a full account of his socio-sexual relationships, fantasies and offending behaviour. He must also take part in the work assignments and social and recreational activities of the therapeutic community and learn to live in intimate proximity with others who know about his problems and oversee his reactions with a sympathetic but critical eye. The aim is to promote in the offender recognition of the hurtfulness of his behaviour, an understanding of how his offences come about and an acceptance of responsiblity for changing his ways. Practice in breaking down social isolation and developing more constructive relationships is considered essential. The offender has to demonstrate before a sophisticated audience real progress in all these respects before he is eligible to begin the first steps towards release.

The regime is meant primarily for men whose sexual misconduct stems from poor socialisation or inability to sustain fulfilling adult relationships, rather than for those whose prime problem is a deviant fixation. Nevertheless, exercises in orgasmic reconditioning by manipulation of masturbation fantasies are encouraged in selected cases. Most of the clients are adults in their 20s or 30s with a history of repeated sex offences and consequently a high risk of recidivism. The great majority of their victims are young females or children. A recidivism rate of 22 per cent in a follow-up period of from 1 to 12 years has been reported (Saylor, 1980), which is considered significantly less than expected. Unfortunately, as with so many other promising treatment programmes, there is no adequate control group with which to compare this statistic. Moreover, when, as must happen sooner or later if large numbers of offenders pass through, one of the subsequent offences is sufficiently serious to attract notoriety and unfavourable comment in the media, there is a great risk of the sacrifice of the whole scheme from loss of public confidence and of judicial support. This nearly happened on more than one occasion in Washington State. When such an event occurs commentators rarely stop to consider whether, without the treatment efforts, incidents of a similar kind following release from ordinary imprisonment might not be still more frequent.

7.37 The best known of American treatment enterprises operate with imprisoned or hospitalised offences, but some specialise in providing alternatives to incarceration. A scheme of this kind was begun in Albuquerque, New Mexico, in 1972 in response to the concern of some local judges who found they had no suitable way of dealing with the more pathetic and non-violent exhibitionists and child seducers. These men seemed to need help rather than a possibly counter-productive sentence of imprisonment. So a community service was set up which aimed to help its offender clients to improve defective social skills, to develop concern for the interests and feelings of potential victims, to achieve self-esteem and to build up strong conditioning against committing further offences. Clients were required to enter into a contract specifying the services to be received, the length of time during which these would be provided and the conditions they would have to agree to fulfil. The system tends to cater for youngish and mostly single men, many of them lonely drifters in the city. It includes a walk-in counselling service for moments of crisis. The reconviction rate of co-operative clients is surprisingly low. The Albuquerque system has gained a considerable reputation, done much to change local community attitudes and even influenced the state laws on sex offending.

7.38 Another community based effort, the Santa Clara Child Sexual Abuse Treatment Program, organised by the Juvenile Probation Department in San Jose, California, has already been mentioned (see para 4.20). This is a counselling programme begun in 1971 to help families who might otherwise be broken up following the disclosure of an incest offence and the subsequent 'explosive reaction' of the traditional criminal justice system, which often deals 'a knock out blow to a family already weakened by internal stresses' (Brecher, 1978, p.26). The initial contact is made by a volunteer from 'Parents United', a group made up of families who have been through similar experiences. Wife, husband and child are each provided with counselling and also with practical help with the allied problems of housing, finance, and legal aid. At a later stage of treatment the whole family meet for counselling as a group. Giarretto, the Director of the project, is content that the effort is coupled with a criminal justice system that is humane and flexible enough to encourage participation in treatment. Offenders are often given relatively short sentences in open conditions so that they can attend counselling sessions and continue work to support their families while residing away from home. The shock effect of legal intervention helps to motivate men to change. It also reinforces the idea of personal responsibility for transgressions. The goal of the treatment is to re-unite the family where possible, and this is accomplished in some 90 per cent of cases.

One consequence of the availability of treatment programmes such as this, with the attendant publicity and increased talk about 'sex abuse', is a rapid escalation of referrals. This does not mean that sex abuse is necessarily increasing, but rather that the problem is being more openly recognised and tackled.

7.39 Complete 'cure' is not always a realistic aim in the treatment of sexual problems. At Atascadero State Hospital in California, where many sex offenders used to be committed under the recently repealed 'mentally disordered sex offender' statute, and where some hundreds still reside pending decisions as to their release, attempts are made to modify the behaviour of homosexual paedophiles without necessarily changing their sexual orientation. The retraining programme aims at encouraging sexual contacts with adult males. Student volunteers from local gay groups help in role-playing sessions to instruct the patients in techniques of socialising in gay bars and securing appropriate sex partners without causing offence to society (Serber and Keith, 1974).

The repeal of the sexual psychopath laws in the United States has not been an unmixed blessing in relation to the securing of treatment for sex offenders within the penal system. In California, for example, there is now legal provision for prisoners wanting treatment to request transfer to hospital in the last two years of their sentence. Atascadero, although well equipped to deal with such cases, has received none and expects none under the new system, for the reason that prison authorities prefer to take up the limited number of places allocated for inmates who are more troublesome in prison than the sex offenders (Kiersch, 1983).

7.40 A particularly interesting American development is the proliferation of treatment centres specialising in teenage sex offenders. A recent publication describes 9 such schemes and lists 26 others (Knopp, 1983). Some are residential programmes, others community based. They are inspired by the belief that it is better to tackle deviant sex behaviour before habits have become too ingrained. The techniques include counselling, social skills training, sex education, group discussion, family therapy and emotional re-orientation through experience of a kind and caring therapeutic approach. Therapists identify family conflict and disruption, and physical and sexual abuse of children as important causes of the feelings of bitterness and impotent rage that seem to motivate many aggressive young sex offenders.

There is little in the United Kingdom to compare with all these impressive American projects, but there are avenues by which a favoured few of our sex offenders manage to secure treatment. These will now be described.

HOSTEL PLACEMENTS FOR SEX OFFENDERS

7.41 One of the most serious impediments to the provision of treatment for sex offenders in the community, or for the development of schemes to help the rehabilitation of offenders after discharge from custody, is the difficulty of finding accommodation for those who are either without homes or relatives or who have been excluded from their families because of the nature of their misconduct. Hostel placement is often essential because so many sex offenders, especially following imprisonment, become 'of no fixed abode' and, by the nature of their crimes and reputations, find themselves unable to secure anywhere to live. Hostels, however, even the statutorily established probation hostels, are, in general, very wary of accepting offenders with special peculiarities, such as drug, drink or sex problems. The latter are especially unwelcome because of fear, sometimes unrealistically magnified, that they may pose a threat to children.

7.42 The great majority of the hundred or so probation and bail hostels in England and Wales are run individually by the Probation Committees, who determine the character of the clientele, taking into account the location of the hostel and the nature of the offences. There is no national policy as to the types of person hostels can accept. Some will admit both sexes, 5 are for women only, and some have a section for offenders on bail. The wardens, who are very often probation officers, sometimes live on the premises with their families. If a child is living at a hostel a paedophile would be unlikely to be given a place. This kind of decision is in practice usually taken by the warden. An offender on probation, with a condition in his order not to contact his victim or his family, will not often be given a place because this presents the hostels with particular complications, over and above those associated with ordinary non-sex offenders. Nevertheless, there are some hostels (in Avon for example) willing to house sex offenders, both at the stage of remand on bail and later under a probation order.

Some probation areas with accommodation officers have recruited pools of suitable 'landladies', usually without children, some of whom are willing and able to manage sex offenders. They can probably do so in a more helpful way than is possible in a hostel, where there are more people around ready to scapegoat or persecute sex offenders.

7.43 Hostels run by voluntary agencies, of which there are approximately 2,000 in England and Wales, include both privately and committee-run establishments. They are very varied in their admission policies, some taking offenders only, some allowing only short stays, some accepting clients only from particular referring agencies and some taking a mixture of clients from many sources. The National Association of Voluntary Hostels are funded by the Home Office, the Department of Health and Social Security and the Department of the Environment, but these three departments do not have detailed control over the allocation of resources to individual hostels. Referrals to voluntary hostels under the National Association are made by experienced and trained placement officers who usually have a close relationship with the individual wardens, although of course they do not have the final say in the admission of a particular client. Rulings on the admission of sex offenders to voluntary hostels are similar to those operated by probation hostels and are sometimes very restrictive. Decisions are much affected by local attitudes and are sometimes taken on emotional rather than on rational grounds.

SECURING TREATMENT IN THE HEALTH SERVICE

7.44 Sexual offenders, or persons with sexual problems that they fear may lead them to the commission of an offence, sometimes present themselves voluntarily to a general practioner or to a counselling agency such as the Samaritians. If it seems appropiate, they can be referred to a psychiatric consultant in the National Health Service.

Unfortunately, although all psychiatrists have training and experience in the field of sexual problems in general, relatively few have specialist knowledge or skills in the assessment and treatment of sex offenders or potential offenders. Moreover, they may not have access to the necessary facilities. If group counselling is required, they may not have enough suitable clients to form a specialised group. If in-patient care is indicated, they may find their nurses object to the admission of men whose sexual misconduct could pose a threat or embarrassment to other patients or staff. If behaviour modification is wanted, this is usually carried out by a clinical psychologist, but few psychiatric departments have personnel skilled in these specialised techniques. If long-term social and psychological support is needed, there may be nobody available with the time and interest to carry it through.

7.45 Individual clinicians or departments within the National Heatlh Service, such as the Midland Forensic Service in Birmingham, possess the necessary expertise and facilities, but they are often remote from, or not available to, persons in the catchment area where the would-be patient happens to live. It has been suggested that specialised units for sex offenders might be set up able to take patients from any area. That would not solve the problem of the client who would be best served by out-patient treatment within reach of his own home, but it would represent an improvement on the presently existing facilities.

7.46 The stigma inseparable from sexual deviation or sexual offending is considered by some authorities as a sufficient reason for resisting the establishment of special units. The special clinics which deal with sexually transmitted diseases or opiate addiction have to contend with a similar social stigma. Clients do not like to be seen entering, and some are deterred from seeking necessary treatment by the idea of being registered and labelled a venereal disease patient or an addict.

One method of reducing patients' anxieties about stigma is to make the contact as informal as possible. A 'walk-in' clinic that does not demand a referral note from a general practitioner might attract men who would be reluctant to confide their sexual secrets to the same doctor who sees their wives, parents or children. Some might be prepared to seek advice provided they were not obliged to give their name and address. A facility dealing with a range of problems, including for example marital difficulties and frigidity, might develop a more acceptable image than one dealing exclusively with sexual deviations and sexual offending. All of these methods have in fact been tried out with success in some places, for instance at the Brook Counselling Service in Birmingham.

7.47 Most often sexual offenders' first requests for help to control their behaviour are made after they have been charged with an offence. Either spontaneously, or on the advice of their solicitor, they may then seek a psychiatric assessment with a view to the production of a report calculated to influence the court against a severe sentence. For example, the report may suggest that the behaviour was out of character and a temporary aberration, brought on by special stress or provoking circumstances and therefore unlikely to be repeated. The defence can submit such an opinion at their discretion, quoting the report either in whole or in part, in the course of a plea for mitigation of punishment. Alternatively, the psychiatric report may suggest a need for treatment, and the court may decide that treatment is more appropriate than punishment. The court may also, on its own initiative, order an investigation into the need for treatment.

TREATMENT BY COURT ORDER

7.48 If a magistrates' court is satisfied that a person accused of an imprisonable offence – and most sex offences are imprisonable – 'did the act or made the omission charged but is of the opinion that an inquiry ought to be made into his physical or mental condition before the method of dealing with him is determined' it may invoke section 30 of the Magistrates' Court Act 1980 and adjourn the case and remand the offender, either on bail or in custody, to enable an appropriate examination to be made and a report prepared. Most such remands are for psychiatric reports. If the demand is on bail, either the probation service of the justices' clerk arranges an appointment for the offender at a local National Health Service psychiatric clinic. Some psychiatrists are willing to see such referrals, but not at their N.H.S. out-patients service, in order to avoid the complaint that alleged criminals are allowed to jump the queue for an interview. If the offender is remanded to prison, the examination is normally carried out by a prison medical officer. The courts may also remand for a social enquiry report on the offender's history and current circumstances to be prepared by a probation officer. When a psychiatric report on a bailed offender is requested, a social enquiry report is usually required as well.

7.49 Overall, the proportion of sex offenders among men remanded for a psychiatric report is over five times what would be expected if all types of offender stood an equal chance of being so remanded (Salem, 1983). However, surveys have shown that the frequency with which courts make use of their power to remand for a psychiatric report varies considerably from one locality to another (Bowden, 1978; Gibbens *et al*, 1977; Prins, 1976). Magistrates naturally vary in their opinions as to the utility of reports. The availability of a local psychiatric clinic or consultant willing to produce a report in time for the scheduled reappearance in court, and if necessary to offer treatment, also greatly influences the likelihood of a report being requested. Where a smooth working relationship exists between the probation service and the local psychiatric service, this encourages referrals from the courts. Sometimes probation officers are able to make their social inquiries and share their findings with the psychiatrist in advance of his examination. This avoids a duplication of interrogations, and means that the psychiatrist can take into account information from an officer who may have had direct contact with the offender's household. Unfortunately, pressure of work and the shortness of the remand period often precludes the regular adoption of this procedure.

7.50 Sexual offenders whose misconduct involves children or homosexuality or indecent exposure, and is suggestive of sexual deviancy, are particularly likely to be remanded for reports. The magistrates may be puzzled by motivations difficult to understand, or believe that sexual abnormality calls for medical help, or want to know whether treatment is likely to reduce the risk of re-offending. Often the need for a medical report is suggested to the magistrates by police or probation officers who know the offender's peculiarities, but even more often the suggestion comes from the defending solicitor. Some magistrates may be reluctant to refuse, because to do so might provide grounds for an appeal. If the remand is in custody, this gives the offender 'a taste of prison', but that is never the official reason for seeking a prison medical officer's report.

7.51 Given the appropriate medical recommendations, the courts have two possibilities for making a formal treatment order in lieu of passing a punitive sentence: the probation order and the hospital order. Under section 3 of the Powers of Criminal Courts Act 1973, if a court receives a recommendation from an approved practitioner that 'the mental condition of an offender is such as requires and may be susceptible to treatment', and provided a named hospital or psychiatrist is prepared to undertake it, a requirement that the offender submits to the treatment can be made a condition of a probation order. In a formal sense this is a voluntary system, for the offender has to agree before the order can be made, but of course he is in a situation of duress, knowing that a punitive sentence may be imposed if he refuses. Once having agreed, he may commit the offence of 'breach of probation' if he fails to co-operate. In practice psychiatrists do not usually report non-co-operation, and clients are apt to drift away without being prosecuted. The court prescribes the duration of treatment, up to a maximum of three years (which is the limit of a probation order), and whether it is to be carried out in hospital or as an out-patient. The psychiatrist, however, can terminate the treatment whenever he thinks fit, but he should notify the probation officer so that the court can formally rescind the treatment requirement. Unfortunately, liaison between psychiatrists and probation officers is not always very satisfactory (Lewis, 1980).

At present about 13 per cent of persons convicted of indictable sex offences are put on probation, but not necessarily with a treatment requirement. The use of probation by the courts showed some decline during the 1970s, but has considerably increased more recently (Home Office, 1983, Table 7.1).

7.52 The varying chances of an offender being remanded for a medical report and being offered treatment were exemplified by the findings of a research team (Gibbens *et al*, 1977) who compared the practice of 18 inner London magistrates' courts and 34 magistrates' courts in the Wessex Regional Health Authority region during the year 1969. Of males charged with indictable offences of all kinds, 9.3 per cent were remanded for a medical report in London, 4.3 per cent in Wessex. Of male indictable sex offenders, however, a much higher proportion was so remanded, about a fifth in both areas.

Among the much commoner non-indictable offenders, the tendency to select sex cases for medical reports was even more striking. Among the generality of male non-indictable offenders very small proportions were remanded (1.2 per cent in London, 0.3 per cent in Wessex) but of the non-indictable male sex offenders, most of whom were charged with indecent exposure, 29.1 per cent were remanded for medical reports in London and 10.5 per cent in Wessex.

The proportions of offenders who ultimately received a formal treatment order were much smaller than the proportions remanded for a report. Among indictable male sex offenders in Wessex 6.74 per cent received a treatment order compared with only 2.04 per cent in London. Of the non-indictable male sex offenders, 2.69 per cent received a treatment order in London, and 2.10 per cent in Wessex.

The likelihood of treatment being recommended and offered was much greater for sex offenders remanded on bail than for those examined in prison. Since the London courts made much greater use of remands in custody than did the Wessex courts, this accounted, at least in part, for fewer of the London reports leading to a treatment order.

7.53 There are several obvious reasons why an offender remanded for examination on bail stands a greater chance of being recommended for treatment than one remanded to prison. First, the prisons deal with more socially alienated, poorly motivated and recidivistic offenders who are less likely to respond to treatment. Second, the prison medical officers cannot offer treatment themselves, but must arrange it by calling upon a National Health Service colleague. This can involve protracted and sometimes frustrating negotiations, which are likely to be undertaken only in very serious cases or where offenders have some florid psychiatric illness. Prison medical officers rarely recommend out-patient treatment on probation, perhaps because they are in less close touch with facilities in the community than are the consultants working in the locality. The nearest remand prison is often many miles from where the offender lives. Relatively mild psycho-sexual problems, such as might alert an outside consultant to a need for treatment, are easily lost sight of against the background of an inmate population with a high incidence of psychiatric disorder. While theoretically a custodial remand allows opportunity for observation, in fact the pressure of work at a busy remand prison is such that the interview with the doctor probably takes place only in the third and last week of the remand period, and often without the benefit of much information from the probation service about current social circumstances, previous treatments or assessments of personality.

7.54 The regional differences in medical remands, and the contrasting outcome of remands to prison and remands on bail, suggest that there is scope for improving procedures and increasing the numbers of sex offenders who receive psychiatric treatment. As the authors of the Gibbens (1977, p. 37) survey point out, in busy London courts where speed is important the custodial remand is dangerously easy to administer. A quarter of those remanded in custody by London courts had had either police or court bail at an earlier stage, so the decision to remand in custody must often have been unconnected with the defendant's liability to disappear.

7.55 Offenders found guilty of an imprisonable offence who are mentally disordered to such an extent as to warrant compulsory detention in a psychiatric facility may be committed by the courts by means of a hospital order under s. 37 of the Mental Health Act 1983. Since the offender will lose his liberty, this is a more formal procedure than the probation order and two independent psychiatrists have to examine the offender and agree that he is suffering from a specified form of disorder within the meaning of the Act namely mental illness, psychopathic disorder, mental impairment (formerly subnormality) or severe mental impairment. The disorder must be of such a degree as to warrant involuntary detention for medical treatment. Sexual deviation or sexual misconduct, in the absence of mental disorder, is not in itself a valid criterion for a compulsory hospital order.

Hospital orders are rarely used for sex offenders unless they are seriously disordered or have committed grave crimes. For example, a sex offender charged with murder who escaped a mandatory life sentence by successfully pleading 'diminished responsibility' (under s. 2 of the Homicide Act 1957) would be likely to receive a hospital order, whereas an exhibitionist would not. When a Crown Court makes such an order the judge may, if he has evidence that it is necessary for the protection of the public, add a restriction, under s. 41 of the Mental Health Act 1983, to prevent the responsible medical officer from granting leave of absence, transfer or discharge of the patient without the consent of the Home Secretary. Otherwise, the responsible medical officer can discharge a hospital order patient at any time he thinks fit. The Mental Health Review Tribunals also have the power to terminate a hospital order and release the patient if they find that his mental condition no longer warrants continued detention. Since the coming into force of the Mental Health Act 1983 they have been able to do so even when a restriction order is in force, but such proceedings are now always chaired by a judge.

7.56 The use of hospital orders has declined in recent years, largely because of the unwillingness of consultants and nursing staff in the National Health Service to agree to admit to their hospital wards offender patients who are potentially dangerous or who require restraints incompatible with the 'open door' policy with mixed-sex wards and mixed-sex staff, that has become almost universal. Consequently, unless places can be found in the special high security hospitals (Broadmoor, Rampton, Moss Side, Park Lane) run by the Department of Health, or in the new 'medium secure units', mentally abnormal sex offenders are increasingly liable to be sentenced to imprisonment, either for a fixed term or, in serious cases, for life, which means detention of indeterminate duration with release only at the discretion of the Home Secretary and the Parole Board. However, in making their recommendation for release, the Board does have up-to-date medical reports.

7.57 The number of sex offenders admitted to the special hospitals is quite small. A personal communication from the Special Hospitals Research Unit records a total of 154 admissions of male sex offenders to the four special hospitals during the eight years from 1972 to 1979. Their offence category and their Mental Health Act diagnosis is shown in the following table:

Table 7.57
Numbers of Male Sex Offenders Admitted for the First Time to Special Hospitals in 1972–1979.

	Offence Type:-				
Diagnostic Group	Buggery/indecent assault on male	Rape	Indecent assault on female	Other (eg indecency with a child, unlawful sexual intercourse)	Total
Mental Illness	4	12	21	3	40 (26%)
Psychopathic Disorder	11	19	44	8	82 (53%)
Subnormality	6	6	14	4	30 (20%)
Severe Subnormality	1	0	1	–	2 (1%)
	22 (14%)	37 (24%)	80 (52%)	15 (10%)	154 (100%)

It can be seen that psychopathic disorder is the commonest diagnostic category. Because this diagnosis is becoming increasingly unpopular as a justification for a hospital order, and because the total number of hospital orders has been declining in recent years, it is evident that the chances of a serious sex offender receiving treatment in hospital rather than a sentence of imprisonment are diminishing considerably.

7.58 The new system of 'interim hospital orders', introduced by the 1983 Act for implementation in October 1984, may do something to counteract the trend. These orders are intended to give offenders a trial period in hospital before the court finally decides how to deal with them. It will not make a hospital order if the hospital finds the offender untreatable. This new system may encourage psychiatrists to allow more offenders at least a chance of treatment.

The 1983 Act also makes provision for seriously disturbed offenders to be remanded to hospital rather than to prison, but the numbers so dealt with will be limited by the level of security available at hospitals.

ETHICAL PROBLEMS OF CONSENT

7.59 Ethical problems relating to treatment are not peculiar to sex offenders, except in so far as controversial methods are more likely to be used in their case. Three aspects present particular problems: how to obtain valid consent, what conditions should be satisfied before giving treatment without consent, and what special safeguards are required in the light of the controversial nature of the treatment approach to sex offenders.

A person cannot give realistic consent to treatment unless he fully understands its nature and purpose and has not been induced to agree through any form of duress or fraud: consent should be both informed and free.

A doctor or psychologist proposing treatment to a patient or prisoner has a duty to make the best assessment he can of the likelihood of benefit and of the possibilities of adverse side-effects and to explain these as fully as possible. In view of the complexities of real life situations these requirements cannot always be met in an ideal fashion; for example the amount of information given may have to be adjusted to what the individual can understand, and side effects may have to be described in a reassuring way to over-anxious individuals who might otherwise be unnecessarily frightened. The complexity of clinical situations can never be completely encompassed in statutory formulae. Recourse to more general concepts, such as 'good faith' and 'negligence', will always be needed in disputed cases.

7.60 In order to make an informed and properly motivated decision to undertake treatment a prospective patient needs to have an open discussion of what is involved, to be told the advantages and difficulties of any programme that is on offer, and to be given a clear idea of the prospects of a satisfactory outcome, so far as the current state of knowledge allows. With a sex offender on remand there is a risk that treatment, either unconditional or as a requirement of probation, may be seen as preferable to a prison sentence and thus accepted without genuine motivation to change. Although such consent is not entirely free, this is true of many decisions taken in ordinary life, and there are many clinical situations in which treatment is accepted under a variety of pressures.

It may be that absolutely free consent is an unattainable ideal and that it would be preferable to replace it with agreed criteria for acceptable practice. For example, if it could be decided by courts, probation officers and therapists that certain treatments would be on offer as alternatives to imprisonment in suitable cases, provided that the offender attended for an agreed length of time, this might be regarded as in itself an ethically acceptable arrangement. There would then be no need to question whether the offender's formal concurrence amounted to valid consent in an absolute sense. The guidelines for acceptable treatment alternatives could then be amended to meet any changes in scientific ideas and social values.

7.61 Offers of help to offenders serving sentences of imprisonment also raise problems because consent may be thought to improve their prospects of parole. It has to be made clear that earlier parole as a result of consent to treatment can be neither guaranteed nor even expected. Although a prisoner might be swayed into giving consent by misplaced hopes of parole, it is a more common experience of therapists working in prisons that men who want to accept treatment fear to do so because of the serious consequence of being labelled a sex offender while living among the general inmate population.

Treatment Without Consent

7.62 Unless some dramatic new form of treatment for sexual deviations were to be discovered, compulsory treatment for sane sex offenders would rarely, if ever, be proposed. Exceptionally, a psychiatrist might want to give treatment to a compulsorily detained mentally disordered patient who happens to be a convicted sex offender and who is unable or unwilling to give consent. The Department of Health and Social Security's legal advisers used to take the view that the responsible medical officer had the authority to treat a detained patient without consulting anyone else, but after prolonged controversy and public debate new procedures have now been embodied in legislation. Part IV of the Mental Health Act 1983 now requires that if the consent of a detained patient cannot be obtained, for certain treatments a second opinion must be sought before proceeding with them. The treatments in question include 'the administration of medicine to a patient by any means' for over three months and any other forms of treatment that may from time to time be included in regulations issued by the Secretary of State. The second opinion must be obtained from a medical practitioner appointed for the purposes of this Part of the Act by the Secretary of State. This practitioner, before providing a certificate permitting the treatment to go ahead, must consult two other persons who have been professionally concerned with the patient's medical treatment, one of whom must be a nurse and the other neither a nurse nor a medical practitioner. However, in the circumstances of urgent necessity set out in s. 62 – such as to save life or prevent serious deterioration – treatment may still proceed on the authority of the responsible medical officer alone.

7.63 Because the Mental Health Act 1983 requires that a second opinion must be obtained before a patient is given treatment against his will, the new Act may be seen as providing safeguards for the patient which were not explicit in the previous legislation. These safeguards operate for the mentally disordered patient whether he is convicted of a criminal offence or not, and it is only in the emergencies specified by s. 62 that they may be over-ridden. If the responsible medical officer acts alone he may subsequently be asked to account for his decisions.

However, it is worth pointing out that the second opinion in a case of imposed treatment will be provided by a State-appointed medical practitioner. Thus, if at some future time the ethical standards of some members of the psychiatric profession were to fall short of those to which we are now accustomed, the obtaining of two apparently independent opinions could act to facilitate the imposition of treatment on competent patients against their will. The pressure to apply any form of treatment that claimed to render sexual offenders harmless, such as chemical castration or whatever new techniques might be developed in the future, could then become difficult to resist. However hypothetical that may seem today, we feel it right to note this dangerous possiblity.

CONTROVERSIAL TREATMENTS REQUIRING SPECIAL SAFEGUARDS

7.64 S. 57 of the Mental Health Act 1983 deals with controversial or potentially hazardous treatments for mental disorder that may not be given to any patient, consenting or otherwise, without the agreement of an authorised second opinion. This applies to 'any surgical operation for destroying brain tissue or for destroying the function of brain tissue' as well as to such other treatments as may be specified in regulations made by the Secretary of State. Regulation 16 specifies 'the surgical implantation of hormones for the purpose of reducing male sex drive', but does not include the similar use of tablets by mouth. Brain surgery has not been used for sex offenders in this country, but it has been applied in some places as a voluntary treatment for sexual deviations (Dörner, 1976). With increasing understanding of brain mechanisms and localisation of functions it is possible that psycho-surgery for sexual disorders may attract more advocates in the future.

7.65 Apart from brain surgery it is possible that other forms of treatment might in time come to be included under this section. For example, behaviour modification for sex offenders continues to be controversial and gives rise to comments in the press and on television, so it could at some time attract attention from the Secretary of State.

Behaviour modification using aversion as an element in the reconditioning process causes concern to see that the method gives worthwhile results without being excessively punitive. Some ethical guidelines for National Health Service programmes have been produced by an official working party (Zangwill, 1980). One recommendation is that aversion with electric shocks should be used only after other methods have failed, and after full discussion, explanation and written consent. For some clients, however, conventional aversive techniques can appear more rational, and thus more readily acceptable, than more 'positive' alternatives such as social skills training.

As the law now stands, no second opinion is required for behaviour modification programmes, but the issue of consent is a complicated matter. The Zangwill Working Party Report (1980) envisages the possibility that such programmes might be proposed for detained patients, but advises that they should have some right of appeal.

7.66 The decision to try to suppress sexuality by hormone manipulation or implantation should never be taken lightly, particularly in view of known side-effects. Although at one time favoured by a few practitioners in the prison medical service such work has always been regarded as controversial. Dr. Fitzgerald, who was at one time using these methods at Dartmoor, reported to us that the results were variable. Hormone treatment may well be justified for individuals whose propensities are likely to result in the commission of seriously antisocial sexual acts, where no other measure would suffice. Research into the effects of long-term anti-androgen administration, the possible development of new synthetic compounds with fewer undesirable side-effects, and the integration of hormonal medication with other forms of therapy (so that it can be used as a temporary and reversible procedure while other treatments have time to take effect) may alter the ethical consideration for the future.

The use of anti-libidinal medication against a patient's wishes can hardly ever be justified, but if the drug is surgically implanted s. 57 of the Mental Health Act 1983 still applies even if a detained patient gives his consent. This requires that two non-medical members of the Mental Health Commission must see the patient and agree that his consent is valid before the treatment is initiated. In addition one medical member must see the patient and come to the same opinion and must also interview two people who know the patient, one of whom is a nurse and the other not a doctor or a nurse – a social worker or occupational therapist for example. In all, a minimum of five persons in addition to the patient and the doctor must be involved and all agree.

PART II

WHAT SHOULD BE DONE?

CHAPTER 8

The criminal law

INTRODUCTION

8.1 Having reviewed social, legal and penal attitudes and practices about sexual offending, we are now in a position to make some proposals about what ought to be done. As we mentioned at the outset, we do not pretend to offer complete solutions to what are, after all, perennial human problems, but there are some steps which could be taken to deal with these matters more rationally and practically, in the hope that this would reduce, at least to some extent, the risks of sexual victimisation and exploitation, and the suffering that follows the commission of sex offences.

The considerations from which our recommendations emerge have been set out in Part I. Here, therefore, we only summarise the reasoning behind them, fuller discussions and justifications having been given previously in Part I. This accounts for the rather frequent cross-references.

Proposals of this kind tend to fall into two broad categories; those that can be implemented quickly without any great upheaval, controversy or expenditure; and those that are ideally desirable if only there were enough resources and enough public support. Most of ours are of the former kind, but we have included a few suggestions of the latter also, to indicate the direction of our thinking.

LEGAL ANOMALIES

8.2 We drew attention, in Chapter 2, to some of the anomalies in the substantive law about sex offences. That law does not distinguish consistently between different kinds of anticipated harm: for example, violent acts, non-violent indecencies, and sex play between juveniles are all included under sexual assaults. The maximum penalties for different sex crimes bear no obvious proportion to their gravity. There is a great deal of overlap between different offences. The law discriminates inexplicably between males and females, both as victims and offenders. Finally, there are still some very odd or obsolescent crimes.

We think that at least some of the more blatant legal anomalies ought to be removed, and not just for the sake of tidiness or logic. The public is only too ready to pin asses' ears on the law, and laws that are open to mockery lessen the respect for the whole legal system. It must therefore be in the general interest to reduce absurdities and incongruities to a minimum. That seems also to be the view of the CLRC.

8.3 Apart from the oddities already listed in para 2.2, here are a few more examples of the kinds of legal anomaly we should like to see rectified:-

(1) An indecent assault by a woman on a man carries a maximum penalty of ten years' imprisonment, but an indecent assault by a man on a woman carries only two years.
(2) It appears to be no offence if a woman procures a man to have intercourse with her by fraud, or by drugging him, but it is a serious offence if a man does this to a woman.
(3) If two men and a woman make love to each other, it is a crime; but if one man and two women do so, it is not.
(4) The maximum penalty for having sexual intercourse with a consenting girl of 13–15 is two years' imprisonment, but for having intercourse with an animal it is life imprisonment.

8.4 One cannot expect full rationality about so highly emotive a subject, but some of the crassest anomalies in the law are simply left-overs from times when values and opinions used to prevail, which have long since been abandoned. For example, male homosexuality was once regarded with universal abhorrence, and all its manifestations were criminal, if not capital, offences. The act of anal intercourse, the only form available between men, was included in the general condemnation, even when committed by a heterosexual couple. Now that intercourse between consenting adult males is no longer criminal, there is surely no reason for consenting heterosexual anal intercourse to be retained as a crime.

Again, women were once regarded as psychologically weaker and more easily swayed than men, needing to be protected by law from their own frailty as much as from the sexuality of men. This paternalistic, if not chauvinistic, view fits ill with modern attitudes about the equality of rights between men and women. We see no reason why the law should continue to discriminate, either for or against one gender or the other in the field of sexual offences, whether as victims or offenders. Although the Criminal Law Revision Committee (1984, para 1.6) formally subscribes to the general principle, it still seems to take the view (para 7.5) that girls stand in greater need of protection than boys from heterosexual approaches by adults, but that boys require protection from homosexual contacts to a later age than girls (para 6.18).

8.5 With those considerations in mind, we recommend that the whole of the substantive law about sex offences should be reconsidered more radically than the CLRC seems to have been able to do, not in order to 'decriminalise' anything that is now an offence and ought to remain one, but in order to introduce greater rationality and coherence into a system which at present provides an unrealistic scale of maximum penalties and makes unnecessary distinctions based upon the gender of victims or offenders. Here are our own proposals.

OFFENCES INVOLVING VIOLENCE

8.6 First, we think it important that a clear distinction should be drawn between acts committed with the full and free consent of both parties, and acts which are not. There are indeed some consensual sexual acts, especially if they involve immature young people, which should continue to be punishable as criminal offences, and we shall return to these later. But where there is no consent, what is primarily objectionable is the use of violence, fraud or undue influence, rather than the motive of the offender. Violent assault is no better and no worse if it is motivated by sexual desire rather than anger. An act of deliberate deception is no better and no worse if the objective is to obtain sexual gratification rather than financial enrichment. Because the term "sexual" amplifies the emotive content of the offence, and therefore the harm suffered, we believe it would be better for the law to deal with non-consensual sexual activities in exactly the same way as it already deals with any other acts of violence, fraud or undue influence. As we shall show, the existing law already covers all these things with very few exceptions, so that there is in fact no need to maintain a separate set of specifically "sexual" offences of that kind.

8.7 All intentional physical contact with a non-consenting individual constitutes an assault (strictly a 'battery') punishable by law, whether it is decent or indecent, with whatever part of the body it takes place, and however it is motivated. If it is a simple assault, the maximum penalty at present is twelve months' imprisonment; if it causes actual bodily harm, it is five years; if it causes grievous bodily harm, it is life imprisonment. The laws against personal violence, therefore, are already largely adequate to punish all sex offences involving force or the threat of force. To maintain separate statutes to cover violence in a sexual context creates unnecessary overlap and emotion. The specific sex offences already covered by the laws against personal violence could therefore be safely removed. This would do away with some of the inconsistencies in maximum penalties, such as that between indecent assaults on men or women. We emphasise, however, that on this proposal the use of force without their free consent, would continue to be a criminal assault, aggravated if it causes actual or grievous bodily harm.

RAPE, ANAL PENETRATION AND ASSAULTS ON CHILDREN

8.8 An exception must be made for rape, because the penalty would be far too low if, in the absence of evidence of 'actual' or 'grievous' bodily harm, it could only be charged as a simple assault. That difficulty can easily be overcome, however, by providing that any offence which involves vaginal penetration by the penis shall be treated as having occasioned grievous bodily harm, and so will continue to be subject to a much higher maximum penalty (at present life imprisonment).

8.9 In our view anal rape is as serious an offence as vaginal rape. We therefore propose that an assault involving anal penetration by the penis should also be treated as having occasioned grievous bodily harm, whatever the gender of the victim.

8.10 At present, if the forcible penetration of anus or vagina is not by the penis, but by a hand or other part of the body, or by some object, the offence is a mere indecent assault, as are forced genital-mouth contacts or anal penetration. We think this is inadequate and propose that all these assaults should be treated as having occasioned actual bodily harm. This would overcome the frequently raised and often justified criticism that the present maximum penalty for indecent assault on a female is inadequate to deal with the more serious cases. Assaults of such violence as to result in genital or other injuries, however produced, would of course constitute the infliction of actual or grievous bodily harm.

8.11 Any form of sexual molestation of a reluctant child, however harmless in terms of manifest physical damage, must be regarded as serious because of its potentially adverse psychological consequences. This, however, can best be dealt with at the sentencing stage, by increasing severity of punishments for offences against victims of increasingly tender years. There is in any event a strong case for increasing the present maximum penalties for assaults on children.

8.12 It does not appear to us that any of these assaults differ in gravity if committed on a man rather than a woman. Accordingly, we propose that no distinction should be made in regard to sexual assaults, any more than it is for other forms of personal violence, for the gender of the victim.

These proposals are broadly similar to recent changes in Canadian law introduced by: 'An Act to amend the Criminal Code relating to Sexual Offences', which was passed in August 1982 (C–127). This abolished the crime of rape, substituted sexual assault, which could be committed by either males or females, and introduced three levels of seriousness. The third and most serious category involves wounding, maiming, disfiguring or endangering life, and carries a maximum of life imprisonment. The second level, where there is bodily harm, use of a weapon or threats to a third party, carries up to fourteen years. The first level covers everything from touching to forced sexual intercourse with a minimum of violence, and carries up to ten years (Greenland, 1983).

8.13 On the vexed question of rape within marriage (para 4.50), we fully appreciate the difficulties which have exercised authorities both here and in the United States (Marsh *et al*, 1982). The Criminal Law Revision Committee also considered the question, devoting eight pages to the topic. We agree with their recommendation that a husband should not be immune from prosecution if the couple are living apart, but that otherwise it should be left to matrimonial rather than criminal law to provide the main protection against unreasonable sexual demands.

NON-VIOLENT OFFENCES

8.14 Where an act is committed with the consent of the parties concerned, that is, without any force or threat of force, its prohibition by law, and the imposition of penalties on those who commit it, calls for some justification. Since approval or disapproval of various kinds of sexual activity differ so much between individuals and between sections of society, it is difficult to find common ground on what seems reasonable justification for prohibition. Nonetheless, we believe that quite a wide measure of agreement might be found on some issues.

For example, we should not wish to alter the principle set by the Appeal Court in a classic case of brutal sexual flagellation (Donovan, 1934) that it is an offence to commit bodily harm for sexual purposes even if the person consents.

8.15 Apparent consent may not be real if it is procured by threats, false pretences or the administration of a drug. Procuring sexual intercourse with a woman by such means is rightly now a criminal offence (s. 3 and s. 4, Sexual Offences Act, 1956). But we see no reason why it should not also be an offence if the victim is a man and we therefore recommend that in this, as in other forms of sexual misconduct, the law should not distinguish between the genders of the victims. Furthermore, we think the offence should be extended to include anal, as well as vaginal, intercourse.

8.16 Similar considerations apply to the severely mentally impaired who may be capable of only apparent and not real consent. It is already an offence for a man to have intercourse with a woman who is severely mentally impaired (s. 7, Sexual Offences Act, 1956) and once again we see no good reason why this law should distinguish between the gender of the participants or between vaginal and anal penetration. As the Criminal Law Revision Committee pointed out (1980, para 101) the present law appears to deny the severely mentally impaired 'opportunities for tender and close relationships which it is a fundamental right of all people to enjoy', and which the Committee was anxious to encourage, so long as no exploitation was involved. It puts those in charge of institutions for the mentally impaired into a difficult position about the control of the sexual responses of inmates to each other. We ourselves have no strong views on this, but we are inclined to agree with the suggestion by the CLRC (1984, para 9.9) that sexual activity between a man and a woman who are both severely mentally impaired should not be a crime. However, in conformity with the general principle of disregarding gender, we should also exclude sexual acts between severely mentally impaired persons of the same sex.

8.17 Another variety of disapproved behaviour that requires legal control is the unscrupulous exploitation of the sexual proclivities of others for personal financial gain. Some of the abuses of pimps, brothelkeepers, procurers, blackmailers and pornographers fall into this category, but, as we said at the outset (para 2.6), we have excluded them from our consideration in this report.

RESPONSIBLE ADULTS

8.18 We must next consider acts between adults which take place with the full and free consent of all the parties concerned, without force, fear or fraud, but which are still criminal offences. These include heterosexual anal intercourse, homosexual acts committed in private if more than two persons 'take part or are present', and intercourse with animals. All three are potentially punishable with life imprisonment.

It seems to us quite unwarranted to retain the first of these as a crime. Heterosexual couples who engage in anal intercourse do no demonstrable harm. To brand them as criminals, subject to the same penalty as murderers and rapists, can only bring the law into disrepute. The Sexual Offences Act 1967, which legalised anal intercourse between consenting adult males, inexplicably left out consenting adults of the opposite sex. We believe that action should be taken at the first opportunity to put this right, and we are glad to note that the Criminal Law Revision Committee (1984, para 6.7) would also like to see consensual buggery with women over 16 no longer punishable.

8.19 Though some people may disapprove of private sex parties, it is questionable whether there is any strong support for making such activities criminal, still less for making only some of them criminal, depending on the gender of some of the participants. In conformity with the general principle that the law should not discriminate according to the gender of offenders, we recommend the abolition of the prohibition against male homosexual acts in private when more than two persons 'take part or are present'. This recommendation too now has the support of the CLRC (1984, paras 10.4–10.15), although they were careful to advise (para 10.21) that this dispensation should not cover homosexual clubs or other places of common resort.

8.20 As to what the law calls bestiality, that is, sexual intercourse with an animal, we fail to see why this ancient offence, which is rarely prosecuted nowadays, should be maintained. If an animal is treated with cruelty, the law already provides appropriate penalties. In a recent decision about a man imprisoned for attempted bestiality with a bitch, the Court of Appeal commented that to uphold the sentence would leave the Court without any sensible scale of reference for the punishment of buggery with human beings: it was the appellant, not the dog, who needed help. A probation order was substituted (*R v Higson* [1984] 4711 / A /83). Both the Policy Advisory Committee and the Criminal Law Revision Committee were divided on whether the offence should be retained, but we are firmly of the opinion that it should now be abolished.

8.21 The offence of soliciting by women applies only to soliciting for purposes of prostitution, and has recently ceased to be imprisonable. However, soliciting by men is still imprisonable and is treated as a crime when the purpose is to obtain a partner for homosexual activity, even when no element of prostitution is involved. It has been suggested in some quarters that soliciting should be prosecuted only if annoyance is caused to a complaining member of the public other than a policeman. Since we have excluded prostitution from our considerations, we make no comment on that issue, but in accordance with our general principle that the gender of an offender should not determine the definition of a crime, nor the penalty imposed, we should like to see whatever laws are applied to soliciting by women to be applied in the same way, and neither more nor less strictly, to soliciting by men. For instance, the cautioning procedures under the Street Offences Act that are applied to women soliciting for prostitution might also be used for male prostitutes.

8.22 Similar considerations apply to the offence of 'procuring'. It is no offence to procure (ie introduce) a woman to a third party for sexual intercourse if she is over 21, not a prostitute or mentally impaired, and genuinely consenting. However, it remains an offence for anyone to procure a man for homosexual activity with a third party, even though the two who actually perform the activity commit no crime. Again, we think this is unnecessarily discriminatory, and we believe that the offence of procuring should be defined similarly, regardless of the gender of the person procured, and whether the purpose is heterosexual or homosexual. This may seem trivial, but it matters because of the possible liability to prosecution of persons who run counselling groups, discussion sessions or social gatherings attended by homosexuals.

THE CONSENTING YOUNG

8.23 We now come to the most difficult topic of all: consensual sexual activity by or with the young. As we have already said, the use of any force, threat or fraud to procure sexual contact with children or young people must remain in the category of a serious criminal assault, visited with severe penalties. But we are now considering activities of the young with each other, or with older persons, which involve no violence, force, fear or fraud of any kind. Nonetheless, disapproval is strong, widespread, and must be taken into account. Many people are convinced that young participants in sexual acts may suffer serious harm, especialy when adults are involved with them. As we have reported earlier (see paras 4.1–4.10), such incidents are far commoner than is generally supposed, and the general trend of the evidence suggests that it is any associated coercion, or the adverse reactions of parents or others when matters come to light, rather than the sexual experience itself, which seems to cause the most harm.

However, some people are very easily influenced, persuaded or seduced by people older than themselves, especially when they are at a stage of having to contend with their own sexual impulses without yet having acquired the strength or the wisdom to control them, or to resist sexual pressures from others. The law therefore has good reason to seek to protect young people of both sexes from the advance of older, more powerful and more experienced people of either gender. It seems to us, however, that it is not simply the ages of the participants, but more particularly the size of the age difference, and the nature of the relationship between them, that determine the seriousness of these incidents. The young need particular protection from adults, and especially from those who occupy some position of responsibility or authority over them, such as parents, teachers, employers, physicians, youth workers and so forth.

8.24 At present, the young are protected by the unreal legal fiction that boys and girls under 16 are incapable of consenting to any sexual acts whatsoever, and that young men under 21 can give no valid consent to homosexual acts. In reality they may be perfectly capable of giving full consent at earlier ages, and they frequently do, but the law 'deems' any such consent to be invalid. One of the unrealistic features of these provisions, apt to bring the law into disrepute, is that on their sixteenth or twenty-first birthdays (or, in strict law, at midnight on the previous day) girls and boys are suddenly supposed to become capable of giving a consent that they were unable to give the day before. In the case of girls, the effect is to remove legal protection at an age which many people, including ourselves, consider premature, because they may still be under the authority of a variety of older persons and may not yet be capable of withstanding undue pressure.

Any age of consent implies some threshold, but a two-tier system, allowing for some protection between the ages of absolute freedom and absolute prohibition, would be a substantial improvement.

8.25 In our view, protection against older people, and against persons in positions of authority, is needed beyond 16, and up to 18. But we do not believe that the same protection is needed for dealing with two young people of roughly similar age, neither of whom is in authority over the other. A great deal of sexual experimentation has always gone on amongst children and young people, probably much more than some parents realise, or could stop if they knew. To brand it all as criminal and lacking consent – when plainly it is not – while doing little or nothing to stop it in practice, is no way to encourage the young to respect the law.

8.26 We think that the best way to overcome these problems is by a modification and extension of the provisions of the Indecency with Children Act 1960. This sensible statute makes any act of indecency, or incitement to indecency, with or towards a child under 14, regardless of the sex of either the child or the offender, punishable with up to two years' imprisonment. The wording covers indecent behaviour in the presence of a child even if the child is not actually touched, or if the child is induced to touch the offender. We propose that these provisions should be extended to protect young persons from 14 up to 18 by introducing a single, comprehensive offence of 'unlawful indecency' with a person of either sex who is under 18. A separate and graver offence of 'unlawful sexual intercourse' with anyone under 18 should also be added.

8.27 Whether these offences are deemed to have been committed, however, should depend upon certain qualifying factors. In order to avoid making crimes out of the sex play of children with each other, we propose that the offence of unlawful indecency with a child under 14 can only be committed by a person over 14.

As regards sexual contact with young persons between 14 and 18 we would propose, for the reasons already explained, that the offences of unlawful indecency and unlawful sexual intercourse would be committed only if the offender is two or more years older than and is not the husband or wife of the young person in question, and has either abused a position of trust or authority (such as that of a parent, guardian or older relative), or exerted some undue influence over the young person. The law might usefully here provide a presumption, in the absence of evidence to the contrary, that undue influence applies in the case of teachers, employers, youth workers, hostel wardens and so forth, or if the accused is 7 or more years older than the young person, or if the young person has been offered some material inducement, or been kept away from home against the wishes of parents or guardians.

8.28 These proposals for maintaining absolute protection for children under 14 and protection, in many cases, for all young persons up to 18, are very similar to the suggestions put forward by the Canadian Law Commission (1978). The notion of providing special protection for persons in situations of dependency is already found in some European legal systems, for example in the Swiss Penal Code, section 192. These proposals would not of course affect the right to marry at sixteen.

8.29 We do not imagine that these proposals would solve all problems, or meet with instant or universal approval. There is no perfect solution, and this is a compromise which some may see as encouraging the corruption of the young and others as a return to the Victorian age. But we believe that this scheme, or something like it, would better reflect the realities of life than does the present archaic law.

One advantage consequent upon our proposals is that the age of protection would be the same for both sexes. The only conceivable justification for maintaining it for men at the present level of 21, the age below which all male homosexual acts are criminal, would seem to be the belief that inherently heterosexual young men between 18 and 21 might be converted into homosexuals by exposure to the possibility of that kind of activity. In fact, as we pointed out earlier (para 4.17), there is good evidence that this is not a significant cause of homosexuality. Most fixed homosexual orientations seem to develop at a much earlier age and are not influenced by any attempt to use the criminal law to enforce chastity up to age 21, and indeed the Policy Advisory Committee on Sexual Offences (1981) has already recommended that this age should now be reduced to 18.

We believe that our scheme comes closer than the present law to meeting the real needs for protection of the young at various ages and at various stages of development, both of sexuality and of maturity of judgement, without uselessly making criminals of thousands who can never in practice be prosecuted.

INCEST

8.30 Incest only became a criminal offence as recently as 1908 as the result of the activities of crusading pressure groups against immorality and child abuse (Bailey and Blackburn, 1979). Relatively few cases come to light, and fewer still are prosecuted. If the proposals we have outlined were adopted, the separate offence of incest could in fact be safely abolished, for our scheme would provide protection for the vulnerable young from their parents as much as from anyone else. The presumption of abuse of authority or undue influence would clearly apply to parents, and also to step-parents adopting parents and adults *in loco parentis*, who cannot be guilty of incest under the present law. Moreover, indecencies and assaults not involving sexual intercourse, which are presently not covered by the incest law, would also be adequately covered.

8.31 Under our scheme, consensual acts of incest between adults would escape prosecution. One argument for maintaining these as crimes is the risk of congenital defects in the children of such unions, which we mentioned in Chapter 4. However, the criminal law is not used to prohibit intercourse by persons known to be carrying genetically transmitted diseases, where the risk of producing defective children is sometimes much greater, so that argument cannot carry much weight. The CLRC (1984, para 8.22) does not propose abolition of the specific crime of incest, but on a majority view proposes that consensual incest between a brother and sister both over 21 should cease to be an offence.

8.32 As for consensual sexual behaviour between young persons or children and their brothers or sisters, our proposals would cover this in the same way as other consensual conduct by or with the young. Many people would, in any case, consider that the control of such conduct between children within the family is best left to parents, supported when necessary by social workers (who have the power, when other measures fail, to apply for the removal of a juvenile from a household where there is exposure to moral danger), rather than to the awesome processes of criminal justice.

It might be objected that loss of the legal label 'incest' would mean that insufficient account would be taken of the special revulsion felt against parents who offend sexually with their own children. We believe, however, that the powers of the courts to take this aggravating circumstance into account when sentencing is an adequate safeguard. Furthermore, the proposals we make later (see para 9.12ff) for dealing with some cases of intra-familial sexual abuse outside the criminal courts, so as to spare the child victim further damage, would be inequitable if other, not dissimilar cases, were dealt with by means of the particularly emotion-laden charge of incest.

Finally, it may be noted that some other countries, such as France and the Netherlands, do not find it necessary to have a specific crime of incest separate from other provisions which protect the young (Freeman, 1979).

PROTECTION FROM PUBLICITY

8.33 Since the passing of the Sexual Offences (Amendment) Act of 1976 the press, radio or TV may no longer publish the name of a victim in a trial for rape, or publish particulars that might identify her (see 4.49). The Act serves to protect the victim from becoming a focus of malicious gossip or being shunned by acquaintances or prospective boy friends, some of whom may regard her as somehow defiled or who may say to themselves, or to each other, 'There's no smoke without fire; she probably led him on'.

We think this is an excellent provision as far as it goes, the more so as the law generally does far too little to help victims of crime to rehabilitate themselves after the event: its concern for them usually ends when they have given their evidence at the trial. Juvenile victims of sex offences of all kinds are already substantially protected by s. 39 of the Children and Young Persons Act, 1933, (as amended by s. 57 (4) of the Children and Young Persons Act 1963), whereby the courts can prohibit publication of 'any particulars calculated to lead to the identification of any child or young person'. If, however, a court fails to make such an order – in an incest case for example – the press are free to publish the offender's name, thus making known the child's involvement to neighbours and schoolfellows, with consequences that can all too easily be imagined, not least at the hands of their schoolfriends' parents, who may forbid them from having any contact with the child. To give just one example, in 1981 a Northamptonshire newspaper gave the name and address of a man convicted of sexual assaults over a twelve month period on a girl of twelve. It was not mentioned that she was in fact his daughter, but the information was quite enough to identify her to schoolfellows and neighbours. According to social workers' records, the family received abusive telephone calls, the mother was rejected by neighbours because she allowed her husband back, and the girl did not return to her school because of the publicity (Cooper, 1984).

In the case of older victims, we see no reason for confining protection from publicity to rape victims: in our view it could usefully be extended to the victims of other sex offences, who are just as exposed to the risk of undeserved obloquy. The Criminal Law Revision Committee (1984, para 2.99), however, do not recommend that anonymity for complainants should extend beyond 'rape offences'. As for child victims, the publication of identifying particulars should be prohibited always, and not only when a court makes a specific order.

8.34 Section 6 of the Act extends a similar protection to the accused, but only if he is acquitted. The reason is that, like the victim, he too is exposed to malicious gossip and irrational responses of this kind, and it would be inequitable to protect one innocent party and not the other. That seems to us entirely sound, and we would therefore also recommend the extension of the provisions of this section of the Act to persons accused of any sex offence, and not only rape.

It could be argued that these two protections should be extended to all offences, and not remain confined to those involving sex. If there is a case for this, we do not believe it to be very strong in the case of the victims: even ill-motivated people do not generally shun the victims of theft, burglary, street mugging or other crimes. It is the sexual element which is most apt to precipitate this kind of irrational malice. The case is probably stronger here for protecting the innocent accused, about whom people may still say later, 'Wasn't he the man who was involved in that robbery case?', or just 'He was lucky to get off; I'll bet he really did it'. But this question is beyond our terms of reference.

8.35 There is something to be said for protecting even some guilty persons from disproportionate suffering caused by indiscriminate publicity. Minor offences, such as indecent exposure or lavatory indecencies, which commonly attract no more than a small fine, can ruin a promising career if reported in the local press, break up a family, and even lead to suicide. This chance targetting of individuals, selected by the press with little regard for the consequences, scarcely serves the public interest. On the other hand, the threat of publicity is widely regarded as a useful deterent, and the principle of public hearings and free reporting is a treasured part of our system of justice. However, in many European countries the press themselves have adopted rules which prevent the publication of the identities of accused persons in cases where the sentences fall below certain levels of severity (Jones, 1974, p. 160).

We recognise the undesirability of any statutory system, whether imposed on the press or the courts, intended to conceal the identity of specified classes of adult offender. On the other hand, it is reasonable to expect the press to adopt a more responsible attitude, and for the Press Council to give a lead, by laying down guidelines to prevent the inhumane, unfair, and unnecessary practice of publishing the names and addresses of selected petty offenders, especially first offenders in cases of minor indecency.

CHAPTER 9

Social policy

EDUCATION AND TRAINING

9.1 The operations of the criminal justice system are costly, its decisions sometimes have very destructive side-effects, and it is not outstandingly successful in controlling crimes, especially the kinds of crime that often go unreported. It is a necessary agency of last resort, but less formal methods of discouraging crime need to be further developed. Here, education has an important part to play.

9.2 A child brought up to know and care about responsibilities towards others, in sex as in other aspects of life, is less at risk of developing anti-socially. We believe that every encouragement should be given to parental efforts to inculcate informed and reasonable attitudes and standards in sexual matters. Naturally, in a pluralist society, differing cultural backgrounds will determine parental ideas of morality, and there must be a very wide measure of tolerance for parents' rights to pass on their own deeply held values. But young persons today are confronted with a multiplicity of conflicting examples and pressures in the sexual sphere and stand in need, as never before, of the ability to make educated choices.

9.3 One reason why sex education in early years is important is because research has shown that many sex offenders, more especially those whose behaviour is sexually deviant, have been reared in prudish homes that kept them sexually ignorant, thereby promoting guilt feelings, anxieties and revulsions that interfered with the normal course of heterosexual development. Apart from embarrassed avoidance, sheer parental neglect which leaves children to learn from hints haphazardly picked up outside the home, can also lead to the acquisition of distorted ideas. A strong body of expert opinion advocates a more straightforward approach to childhood sex instruction. Children are sensitive to furtiveness, embarrassment, avoidance, intimations of disgust or condemnation and unwillingness to answer questions frankly. The fact that so many of the children who have been troubled by some unpleasant sexual encounter fear to tell their parents about it points to a sad lack of communication (see para 4.9).

9.4 Sex information is best acquired gradually and naturally in the course of everyday family interchange. Difficulties arising from their own unresolved anxieties prevent some well-meaning parents from fulfilling this need adequately. It is important, therefore, that parents should be backed up by a sensible programme of sex education in the schools, covering not just the anatomy and physiology of sex, but also the social, psychological, emotional and moral aspects which are likely to cause young people the most problems. This is no easy task, since teachers' ideas on matters such as teenage sex contacts, contraception, masturbation and homsexuality will inevitably vary. Nevertheless, as in religious instruction, it should be possible to provide basic information and promote awareness of contrasting views without seeking to impose a system of morality that might conflict with parental wishes. It would be advantageous if means could be devised to secure some parental input or involvement in the schools' efforts at sex education. We believe that informed choices, whether towards a strict code of conduct or a more permissive one, are sounder, healthier and more likely to prove successful than attitudes built upon ignorance or unspoken fears.

9.5 Crude macho attitudes which relegate women to a second class of humanity are still regrettably prevalent, more especially among the less educated. It is more than coincidence that sexual attacks upon women are commoner among groups in which adolescent males learn to treat girls as objects to be possessed, boasted about and fought over, and in which domination of women, sexually and otherwise, is seen as a mark of masculine achievement.

The secondary schools can do something about this. They have a responsibility for educating the young in the practical skills of social living as well as in academic subjects. Every young person needs to have some preparatory training for home-making, marriage and parenthood and to have guidance in appreciating the different emotional and material expectations of the two sexes.

9.6 Education about contraception should emphasise the element of personal responsibility, more especially the responsibility of the male partner, who too readily assumes that it can all be left to the girl. The known risks of the use of hormonal contraceptives by young girls may bring about a return to the use of the male condom, but an amount of irrational prejudice against this, as being 'unmanly', needs to be overcome.

Whether contraceptive advice and material should be made available to young people on demand is a difficult issue. We are quite clear that we do not wish to suggest anything that might encourage sexual promiscuity among the young, or even to condone sexual intercourse between young persons who could not cope properly with a pregnancy. Nevertheless, given that the present arrangements fail to prevent some 4,000 girls under 16 from becoming pregnant each year, and given that abortions and unwanted births in these girls are such tragic events, we think, on balance, that the sexually active young should have the right to obtain the necessary aids from doctors and clinics. The main practical objection is that some youngsters who might otherwise refrain from premature sexual intercourse would take advantage of a liberal policy. We do not consider this an overriding consideration. Experience suggests that it is the irresponsibly promiscuous or impulsive who cause most of the problems, and they are unlikely to bother about contraceptives unless access is made comparatively easy. Those whose personal morality or social background make avoidance of early sex the norm do not need to be given contraceptives.

All too often, young girls who are known to social workers and teachers to be at risk of pregnancy, and who have agreed to visit a family planning clinic, never get round to doing so. Given more resources, workers at such clinics could go out to meet these prospective clients, much as the 'contact chasers' from V.D. clinics are able to do.

9.7 Education may also help young children to protect themselves from potential molesters. Parents frequently give warnings not to accept invitations from strangers, but explanations can be difficult or alarming if sex has otherwise been a taboo topic. The police have produced a helpful film which puts the lesson over in ways that are realistic, not too frightening, and in a form children can readily grasp. It depicts actual situations of risk, how to avoid them, and how to resist the plausible stories that molesters sometimes invent to overcome distrust. We endorse efforts to put this message across in schools.

9.8 The mass media have an important role to play in educating the public. We commented in Part I (see paras 6.2–6.4) on the undue emphasis on crime, especially sex crime, and the use of exaggeratedly emotive language in certain popular newspapers. The inordinate amount of space devoted to sex scandals, especially if politicians are involved, surprises foreigners. It is as if the British public is assumed to have an insatiable desire for purient titillation to which some newspapers are all too willing to pander. The high moral tone which the same newspapers adopt to condemn the lapses they so eagerly report is thoroughly hypocritical.

We deplore such exploitative sensationalism, especially by papers with a mass impact on millions of readers. It promotes moral panic, encourages over-reaction to all categories of sex offender, and causes unjustified anxiety, based on misleading impressions of the likelihood of either adults or children becoming the victim of a serious sexual assault. Freedom of the press is a treasured feature of our society and abuses of that freedom carry the danger of provoking demands for tighter control. Except for occasional programmes from local radio stations, broadcast material does not offend in this way, possibly because radio and television are subject to more central regulation. In the end, the curbing of sensationalism is a task for responsible editors and journalists and for the influence of a better educated public who may learn to become more critical. The reforms we have already proposed (paras 8.33–8.34) for the protection from public identification of victims of sex crimes and of persons acquitted should limit the scope for press abuse of individuals, and should encourage the Press Council to condemn unnecessary campaigns against individual offenders unfairly singled out. The Press Council might also take a lead in promulgating desirable standards of reporting and commentary in this sensitive field.

9.9 Education and training is of crucial importance for police, prison officers, police surgeons, social workers, probation officers, magistrates, counsellors and voluntary workers, all of whom have professional dealings with sex offenders and may need to make decisions that can be of momentous significance in the lives of the individuals affected. The need is particularly great in the case of prison officers, in order to combat the abuses to which sex offenders are subjected by fellow prisoners when appropriate discipline and good example are deficient (see para 4.57). Evidence that the more experienced police surgeons give more credence to victims (see para 6.15) suggests that their task, as well as that of police interrogators, would be helped by introductory training. The information we have received from the probation service (see paras 7.32 – 7.33) has highlighted the need for workshops to disseminate information about different types of sex offender and how to deal with them.

9.10 We remarked in Part I (paras 7.41 – 7.43) on the difficulty of finding accommodation in hostels or elsewhere for sex offenders. Exaggerated fears generated by press sensationalism cannot but have some deterrent effect on prospective landladies. Hostel wardens, however, are a more accessible group. Brief educational courses for them, followed by sustained professional back-up from the psychiatric services in the handling of problems arising from the management of individual sex offenders, would be a valuable development. The voluntary hostel sector, which is larger and possibly more likely to expand than the probation hostels, might well be receptive to an eductional drive, through the National Association of Voluntary Hostels, directed towards greater understanding of the particular needs of sex offenders and greater willingness to try to cater for them. One good example that already exists is the St. Christopher's Fellowship, a charity running hostels for boys, which has set up a specialist project that offers accommodation to young people with sexual difficulties who might be helped. The staff receive supplementary training and have a consultant psychiatrist to assist and support them.

PROSECUTION POLICY

9.11 Imprisonment, and indeed the fact of prosecution itself, is a particularly severe punishment for many non-violent sex offenders, who afterwards find themselves social pariahs, estranged from family and friends and, through loneliness and loss of self respect, at increased risk of offending. If the misconduct is not very serious, the police can deal with the matter by means of an official caution. This could be done more often than at present, especially with juveniles, with first offenders who freely admit culpability, and with men who recognise the need to change their habits and who are willing to follow advice from some responsible social worker or therapist. The extension of helping services for sex offenders, which we recommend later (see para 9.36ff) should enable this procedure to be used with safety in a larger number of cases. The interests and wishes of victims, particularly child victims, are often against a formal prosecution if this can reasonably be avoided. We note with satisfaction the suggestions in a recent consultative document for an extension of cautions for offences by adults, including sexual offences where a girl or youth has been a willing partner (Home Office, 1984, para 5.27).

9.12 In the ordinary course of events persons alleged to have committed serious offences should be tried in public, and sentenced if they are found guilty. There is a special problem, however, when the essential witnesses are child victims who can be made to suffer greatly during the process of investigation, and by having to appear at the trial in contested cases. The stress is especially acute if the accused is a number of the family, since the consequences may include the loss of a parent or the victim being taken into the care of the local authority. In contested cases the police may tell those in contact with the child not to discuss the alleged offence as this could amount to interference with a prosecution witness. That makes it difficult for social workers or doctors to help the child come to terms with an unhappy situation during the long and difficult period of waiting for a Crown Court hearing. We have discussed these and other adverse side effects of prosecution upon the child of sexual abuse at some length in Part I (see para 4.19ff) but they are worth reiterating because they affect policy.

9.13 Because proof is often difficult to establish in these cases, an accused parent is sometimes acquitted in spite of the child's evidence. If the defendant is found guilty he may receive a sentence, in accordance with the serious view taken by the courts of sex offences involving children, but much in excess of what the victim or other family members may think he deserves. In both instances the victim suffers added distress, either through being apparently disbelieved and perhaps exposed to retaliation, or through guilt at being the unwitting cause of a parent receiving a long prison sentence. Apart from the consequences to the child, the prosecution of such cases often results in the break-up of the home, and economic and other deprivations which affect all family members, including other children in the household.

9.14 Child sex abuse within a family often occurs when marital and parental relationships are already disturbed. A strong body of opinion favours treating such situations as family problems, rather than criminal acts. Evidence from places where a therapeutic rather than a punitive approach is employed where possible (see para 4.20) suggest that such a policy, by preserving the affected families intact, or reuniting them after a temporary separation to allow counselling or other treatment to take effect, often succeeds in resolving the situation without subjecting the child victim to further stress or serious deprivation. Experience also shows that this kind of policy results in many more cases being disclosed and dealt with, so that many more victims obtain protection.

9.15 There must always remain some cases where the sanction of criminal proceedings is the only way remedial action can be secured.

Nevertheless, we believe that prosecutions of sex offences involving children should only take place when they are clearly necessary, in the public interest and for the protection from serious harm of actual or potential victims. This policy is already widely agreed and practised in cases of non-sexual physical abuse of chidren, but not in cases of sexual abuse, where there are even stronger reasons for it. In intra-familial sexual misconduct, where the perpetrator acknowledges responsibility and collaborates with social work or other treatment interventions, and the situation can be resolved to the satisfaction of the professional workers dealing with the case, such prosecutions should in general be avoided. To achieve this, there should be much closer collaboration between agencies receiving reports of suspected child abuse (notably local authority social workers, doctors and officers of the National Society for the Prevention of Cruelty to Children) and the prosecuting authorities. A good working relationship with the police already exists in some areas (such as Northampton and Devon), but a uniform national policy should be adopted.

9.16 The system operating in Scotland is more appropriate to these cases. The prosecuting authorities, the Procurators Fiscal, are legally qualified civil servants who are independent of the police, the courts and the local authority. They are able to weigh up information from all sources and make impartial decisions which take into account the interests of everyone concerned. The Social Work Department can invite a Procurator Fiscal to participate in case conferences about children considered at risk. He is able to learn at first hand and at an early stage how the matter came to light and what is known about the background of the alleged or suspected offences, the characteristics of the family and the condition of the child, and the probable effect upon the child of appearing in court to give evidence against a parent. He can also discuss with other professionals their assessment of the situation and their views about what ought to be done. This close liaison enables the Fiscal to assess better such legal considerations as the strength of the available evidence against the suspect, whether there is any suggestion that the accusations could have been inspired by malice, and whether the alleged acts are of sufficient gravity to justify proceedings in a lower or a higher court (Moody and Tombs, 1982). We hope that, once an independent prosecution service is established in England and Wales, that excellent example will be followed.

9.17 When doctors hear about such cases professionally, they usually feel bound by their obligations of confidentiality to advise and help the family on their own, without reporting the matter to any other authority. We agree that the confidence should not be broken without the patient's consent, but we believe that, unless there are sound reasons to the contrary, doctors should try in such cases, without imposing undue pressure, to obtain their patients' agreement to bringing in the help of the local authority social services, who have statutory obligations in regard to child welfare. They are in a position to bring to bear expertise and consistent policy, to organise long-term supportive help and surveillance, and to call upon psychiatric services where necessary. One reason for involving the social services is the tendency for initial disclosures, whether by a complaining child or a confessing offender, to be retracted later as guilt about what has happened mounts, fear of the consequences of discovery takes over, or difficulty in changing established patterns of behaviour is experienced. The social services have the advantage that they can insist on continued contact with such families as long as they perceive the children to be at some risk.

Some Social Service Departments deal with child sex abuse by placing the victims on the same 'at risk' register as cases of physical abuse. This ensures that the case receives continued attention. However, a

Department of Health circular (August, 1978, LASSL (80) 4), while explaining that the issues are being examined, 'does not recommend that sexual abuse be included . . .' We see no good reason for this, and would like to see this practice made uniform throughout the country.

9.18 Immediate reporting to the police with a view to arrest is obviously necessary where there is risk of violence, or where the offences have not stopped after disclosure. The police are the only competent authorities to collect physical evidence or formal testimony, or to make additional inquiries with a view to building up a prosecution case or to confirm what otherwise might be unfounded suspicion. These necessary tasks need to be carried out speedily, and consultation with other agencies may not be feasible. In most cases, however, the offender does not deny his guilt, immediate police action is not imperative, and there is opportunity to hold an urgent case conference with the professionals concerned present, including the police. The decisions taken should be agreed by all parties. The police should participate in the deliberations and not act independently without consultation, except in an emergency.

Since the decisions taken may affect the family profoundly for many years to come, it is right that all its members, including the alleged offender, should be allowed to express their viewpoints. The deliberations of case conferences cannot be open to public scrutiny, any more than the deliberations of public prosecutors, but all those with a close personal interest in the outcome, and particularly the victim and the offender, should have the chance to make representations.

9.19 When it is agreed, after consultation between all the professionals involved, that a family problem can probably be resolved by a treatment approach, then prosecution should be delayed. It should be explicitly recognized that the police have this discretion. The possibility of prosecution should not be dismissed at an early stage (as it would be, for example, by the issue of an official caution), because an offender, once free from legal pressures, may cease to collaborate willingly with the prescribed treatment programme, or may insist on returning home prematurely against advice. When a case has to be prosecuted in the courts, treatment does not always have to be abandoned. A deferred sentence, pending a favourable response from the offender, can avoid imprisonment.

9.20 In deciding whether to prosecute, the police are obliged to refer to the Director of Public Prosecutions if the contemplated charge is one of incest or of homosexual misconduct involving a male under 21. This is a sensible provision which, provided something could be done to avoid intolerable delays, could be extended to all indictable sex offences involving persons of either sex under the age of 14 – at all events until we have a proper system of independent prosecutors throughout the country. Where social workers or others concerned with a case have important information which they think should be taken into account they can, and should, communicate it directly to the Director of Public Prosecutions. If, however, the close collaboration with the police which we have advocated could be put into operation everywhere, there might be no need for such action.

9.21 In order for a prosecution to lead to an appropriate sentence that takes full account of the victim's interests, it is most desirable that the court should be fully informed of the findings of all the inquiries that may have been made before the trial. The probation officer, acting as liaison officer to the Crown Court, is the person most directly responsible, and he should have the duty of ensuring that all relevant social work or psychiatric reports are collected together and made available. In intra-familial child sexual abuse, where the offender is not thought to be a danger to other people's children, where the misconduct has been brought to an end, and where it seems reasonable to try to preserve the family unit intact, a probation order with appropriate conditions, (eg to undertake treatment, or to reside away from the home for a time) can be a useful solution. It ensures some remedial action as well as exercising a measure of control, since legal sanctions can be invoked if the agreed plan of action is not followed.

At present apparent injustices sometimes occur when long sentences of imprisonment are given to certain offenders whilst others, guilty of substantially similar misconduct, are put on probation or, if they happen to reside in an area where the authorities exercise greater discretion, avoid prosecution altogether. This could be prevented by the adoption of a consistent policy of seeking constructive alternatives to imprisonment whenever possible in all forms of indecency with children that come before the courts.

SENTENCING

9.22 Sentencing policy needs to take into account the fact that some sex offenders have overwhelming personal problems which make conformity exceptionally difficult for them and reduce the expectation that straightforward punishment will be an effective deterrent. In addition, it is widely acknowledged that the imprisonment of certain categories of sex offender causes particular difficulties both for them and for the prison authorities. How far sentencers can adjust their decisions in the light of such considerations depends on the availability of realistic alternatives to imprisonment and the tolerance of the public to modifications of the expected tariff of punishments.

9.23 As to the customary tariff, we have no particular comments save to note that some sex offenders are imprisoned for exceptionally long periods. This must reflect the seriousness with which the public, and the judiciary, regard sex offences where there is violence or where the victims are children, and may well include a retributive element. Uncertainty about the risk of repetition, the knowledge that such risk persists over many years, and the impossibility of predicting behaviour after release from prison, means that the gravity of the instant offence cannot be the sentencer's sole consideration. The desire to keep a potential menace out of circulation for as long as possible contributes an element of preventive detention to the fixing of sentences for some sex offenders. Unjust as this may seem, we recognise it to be inevitable. We do not, however, agree with the proposals of the Floud Committee (see para 6.50) who would like to institute a statutory category of dangerous offender for whom longer sentences would be available. For the more serious offender who might be considered dangerous the existing maximum sentences are for the most part more than adequate. In view of the uncertainty of prediction, little would be gained by trying to select, for purposes of protective sentencing, the small minority among comparatively minor offenders who go on to commit more serious offences later.

9.24 We have much sympathy with a proposal by the former Advisory Council on the Penal System (1978) to bring maximum sentences of imprisonment more into line with modern practice by reducing those unrealistically high maxima which are nowadays hardly ever used. Several of the revisions proposed by that body were concerned with the existing high maximum penalties for certain sex offences, such as unlawful buggery (life), incest (life), indecent assault on a man (10 years), indecency by a man over 21 with one under 21 (5 years), and living on the earnings of prostitution (7 years). However, we consider that the proposals already made for rationalising the law (for instance by distinguishing between true assaults and consensual indecencies and by abolishing distinctions based on gender) would go a long way towards bringing the scale of maximum penalties more closely into line with the varying gravity of the offence concerned. Our proposals for deeming certain serious sexual assaults to have occasioned bodily harm should ensure adequate penalties for cases which are now dealt with too leniently.

9.25 Because each legal category of sex offence necessarily covers a wide variety of behaviours and circumstances we would not like to see the discretion of the courts limited by a too narrowly prescribed range of punishments. We therefore wholeheartedly support the traditional English system of not fixing any minimum sentence. This permits the courts to react in a flexible manner to special circumstances and to make use of such alternatives to imprisonment as are available.

The lengths of sentences of imprisonment are largely a matter of tradition. Shorter sentences for all kinds of offence are traditional in the Netherlands (Downes, 1982), and many authorities believe that a move towards shorter sentencing in this country would be an improvement. Insofar as imprisonment operates as a deterrent, it appears that the actual length of a sentence may not be the main factor, and that shorter sentences could be equally effective. We firmly support the Howard League's view that, in general, greater use should be made of alternatives to imprisonment, and shorter sentences for those for whom custodial measures are unavoidable. We emphasis that this principle should be applied to sex offenders as much as to other categories.

9.26 An opposite policy of substantially increased periods of imprisonment is sometimes advocated on the grounds that it would reduce the level of crime in the community by taking offenders out of circulation. Home Office research suggests that this would be likely to have less effect than one might expect. Particularly in regard to some types of sex offence, where the detection rate is uncertain and reporting rates poor, the men who are convicted and imprisoned may well represent such a small minority of the totality of such offenders that their removal from the community would not much alter the incidence of sex crimes (Brody and Tarling, 1980).

These considerations do not apply to the small number of desperately violent or repetitive sex offenders from whom society rightly demands protection at all costs. As already pointed out, they can be sentenced adequately under existing arrangements, either by approaching the high maximum sentence available for the offence, or by the use of the extended sentence for recidivists.

9.27 We suggest that parole could play an increased part in the control of known sex offenders. The risk of offending is much affected by life style, home circumstances and social contacts. Following release from imprisonment these influences can be modified in beneficial ways if the offender comes under the compulsory supervision of a probation officer, with the possibility of recall to prison if he fails to co-operate. We suggest, therefore, that sex offenders should in general be released on parole at a sufficiently early stage in their sentence to allow for a reasonably long period of obligatory supervision. Parole is of particular benefit for the socially alienated who might be at a loss where to live or how to find some human contacts. It is also important for those who need to pursue a prescribed treatment programme, but who might not have the resolve to do so conscientiously if it were not made a condition of their parole licence.

We agree with Professor Hall-Williams (*The Times*, 15 December 1983) who wrote: 'Anyone who saw the recent television documentary on sex offenders in Maidstone prison cannot fail to have been impressed with the need for such prisoners to be released with help and support such as a parole licence might provide'. For this reason we do not support policy recommendations for restricting the granting of parole for prisoners serving long sentences for certain sex offences.

The length of sentence having been determined by considerations of justice, we see no serious ethical objection to varying the proportions of the sentence spent under parole supervision according to the circumstances, attitudes and needs of the individual. The conditions of a parole licence are never degrading, and a prisoner is not forced to accept parole.

9.28 We think it particularly undesirable that serious sex offenders, who are considered too great a risk for parole, should be released into the community without supervision. Accordingly, we propose that the Parole Board should be given a discretionary power, in the case of long-sentence sex offenders who have been denied parole, to impose a period of supervision following release (which, with normal remission, is when two-thirds of the sentence have been served) and extending, if necessary, to the expiry of the sentence. Young prisoners and those under extended sentences are already subject to supervision up to the end of their sentences, and former life prisoners receive compulsory supervision for however long the authorities consider desirable. We see no reason why long-sentence sex offenders identified by the Parole Board as needing it should not be subject to an analogous provision. In their case, the supervision would need to be particularly stringent and directive.

TREATMENT OF COMPLAINANTS

9.29 The police have been subjected to much criticism in recent years for the way they deal with complainants in cases of sexual assault (see paras 4.45, 4.48). The matter has been thoroughly examined in a Scottish Office Social Research Study that concluded with some useful suggestions with which we are in substantial agreement (Chambers and Millar, 1983). Faced with a victim of sexual assault, the primary concern should be the alleviation of immediate distress. All but the most urgent questions and examinations should be postponed until the victim is sufficiently calm to collaborate effectively. The chances of detecting the offender would only occasionally be reduced through this delay, for in most cases his identity is not in doubt.

9.30 Victims often stand in great need of help and reassurance following an assault, and during the processes of investigation and prosecution. Any necessary medical attention, including tests for pregnancy or venereal infection, should be provided. Rape victims should be formally offered a choice of either a male or a female medical examiner. Victims should be advised how to contact helping agencies, such as rape crisis centres and victims support schemes, and told how to apply to the Criminal Injuries Compensation Board. Police handling these cases should receive special training in how to deal with sex victims. This would help to avoid loss of a complainant's co-operation through over-hasty or tactless questioning. Assessment of credibility would not be clouded by mistaken expectations about how a genuine victim should react to a sexual assault.

These improvements would be made easier if more special units were set up for investigation of sex cases – at least in large conurbations where the number of such cases warrants it. The existence of specialised units ensures that as far as practicable sex cases are handled by experienced officers and, where appropriate, by women officers. Collaboration with other agencies, particularly with rape crisis centres, which is at present impeded by lack of understanding or even positive hostility, also becomes easier. Experience in the United States shows that collaboration between special police units and specialised helping agencies is feasible and in the end serves the interests of justice (Sanders, 1980). For such systems to work properly the staff of the special units have to be accorded adequate status within the force and their decisions respected by their colleagues.

CHILD WITNESSES

9.31 When child witnesses are involved and have to be interrogated the advantages of special units within the police are particularly obvious. When prosecution cannot be avoided, every effort should be made to minimise the damage to the child. There is merit in the Israeli system, which permits a designated individual with appropriate training and experience, the child examiner, to conduct the initial interrogations. A police officer with the necessary social work training might well perform much the same function and might also provide highly desirable psychological support for the child during the waiting period before the evidence is heard in court.

9.32 We drew attention in Part I (paras 4.27–4.29) to the problems of children who have to testify at the trial of persons charged with committing sexual offences against them, and the disturbing effects this might have, coming on top of the original episode and the subsequent police inquiry. But the interests of the witness have to be balanced against the risk of unfairness to the accused. Cases of mistaken indentification, charges made out of malice, and misinterpretation or exaggeration in testimony all have to be guarded against. After all, one in five Crown Court trials for sex offences end in an acquittal. Legal technicalities, hesitant witnesses, lack of convincing corroboration to prove the defendant's guilt and irrational juries may account for some of these verdicts, but by no means all. For these reasons, juries must see *all* important prosecution witnesses for themselves, and the accused or his counsel must have the opportunity to ask them questions. Indeed, Article 6(3)(d) of the European Convention on Human Rights, to which the United Kingdom is a party, expressly requires that everyone charged with a criminal offence must have the right 'to examine or have examined witnesses against him'. While fully sympathising with child witnesses in sex cases, we cannot support the suggestion that their evidence should be given in the form of written statements which cannot then be challenged, or that they need not attend the trial.

9.33 It might go some way towards mitigating the stress to which child witnesses are subjected if the forbidding and frightening formality of the Crown Court were temporarily laid aside while a child is giving evidence. The public (but not the press) gallery could be temporarily cleared, or the hearing transferred to a less formal setting with wigs and gowns removed. This is not at all impractical, for the number of persons whose presence is essential – judge, jury, accused, the press and lawyers on both sides – should not exceed around 20. Such procedures are already practised quite often and successfully in divorce courts and occasionally in criminal courts.

9.34 An American has made a ingenious suggestion on similar lines (Libai, 1980). He suggests screening off a section of the court-room with one-way glass. In this small section the judge, child witness, a child examiner and counsel would sit together in seeming privacy, but the accused, the jury and the public outside the screen would still be able to see and hear the proceedings. One objection to this proposal is that it involves deceiving the child as to the degree of privacy, which could cause distress later if he or she realises what has happened, but this is perhaps a lesser evil. Another very material objection is that the traditional structure of most British courts would make it very difficult to erect suitable screens.

9.35 The only certain way to eliminate the stress to the child would be to dispense altogether with attendance at the trial. We have considered whether there are any circumstances in which this might be done, and have concluded that, if it ever were to be allowed, it could only be with the full consent of the accused. For example, if the child has been questioned at some time before the trial by representatives of *both* the prosecution and the defence, and the whole of that session had been recorded on videotape, there might be no objection, in principle, to the tape being played to the jury in place of the 'live' evidence of the child at the trial itself, provided that the accused has consented.

But even this raises difficulties. The judge will not have been present at the examination, and this may create a problem. If one of the lawyers asks the child a question to which the other objects, who is to rule whether the answer is admissible? If the objection is put to the judge at the trial and succeeds, one would then have to edit the videotape before it could be shown to the jury: that would take time, and editing recorded evidence is inherently undesirable. Another difficulty is that, once such a procedure is available, defendants will come under strong pressure to consent to it, even when there may be reasons for not doing so. Their lawyers may point out that they will make themselves unpopular with the jury if they still insist on the attendance of the child at the trial when they could have made use of the alternative procedure. It would probably not be long before juries realised that, if a child is called to give evidence, it must mean that the accused has insisted on it. They may then hold that against him, even if no one has been allowed to mention it during the trial.

All in all, we think that the use of video-recorded testimony would create more problems than it solved, and we therefore confine our recommendations to urging greater informality in the court when children are giving evidence, and perhaps an experimental exploration of the 'one-way glass' idea.

ASSESSMENT AND TREATMENT FACILITIES

9.36 Notwithstanding the scarcity of resources, we recommend a determined effort to increase the availability of treatment for sex offenders. Unlike most thieves, burglars and other common criminals, many sex offenders recognise that there is something wrong with them and are ready to co-operate in treatment. We should not throw that advantage away, for there is good evidence (which we reviewed in Chapter 7), at least in the case of certain important categories of sex offenders, that treatment does indeed make re-offending less likely. As this means saving potential victims from the suffering that would otherwise be inflicted upon them, the effort is certainly worth while. An added benefit is the saving of the considerable costs of renewed court proceedings, even more so when this means renewed imprisonment. The heavy cost of keeping a man in secure custody is in itself only a part of the total cost to the community, which loses the contribution of his work and may have to support his dependants on welfare payments, as well as supporting the man himself if he is released from prison without any prospects of earning an independent livelihood.

9.37 Some other countries, such as the United States and the Netherlands, find it possible to offer sex offenders more attention and treatment than we do. This may be due, in part, to an understandable public resistance in this country to the allocation of scarce resources to people who have committed revolting crimes, when more worthy citizens are in equal need. While we fully appreciate the reasons for this attitude, it is, in fact, short-sighted: it disregards the benefits which the community as a whole stands to gain from successful treatments. As we pointed out in Chapter 7, sex offenders are a very mixed group, with very varied treatment needs and varying degrees of amenability and responsiveness. It is vital to determine the methods most appropriate to each case. Experience provides some guidelines here, but there is, as yet, not nearly enough scientific evidence about the relative merits of different approaches and different combinations of treatment. Further research into these matters is badly needed, especially evaluations of the long-term outcome of treatment interventions. Without this knowledge the available resources will continue to be deployed inefficiently.

9.38 Assessments are of special importance when an offender is brought to court for the first time. We have pointed out (para 3.1) that some sex offences are quite trivial. The majority of defendants on sex charges, however appear for kinds of behaviour which are puzzling, anxiety-provoking, disgusting, and possibly indicative of disturbed sexual attitudes or socially unacceptable sexual proclivities. Remand for social inquiry reports and psychiatric reports are certainly justified and potentially helpful, and not at all to be discouraged. Unfortunately, all too often they fail to provide either sophisticated assessment or constructive recommendations (see paras 7.52–7.54). To rectify this situation fully might require more resources of time and of expertise than can reasonably be afforded. Meanwhile, there are some simple ways in which improvements could be secured.

9.39 So long as resources are limited it may be reasonable to give a low priority to remands for assessment in the case of the less serious first offenders who have a low statistical probability of reappearing before the courts for a further sex offence. Indecent exposure, consensual teenage heterosexual intercourse, and consensual but public homosexual indecency between adults do not normally require assessment unless the behaviour seems uncontrolled and persistent, but any offence by an adult with a young child should alert the court to the need for assessment. Sexual behaviour of a truly assaultive or violent character, whatever the age of the victim, is also serious enough to warrant inquiries, even though, at present, such offenders are often not referred for medical examination because they are considered 'normal' from a sexual standpoint.

9.40 Assessments by the probation and psychiatric services can be carried out more easily and more effectively if the offender is on bail in the community. He can then be examined in a less artificial setting, access to relatives and other informants is made easier, and his interactions with them are more readily observed. Some offenders are understandably suspicious or frightened, and consequently less forthcoming, after removal from home to prison. Specialist assessment services are occassionally needed, such as neurological or psychological tests, and these are more likely to be readily forthcoming in an outside hospital.

Contact between the probation officer and the psychiatrist, when both are involved, is highly desirable in order to co-ordinate information and recommendations, and there is more time and opportunity to do this with an offender on bail. Unfortunately, one study of what happens in practice showed that consultation over selection and recommendation is frequently insufficient. Consequently, when treatment or probation is proposed, the reports are often far from explicit as to the respective roles of the two services in dealing with the offender (Lewis, 1980). It is better to have an extension of the remand period than to have hurried assessments, and of course an extension is less problematic if the offender is not in custody. Finally, if psychiatric treatment, whether as in-patient or out-patient, is appropriate, it is more likely to be recommended and obtained if the offender is on bail and already in contact with the psychiatric service.

9.41 The granting of bail to offenders on remand, pending social inquiries and medical examinations, is influenced by the prospect of cases being adequately managed and necessary treatment secured without the need for a custodial sentence. We have referred eariler (see para 7.28ff) to the advantages of treatment in the community and to the promising experiments by some probation services in providing constructive alternatives to imprisonment. The psychiatric services also have their part to play, and we welcome the development of the discipline of forensic psychiatry and the establishment, albeit tardily, of medium secure units which may enable hospitals to cope with cases that would otherwise be considered too risky. There is a very long way to go, however, before psychiatric services suited to the particular needs of sex offenders are likely to be generally available. The psychiatric hospitals are still reluctant to make places available to offender patients, and, as is the case everywhere, sex offenders are especially unwelcome.

9.42 The apparent success of some American hospital-based units in treating sex offenders (see para 7.34 ff) shows the feasibility of such schemes. As soon as resources become available we should like to see one or two specialised centres set up within the National Health Service (see paras 7.45–7.46). Ideally, such a specialised facility should be available not only to convicted offenders, but also to persons willing to seek help before the stage of arrest and conviction. The existence of a specialised centre would promote research into new methods of treatment and provide a focal point for the development of expertise and the dissemination of knowledge, all of which are badly needed. The Midland Forensic Psychiatric Service in Birmingham provides an example of the beginnings of the sort of comprehensive service we have in mind.

9.43 If resources are to be put into new treatment schemes, evaluation of their effectiveness is a first essential, as much for increasing knowledge and improving techniques, as for convincing authorities of the need to allocate funds. Every serious commentator on the state of affairs deplores the lack of properly controlled trials with a reasonable length of follow-up and a reasonable comparison group (Langevin, 1983, p.66–72). Too often the services responsible for administering treatment lack the support, interest, or commitment to research goals that are required if scientific evaluation is to be carried out properly. Yet without much more effort in this direction progress cannot be expected, investment in treatment schemes will not be forthcoming, and clients, when they are given anything at all, will continue to undergo procedures of questionable validity and uncertain outcome.

While strongly supporting the institution of both traditional and innovative schemes by the National Health Service, the Probation Service and Prison Service, we are of the opinion that no public money should be allocated to such projects unless adequate monitoring and evaluating procedures, preferably by independent research workers skilled in the necessary techniques are included.

CO-ORDINATING EFFORTS AND IMPROVING LIAISON

9.44 Good liaison between the voluntary services and the penal services would improve the quality of help provided. General practitioners, social workers in voluntary organisations and the staff of walk-in services such as the Brook Advisory Centres are sometimes the first to have contact with individuals with sexual problems who are at risk of offending or have already committed as yet unrecorded offences. Some of these clients who are voluntarily seeking treatment could usefully be linked up with the treatment facilities of the Probation Service and the forensic psychiatry clinics. An interchange of voluntary and 'less voluntary' clients would be beneficial, both to ensure that each gets the most appropriate form of help, and also perhaps to diffuse the more positive attitudes of the volunteers among the more reluctant clients under compulsory supervision.

9.45 If treatment of sex offenders in the community or in National Health Service units outside prison is to be promoted, as we hope it will be, it is important that the public should have reasonable grounds for confidence that this will not mean inadequate protection against the repetition of offences. The Probation Order with a treatment requirement is a useful device for ensuring continued supervision and continued collaboration on the offender's part in whatever course of treatment he has agreed to accept. But this is only an effective precaution if those who do not co-operate properly are brought back to court and charged with a breach of probation under secion 6 of the Powers of the Criminal Courts Act, 1973, or brought back under section 8 and sentenced for their original offence if they have committed a further offence while still on probation.

Offenders found in breach of a probation order can be given a custodial sentence, but the courts are usually (perhaps too often) more lenient than that. There is a reluctance on the part of some probation officers to prosecute their clients for breach (Lawson, 1978), especially if the grounds are non-co-operation in psychiatric treatment. There is certainly a serious failure on the part of psychiatrists, whether from simple neglect or for ethical reasons such as breach of confidentiality, to report patients for non-co-operation and to provide evidence for their prosecution. We deplore this laxity in dealing with offenders who do not conscientiously fulfil the requirements they have accepted.

9.46 Too often an offender's apparent enthusiasm for treatment melts away once the court has decided on probation. The psychiatrist is left with a reluctant and unforthcoming patient and sees no point in insisting on frequent interviews, but as there has been no blatant refusal to attend he cannot say that there has been a definite breach of the treatment requirement.

These and similar problems would be alleviated by better communication between psychiatrists and probation officers. As the discipline of forensic psychiatry develops it is to be hoped that more psychiatrists will become experienced in the special needs of offenders and of the courts and readier to share with probation officers the task of assessment and of constructing a comprehensive plan of combined social and psychiatric intervention.

9.47 The role of the probation service in the management and treatment of offenders is paramount, for, even without a change in policy towards less use of imprisonment, there will be more known offenders in the community than in prison. At present there is a quite widespread sense of uncertainty and inexperience in dealing with the many intractable personal and social problems presented by sex offenders. The feeling that somebody else would be better fitted to deal with this type of offender is very prevalent. For this reason we commend the lead taken by some probation areas in the setting up of workshops, education and training sessions and liaison schemes involving a variety of agencies. Attention of a specifically psychiatric nature is required by only a minority of sex offenders. A larger number stand in greater need of the techniques of guidance, control and counselling that probation officers are best qualified to provide.

9.48 Given that facilities for sex offenders provided by the probation service could be expanded and improved, better use might be made of them by ex-prisoners if more were released under a parole licence. The insertion of special conditions into a parole licence, a provision rather little used at present, could facilitate the management of problems hitherto neglected. For example, drug treatments begun in prison would be more likely to be continued effectively if made a condition of the licence.

Regardless of whether they are released with or without parole, there should be better provision for needy sex offenders, especially the homeless or socially alienated, when they emerge from a prison sentence. This would require a system of centralised liaison to negotiate between the various services who might be called upon – hostels, voluntary counselling, social services and medico-psychological facilities. The Probation Service, which has officers both in prison and in the community, would be the organisation best placed to set up such a system. Our enquiries showed that they would welcome the opportunity to do so.

9.49 Lack of liaison between services is a serious impediment to the handling of many of the problems discussed in this report. Lack of liaison between courts and medical facilities, between probation officers and psychiatrists, between prison welfare and voluntary hostels, and between police, social services and therapists dealing with intra-familial offending, have all been mentioned. A particularly glaring example, which militates against providing help for victims, is the lack of contact in many parts of the country between police, victim support schemes and rape crisis centres. In some places police will refer victims to local victim support schemes, but not to rape crisis centres; in other areas it is the rape crisis centres who will handle only self-referrals and refuse to deal with clients sent by the police or to co-operate with support schemes. Some police forces have started training schemes for officers who have to deal with sex victims, and this we certainly commend. If representatives from victim support and rape crisis centres could be drawn into some of these training sessions, it would help to remove unnecessary suspicions and demarcation disputes and make for more effective and better co-ordinated endeavours. Such desirable developments will be impeded so long as certain rape crisis centres maintain a militant ideological stance that prevents co-operation with a predominately male police force.

TREATMENT IN PRISON

9.50 However much facilities in the community are expanded, a proportion of sex offenders will always have to be dealt with in the prisons, and we turn to the problems which they present there. It would be useful if all sex offenders could be assessed as to suitability for treatment both during the period of remand and later, if still in custody, following conviction. There would be difficulties, in that prisoners on remand might be swayed in their views about the desirability of treatment by the hope of an acquittal or a non-custodial sentence, and sentenced prisoners might be influenced by the chances of parole. It should be possible, however, to design guidelines to minimise such problems. Given appropriate training, prison officers could carry out, or at least assist in, these vital assessments.

9.51 Prisoners initially assessed as suitable candidates for treatment could be referred to specialised multi-disciplinary units set up within the prison system, perhaps one in each region. The idea of introducing specialised treatment units is not new. The Butler Committee on Mentally Abnormal Offenders (Home Office, 1975, paras 5.38–5.39) recommended the setting up of special units within the prisons to provide treatment and social training for personality-disordered inmates. They also recommended (paras 3.24–3.27) improving resources for the treatment of sexual deviants and, if suitable treatments could not be provided in prison, arranging for transfer to hospital.

Representatives from any such treatment unit for sex offenders would need to see each candidate and study his records before the final decision to accept him into a treatment programme was made. It might be convenient for the treatment centres to operate at the same prisons as presently house the Rule 43 units, or they might even replace some of these units (see para 4.55 ff). Specialised apparatus would be needed, such as psychophysiological recording apparatus for monitoring sexual arousal patterns, videotape equipment for social skills training programmes, and so forth. Special selection criteria and training programmes would be needed for the staff at these units, which might have to cut across ordinary transfer procedures. Most important, and perhaps most difficult of all, arrangements would need to be made for a gradual transition of the treatment process into the community, perhaps with the help of semi-secure half-way accommodation, near to both the prison treatment unit and the area to which the offender could return after discharge. An exchange of staff and information between the prison unit, the semi-secure units and facilities in the outside community, with prison officers spending time in each setting, would ensure the close liaison upon which an effective programme depends. Probation officers already have an employment structure that permits such flexibility. The example of the programme at Maidstone, initiated by an enterprising probation officer (see para 7.27), illustrates this. Similar arrangements could be made with advantage for psychiatrists, psychologists and other treatment staff involved.

9.52 The operation of these prison treatment centres would present an important opportunity for research and development. It would be helpful to have a national steering group to ensure adequate monitoring and evaluation, to co-ordinate research proposals and to liaise with agencies directly or indirectly concerned with the work of the units, including the Probation Service, the Department of Health and Social Security, the police and the courts.

The costs of these 'ideal arrangements' might appear large, but they could be limited by enlisting accommodation and staff already under the control of the various agencies whose participation is envisaged. It might be largely a matter of redeployment and reordering of priorities, but the costs of some additional staff, of special training, and of travel and other expenses occasioned by the need to establish a bridge between institution and community, could not be avoided.

TREATMENT BY PERSUASION – OR COMPULSION?

9.53 In Part I (para 7.59ff) we mentioned some of the ethical problems inherent in advising, persuading or forcing sex offenders into treatment schemes. With the increase in treatment facilities which we have proposed, these problems would be encountered more often. There are inevitable pressures on some sex offenders – from courts, from relatives or from situations in prison – to agree to participate. Where the treatment is professionally conducted, and the offender is not mentally ill or impaired, the therapist should avoid exploiting such pressures and should not try to coerce him to agree. He should explain, as far as practicable, in the light of the offender's understanding and the limits of current knowledge, the nature of the proposed intervention, including its possible risks and inconveniences, probable effectiveness and what alternative options are available.

9.54 Public concern and legislative and professional safeguards against undue coercion are now well established, but they tend to be directed primarily towards physicians and psychiatrists. They are generally based on a medical model of treatment which, as in the discussion of '*Treating the Troublesome*' by the Council for Science and Society (1981), seems to assume that what goes on between the individual offender and his therapist (who may be a social worker or psychologist) is the crucial factor. Interventions resulting from police policy, sentencing policy or prison regimes are not normally construed as treatment. Social learning theory, however, on which most modern schemes of behaviour modification are based, lays much more stress on the outcome of interaction with the environment than on supposedly immutable or inviolate personality attributes which need to be protected from unethical intrusions. The conditions surrounding the treatment of sex offenders, which are determined by current social attitudes and political and legal frameworks, are often more important than interventions directed towards individuals.

9.55 The modification of unacceptable patterns of sexual behaviour by such techniques as social skills training or exposure to a therapeutic community committed to change, or the manipulation of rewards for conformity, is not without some of the same problems and risks of coerciveness or abuse that can be associated with more strictly medical interventions. The extent of the intrusion which society deems necessary, and the offender wants or is prepared to accept, may or may not match the ideal requirements for effecting change. The safest solution to the ethical problems raised by such conflicting interests is to discusss current practices amongst the widest possible range of professionals and lay persons involved, with the aim of arriving at generally agreed ethical guidelines, as was suggested by the joint Working Party on behaviour modification (Zangwill, 1980). In the last resort it is a question of balance. Where there are genuine ethical doubts, offenders should not be given treatment unless they quite clearly want it and it will benefit them, regardless of whether it will also benefit society.

9.56 As to the forcible treatment of sex offenders against their will, we see no scope for this whatsoever. If the individual is severely mentally ill, and irrational and dangerous, compulsory treatment may briefly be necessary to reduce such primary symptoms as uncontrollable excitement and dangerous delusions, but any improvement in sexual misconduct would be incidental. For these exceptional cases, the present safeguards against abuse, which have been strengthened by the Mental Health Act 1983, seem adequate.

9.57 The question of whether agreement to treatment, response to treatment or acceptance of anti-libidinal drugs, should be allowed to influence the release date of a prisoner is difficult to answer categorically. In so far as detention in prison is for the protection of the community rather than a tariff punishment for the offence, this is a utilitarian consideration that could be affected by response to treatment. In forms of intervention that involve personal interaction between client and therapist, the individual therapist cannot be considered a disinterested party, or one immune from manipulation by the offender, so his recommendations need to be supported by other criteria. If his views and recommendations are to be taken into account by, for instance, the Parole Board, the offender should be made aware of that fact.

The position may be difficult if a court decides to deal with an offender by means of a probation order, if necessary with a treatment requirement added, a solution which we believe could be used more often, especially if facilities for the management and treatment of sex offenders could be expanded. In this event it should be recognised by all concerned, and accepted by the offender and the community, that the duration of the treatment (within upper limits set by the nature of the order) is determined by the progress of the treatment and not by the nature of the offence.

9.58 In the case of a serious sex offender committed to a special hospital rather than to imprisonment, but with a restriction order preventing the granting of release or leave of absence by the Responsible Medical Officer without the permission of the Home Secretary, the patient may still regain his liberty by a successful application to a Mental Health Review Tribunal. Review Tribunals used to be purely advisory bodies, but as a result of an appeal in 1981, the European Court of Human Rights rules that everyone deprived of liberty should be entitled to have the legality of his detention decided speedily by a court. Accordingly, the Mental Health Act 1983, section 73, gives the Mental Health Review Tribunals the final decision on release or continued detention or conditional release subject to recall. Even if the restricted patient does not apply of his own record, his case must be referred for consideration to a Mental Health Review Tribunal within three years of admission or of the last appeal. The Tribunal must direct discharge if satisfied that the offender is not now suffering from any of the forms of disorder recognised in the Mental Health Act or if it appears no longer necessary for the health or safety of the patient or for the protection of others that he should continue to be detained for treatment. Mental state, therefore, rather than the nature of the offence, is to be the prime criterion when considering release. Of course evidence of liability to repeat dangerous sexual behaviour might constitute grounds for regarding an inmate as still psychopathic. The offence can never really be discounted, and is unlikely to be ignored since the new Tribunals are to be chaired by circuit judges or their equivalent. However, the fact that the Tribunals must now consider all restricted patients, and can release them without reference to the Home Office, could have the unfortunate effect of persuading judges to send dangerous sex offenders to prison, even where hospital treatment might otherwise have been seen as more appropriate. We hope that courts will trust to the professionalism and good sense of the Review Tribunals and not allow this to happen.

CHAPTER 10

Concluding Summary

CONCLUSION

10.1 In this final chapter we summarise our main conclusions and recommendations, giving cross-references to the more detailed considerations set out in the body of the report. Our concern throughout has been to find means to reduce the suffering caused by sexual offending in ways that are humane as well as effective.

10.2 The law of England and Wales includes several hundred different sexual offences. All but three of them date from the reign of Queen Victoria, or later. In Appendix I, we give the particulars of most of them, in 43 groups (paras 2.4–2.5; 2.7).

10.3 These present some odd features: they draw no obvious distinction between different kinds of harm; their maximum penalties reflect no coherent scale either of damage or of inherent wrongfulness; there is a great deal of overlap; there are some obvious omissions; and they discriminate strongly between males and females, both as victims and as offenders (paras 2.8–2.12).

10.4 Unlike the television and radio, the popular newspapers are apt to give the impression that sex offences are far more prevalent than they are (para 6.2). Newspaper accounts featuring the most sensational cases, and using cliches like 'sex fiend', give an exaggerated picture of the seriousness of the generality of sex offences (para 6.3). In fact far fewer serious sex offences are committed than the ordinary newspaper reader might be led to believe. Even if one takes only the more serious 'notifiable offences recorded by the police', less than one in a hundred and fifty is a sex offence. Of these, around half are indecent assaults on females, a tenth are indecent assaults on males; rapes are only one in fifteen (0.04 per cent of all recorded notifiable offences); and incest one in eighty-four (0.0075 per cent). Even taking all offenders *convicted* of serious crimes, only 1.4 per cent are guilty of sex offences – nearly half of them with fully consenting partners (paras 3.3–3.6; 3.9).

10.5 Contrary to public belief, notified sex offences generally are *decreasing* : in the decade from 1973 to 1983, they fell by 20 per cent, while offences of non-sexual violence increased by 80 per cent (para 3.14).

10.6 Although the evidence is not conclusive, the degree of lasting harm suffered by victims (including children) seems to flow predominantly not from the sexual nature of the experience, but rather from other sources of shock associated with it, notably the use of violence or intimidation or the abuse of parental powers (paras 4.1–4.10). The subsequent intervention of parents, or other authorities, in order to bring the offender to justice often seems to aggravate the damage caused by the offence itself (paras 4.19–4.29).

10.7 There seems to be no support for the theory that boys can be easily 'converted' to homosexuality if they do not already have an inclination for it (para 4.17).

10.8 Very few of the sex offences committed between consenting teenagers are ever prosecuted (para 4.31), and whether they are depends largely on the attitudes and policies of different police forces (para 6.9). The same is true for public lavatory offences (para 6.8).

10.9 Sex offenders are preponderantly young: nearly half of them are under 30, and just over half of all convicted rapists are under 21. Once convicted, the great majority never appear before the courts again for a sex offence (para 3.17). They fall into a number of quite distinct categories, varying greatly in motivation, background, personality, and the kinds of offence they commit. Many are socially inadequate, and only a very small fraction are men of violence (paras 5.1–5.34). Unlike, say, thieves, burgulars, and robbers, many of the deviant ones realise that there is something wrong with them, and would be glad to have help to change their ways if that were possible (para 7.16).

10.10 There is some evidence, both from Great Britain and from abroad, that *some* types of sex offenders are less likely to repeat their offences if they receive *some* kinds of treatment or management, either in a closed institution or under supervision in the community – but only if this is appropriate for the particular case (paras 7.17–7.40).

RECOMMENDATIONS

The Law

10.11 Our sex laws need to be made simpler, fairer, and more consistent. Manifestly reasonable laws are more likely to attract public respect and to support decent standards of conduct (paras 2.7–2.16; 8.2–8.5).

Unlawful sexual behaviour should be similarly defined, and should attract similar penalties, regardless of whether the victims of the offenders are male or female. Further, the rules for heterosexual and homosexual behaviour should be the same (paras 2.16; 5.23–5.25; 8.29). The principal distinction should be between conduct which involves force, fraud or undue influence, and conduct which does not (paras 3.9–3.10; 8.1–8.5).

10.12 Sexual offences involving violence should be dealt with like any other offences of violence against the person, for which there is already adequate provision. This would have the advantage of removing an unnessarily emotive label from some of these cases. However, certain particularly serious acts such as vaginal or anal rape should be treated as assaults occasioning grievous bodily harm, and certain others as occasioning actual bodily harm (paras 4.37–4.39; 8.6–8.9).

10.13 Fully consensual sexual behaviour between adults should only be a matter of concern to the criminal law where it causes demonstrable harm. Anal intercourse, which is no longer a crime where the participants are both adult men, should cease to be so where one of them happens to be a woman (paras 8.4; 8.18). Intercourse or indecency with a severely mentally impaired adult should continue to be an offence, unless the other person is similarly impaired (para 8.16). The crime of bestiality should be abolished; the law already covers cruelty to animals (para 8.20). The law of incest is unsatisfactory. It fails to cover sexual abuse other than actual intercourse, or to include offences by step-parents. Virtually all the misbehaviour that it does include would be better prosecuted under other statutes. The only exception is consensual incest between adults, which need not be a concern of the criminal law (paras 4.11–4.15; 5.19–5.20; 8.30–8.31). Our proposals for the protection of young persons under 18 would provide a better way of dealing with sexual exploitation by parents or guardians.

10.14 Because of the vulnerability of young people to sexual pressures and coercion, the legal protection from sexual exploitation should be extended up to the age of 18. This could best be done through the introduction of offences of unlawful indecency and unlawful sexual intercourse, which would apply to anyone obtaining sexual contact with young children under 14, or with young persons under 18, if the age gap between the participants was greater than two years and, in the case of young persons between 14 and 18, if some trust has been abused or some undue influence has been exerted. Persons in positions of authority over young people (such as parents, guardians, teachers, employers and youth workers), or 7 or more years older than the young person concerned, should be treated as having undue influence in the absence of evidence to the contrary (paras 8.24–8.27).

10.15 Offences of public indecency or soliciting should be dealt with, unlike other offences, in a uniform manner regardless of the gender of the persons involved. It seem inequitable, for instance, to prosecute soliciting for heterosexual activity only if prostitution is involved, but to prosecute soliciting for homosexual activity even when there is no suggestion of prostitution and no evidence that any member of the public is offended (paras 8.21–8.22). The control of indecency in mens' lavatories, which has become a controversial issue and has exposed the police to accusations of entrapment, would be better accomplished by structural improvements in the facilities than by deploying scarce law enforcement resources (paras 5.23; 6.10–6.11). Adult sex parties in private houses or private clubs should not be a concern of the criminal law, whatever the gender of the participants, unless the venue is one which causes offence or is open to unsuspecting members of the public (paras 5.25; 8.19).

Social Controls

10.16 Education has a large part to play in moulding attitudes and helping individuals to develop a sense of personal and social responsibility. Experience suggests that individuals who are ignorant, uninformed or poorly socialised in regard to sex are at greater than average risk of becoming sex deviants or sex offenders (paras 5.10; 5.21; 7.3; 7.9; 9.3). For various reasons parental guidance in sex matters often falls short of the ideal (4.9; 9.3), so it is important that this should be backed up by realistic sex education in schools, and not only on topics of physiology and contraception (although these are important), but also on issues concerned with personal relationships and family responsibilities (paras 9.6–9.8).

10.17 Social control through the criminal justice system, particularly in relation to matters of sex, incurs heavy material and psychological costs because it attracts shame and stigma to an unusual extent (paras 6.23–6.28; 6.47). This does not mean that any form of sexual behaviour that causes palpable harm should be decriminalised; all such behaviour should be brought swiftly and effectively to a halt whenever it comes to light, but the criminal justice system should be invoked only when this is really necessary in the public interest (para 9.11).

10.18 The welfare of victims, especially young ones, is an essential consideration. Children sexually molested in their own homes arouse particular concern, because the damage done to a child by injudicious intervention can exceed the damage attributable to the sexual incidents themselves (paras 4.13; 4.19–4.27). The interests of the child victim, for whom the preservation of a parental home may be a prime consideration, sometimes run counter to the interests of justice. These situations should therefore be resolved by social work and therapy whenever this is practicable (paras 4.20; 9.12–9.17). Co-operation between social workers and police should be extended (para 9.18). When circumstances permit, decisions about how to handle a case should be taken only after full consultation with all the agencies concerned, and with the goal of preserving as many families as possible. Greater use should be made of cautions, deferred prosecution, deferred sentences and probation orders with treatment requirements in place of custodial sentences for offenders guilty of indecent misconduct with their own children or with other children in the household (para 9.19–9.20).

10.19 The interests of justice are ill-served by any action detrimental to victims which might discourage the reporting of crimes. Means of preventing adverse publicity for victims of sex offences who have to give evidence in court should be strengthened and made to apply to all age groups (para 6.1–6.4; 8.33–8.35. More attention needs to be paid to the sensitivities and needs of victims at every stage from the preliminary investigation of complaints to the final appearance as a witness. Recent improvements in police procedures for the examination of complainants are to be welcomed, but there should be more specialised units with properly trained personnel dealing with sex cases and collaborating with victim support agencies (paras 4.47–4.49; 9.29–9.30).

Treatment

10.20 Treatment that reduces crime is in the interest of victims, potential victims and offenders alike. Much sexual misbehaviour arises at least in part from personal or social inadequacies, sexual disorders or deviant sexual impulses. Many offenders are capable of benefiting from treatment and willing to accept it (paras 7.1–7.15). While there are difficulties in reaching scientific certainty, there are enough promising results on record to justify investment in more treatment schemes and more treatment research and evaluation (para 7.17).

10.21 Community-based treatment schemes, which permit testing of behaviour in real life situations, and the enlistment of the offender's family circle in the treatment plan, are preferable to prison-based systems, which are limited by institutional hostility and restrictions (paras 7.20–7.24). Many sex offenders are non-violent, responsive to supervision, and therefore suitable candidates for such projects (paras 7.28–7.31). For those who have to be in prison, specialised treatment units are badly needed. They could be set up in association with existing Rule 43 units which house many potentially treatable sex offenders (paras 7.27; 9.50–9.52).

10.22 Improved liaison between the different welfare and treatment services, both inside and outside the penal system, is at least as important as the introduction of new facilities. The probation service is well placed to act as a co-ordinator, having contacts with voluntary agencies, walk-in facilities, forensic psychiatry, in-patient and out-patient services as well as with the medical and psychological services in the prisons. Probation officers are also in a favourable position to advise courts on the need for enquiries and assessments and the availability of facilities to carry them out (para 7.50). Since many sex offenders need counselling and guidance in managing their lives or avoiding situations or temptation, rather than any specific medical or psychological regime, the probation service has a key role to play in providing the help they need (paras 7.28–7.33).

10.23 Resistance to accommodating known sex offenders by the public at large, as well as by hostel authorities, psychiatric nurses and others in a position to provide help, is an obstacle largely created by ignorance and misapprehension. The sensationalism of the popular press is partly to blame for creating exaggerated anxiety, but that is something very difficult to control (para 9.8). Better education and training for personnel required to deal with sex offenders is a more practicable proposition (paras 9.9–9.10).

10.24 Compulsory hospitilisation is relatively rarely required for sex offenders, except for manifestly psychotic or severely mentally impaired individuals whose offending is a by-product of their condition (paras 7.55–7.58). Treatment, either inside or outside prison, must therefore be mainly on a voluntary basis (paras 7.62–7.63). Persuasive pressures from relatives, or from the nature of the situation in which their behaviour has placed them, are unavoidable. However, there is a danger of unbridled therapeutic optimism leading to covert pressures to undergo treatment of questionable value (paras 7.2; 7.64–7.66). Therapists should take particular care to explain to offenders the nature and prospects of treatment, and to secure as full and free consent as circumstances permit (paras 7.59–7.60; 9.53–9.58). We wholly support recent trends in public opinion, professional ethics and mental health legislation which combine to make enforced treatment of sexual misconduct by hormones, castration or psychosurgery unacceptable (paras 7.63–7.64).

Punishment

10.25 We support the view of the Howard League that imprisonment should be a measure of last resort when alternatives to custody are genuinely impracticable, that shorter sentences are often as effective as longer ones, and that sentences should be served under conditions that do not unnecessarily destroy family ties, deny access to treatment or expose the offender to physical or mental damage. All these provisos are of special relevance to sex offenders because of the emotions aroused by their crimes, the precarious nature of their contacts in the outside community and the hostile attitudes of other prisoners and of some prison officers (paras 4.51–4.57; 9.9). Some element of protective sentencing in addition to tariff punishment must enter into the disposal of unpredictable and dangerous offenders, but the use of high maximum sentences and the application of the existing system of extended sentences adequately provides for this without the introduction of special laws for offenders deemed dangerous (paras 6.50–6.51; 9.22–9.23).

10.26 In view of the great difficulties they face when trying to find a place in the community after imprisonment, there should be greater use of parole for sex offenders, involving firm supervision and with specified conditions to prevent return to dangerous habits and, where appropriate, to ensure continued adherence to a treatment programme (para 6.54; 9.27). This proposal may run counter to some recent policies to restrict parole in serious cases, but it would in fact provide better protection to the community in the long run. In the case of sex offenders serving long sentences, the Parole Board should have the discretion to order supervision to continue to the end of the sentence instead of to the two-thirds point as at present (para 9.28).

FINAL THOUGHT

10.27 This bald summary of proposals has to be understood in the context of the basic information set out in Part I. Sensible and humane provisions for the handling of both offenders and victims depends upon the public being made aware of the variety and complexity of the problems involved in unlawful sexual behaviour. We have tried to point out the need to avoid reflexive responses of revulsion born of ignorance, to distinguish between behaviour that is a nuisance and behaviour that is truly harmful, to discriminate between remediable inadequacies and wilful violation of the rights of others, to take more account of the interests and needs of victims, and to develop and evaluate improved methods of management and treatment of offenders. It may be an unfortunate time to advocate putting more resources into an unpopular cause, but it requires little more than goodwill and a change of outlook on the part of services already in existence to put into operation many of our proposals.

APPENDIX I

Sex offences in English Law: a Summary

RAPE

Legal source

S.1 Sexual Offences Act 1956; Sexual Offences (Amendment) Act 1976.

Sexual Offences Act 1956
Rape
1.—(1) It is felony for a man to rape a woman.
(2) A man who induces a married woman to have sexual intercourse with him by impersonating her husband commits rape.

Meaning of "sexual intercourse"
44. Where, on the trial of any offence under this Act, it is necessary to prove sexual intercourse (whether natural or unnatural), it shall not be necessary to prove the completion of the intercourse by the emission of seed, but the intercourse shall be deemed complete upon proof of penetration only.

Use of words "man", "boy", "woman" and "girl"
46. The use in any provision of this Act of the word "man" without the addition of the word "boy", or vice versa, shall not prevent the provision applying to any person to whom it would have applied if both words had been used, and similarly with the words "woman" and "girl".

The definition of rape was not further elaborated until the passage of the 1976 Act. At common law it was established that the slightest degree of penetration was sufficient for the commission of the offence. If such penetration is not satisfactorily proven, then the defendant may be convicted of attempted rape; if the necessary intent is not proved then a conviction for indecent assault may follow.

Sexual Offences (Amendment) Act 1976
1.—(1) For the purposes of section 1 of the Sexual Offences Act 1956 (which relates to rape) a man commits rape if—
(*a*) he has unlawful sexual intercourse with a woman who at the time of the intercourse does not consent to it; and
(*b*) at that time he knows that she does not consent to the intercourse or he is reckless as to whether she consents to it;

and references to rape in other enactments (including the following provisions of this Act) shall be construed accordingly.

(2) It is hereby declared that if at a trial for a rape offence the jury has to consider whether a man believed that a woman was consenting to sexual intercourse, the presence or absence of reasonable grounds for such a belief is a matter to which the jury is to have regard, in conjunction with any other relevant matters, in considering whether he so believed.

NB—Following *R v Gaston* (1981) 73 Cr App Rep 164 CA there is no offence of rape per anum known to the law.

Citation, interpretation, commencement and extent

7.—(1) This Act may be cited as the Sexual Offences (Amendment) Act 1976, and this Act and the Sexual Offences Acts 1956 and 1967 may be cited together as the Sexual Offences Acts 1956 to 1976.

(2) In this Act—

"a rape offence" means any of the following, namely rape, attempted rape, aiding, abetting, counselling and procuring rape or attempted rape, and incitement to rape; and references to sexual intercourse shall be construed in accordance with section 44 of the Sexual Offences Act 1956 so far as it relates to natural intercourse (under which such intercourse is deemed complete on proof of penetration only); and section 46 of that Act (which relates to the meaning of "man" and "woman" in that Act) shall have effect as if the reference to that Act included a reference to this Act.

Who may be convicted

There is an irrebutable presumption in law that a boy under the age of fourteen is incapable of committing rape, irrespective of the nature of the evidence against him. However, such a boy, following *R v Williams* [1893] 1 QB 320, may on an indictment for rape, be convicted of an indecent assault under s.9 of the Criminal Law Amendment Act 1885. Following Hale there is a presumption that a man cannot be guilty as a principal of rape upon his wife, since she is deemed to have consented irrevocably to intercourse with him by the fact of marriage. However, over the years the presumption has been weakened, and the present position is that a man may be convicted of rape upon his wife (or his ex-wife) if there is in force a separation order or decree of judicial separation (*R v Clarke* [1949] 2 All ER 448), or a decree nisi of divorce (*R v O'Brien* [1974] 3 All ER 663). Further, an agreement to separate, particularly if it contains a non-molestation clause, may amount to revocation of the wife's implied consent, after *R v Miller* [1954] 2 QB 282.

A husband who has intercourse with his wife against her will is guilty of assault.

Husbands, boys under fourteen, and women may all be found guilty of aiding and abetting another to commit rape, even though the principal may have been acquitted on the grounds of mistaken belief as to the woman's consent – *R v Cogan* [1975] 2 All ER 1059.

Against whom may the offence be committed?

Subject to the special rules regarding inter-spousal rape, the offence may be committed against any female person.

Defences

It must be proved that the accused had sexual intercourse with the complainant without her consent. This applies even to girls under 16 who are below the age of consent, since, following s.1(1) (b) of the 1976 Act, if the man can show either that the woman had actually consented, or that he believed that she had done so, then that is a complete defence to the charge. In *Morgan v DPP* [1975] 2 All ER 347 the argument that an unreasonable belief as to consent could not be a defence was rejected. The test is a subjective one and the reasonableness or otherwise of the belief is probative only of whether or not it was likely in fact to have been held by the accused – s.1(2) of the 1976 Act. Consent obtained by duress or through fear of death is not a defence to a charge of rape; equally, where the woman is unconscious due to drink or drugs, or is asleep when the offence is committed, then that is also rape.

Submission owing to ignorance of, or to a mistake as to the nature of the act done or of the person doing it, and induced by the fraud of the defendant, does not constitute consent, *R v Case* 1 Den 580 (1850); s.1(2) 1956 Act; *R v Williams* [1923] 1 KB 340. A person who has sexual intercourse without consent with a woman of unsound mind who is incapable of expressing consent or dissent is guilty of rape. However, if such a woman consents to the act by reason of mere animal instinct the act does not constitute rape (although it may constitute the indictable offence of unlawful sexual intercourse with a woman who is defective, unless the defendant can establish that he did not know and had no reason to suspect her to be a defective).

Mode of prosecution

Both rape and attempted rape are triable on indictment only (except for the statutory provisions providing for summary trial in certain cases of persons under the age of 17 years – s.6(1) Children and Young Persons Act 1969).

Maximum penalty

The maximum penalty on a charge of rape is life imprisonment, and on a charge of attempted rape is seven years' imprisonment.

PROCUREMENT OF WOMAN BY THREATS

Definition

The term 'procures' includes procurement to have intercourse with the procurer – *R v Williams* (1898) 62 JP 310. A woman is not procured if she acts on her own initiative – *R v Christian* (1913) 78 JP 112. An offence constituted by procuring a woman to have unlawful sexual intercourse is committed only if unlawful sexual intercourse occurs – *R v Mackenzie and Higginson* (1910) 6 CrAppR 64; *R v Johnson* [1964] 2 QB 404.

Legal source

S.2 Sexual Offences Act 1956

Sexual Offences Act 1956
Procurement of woman by threats

2.—(1) It is an offence for a person to procure a woman, by threats or intimidation, to have unlawful sexual intercourse in any part of the world.

(2) A person shall not be convicted of an offence under this section on the evidence of one witness only, unless the witness is corroborated in some material particular by evidence implicating the accused.

Who may be convicted

S.2 refers to 'any persons', thus the presumption is that both male and female persons may be charged provided that they are over fourteen years of age.

Mode of prosecution

Class 3 offence triable on indictment.

Maximum penalty

Imprisonment not exceeding two years – s.37 and Sched 2 para 7(a) Sexual Offences Act 1956.

Punishment for attempt

Class 3 offence triable on indictment. Maximum penalty is imprisonment for period not exceeding two years – s.37 and Sched 2 para 7(b) Sexual Offences Act 1956.

PROCUREMENT OF WOMAN BY FALSE PRETENCES

Legal source

S.3 Sexual Offences Act 1956

Sexual Offences Act 1956
Procurement of woman by false pretences
3.—(1) It is an offence for a person to procure a woman, by false pretences or false representations, to have unlawful sexual intercourse in any part of the world.
(2) A person shall not be convicted of an offence under this section on the evidence of one witness only, unless the witness is corroborated in some material particular by evidence implicating the accused.

Who may be convicted

S.3 refers to 'any person', thus the presumption is that both male and female persons may be charged provided that they are over the age of fourteen years.

Mode of prosecution

Class 3 offence triable on indictment.

Maximum penalty

Two years' imprisonment – s.37 and Sched 2 para 8 Sexual Offences Act 1956.

Punishment for attempt

There is no separate offence of attempted procurement of a woman by false pretences in English law.

ADMINISTERING DRUGS TO OBTAIN OR FACILITATE INTERCOURSE

Description

The essence of the offence is the administering of the drug; therefore, where there has been a single administration only, then only one offence is committed, even if the intention of the administration was to enable more than one man to have sexual intercourse – *R v Shillingford* [1968] 2 All ER 200.

Legal source

S.4 Sexual Offences Act 1956

Sexual Offences Act 1956
Administering drugs to obtain or facilitate intercourse
4.—(1) It is an offence for a person to apply or administer to, or cause to be taken by, a woman any drug, matter or thing with intent to stupefy or overpower her so as thereby to enable any man to have unlawful sexual intercourse with her.
(2) A person shall not be convicted of an offence under this section on the evidence of one witness only, unless the witness is corroborated in some material particular by evidence implicating the accused.

Mode of prosecution

Class 3 offence triable on indictment.

Maximum penalty

Two years' imprisonment – s.37 and Sched 2 para 9 of the Sexual Offences Act 1956.

Punishment for attempt

There is no separate offence of attempt to administer drugs to obtain or facilitate intercourse in English law.

UNLAWFUL SEXUAL INTERCOURSE WITH A GIRL UNDER 13 YEARS

Legal source

S.5 Sexual Offences Act 1956; (see also ss.44, 46 under Rape).

Sexual Offences Act 1956
Intercourse with girl under thirteen
5. It is felony for a man to have unlawful sexual intercourse with a girl under the age of thirteen.

Who may be convicted

The irrebuttable presumption that a boy under fourteen years is incapable of sexual intercourse extends to this offence. Otherwise the offence may be committed by any male person.

Against whom may the offence be committed?

Any girl under the age of thirteen years.

Defences

The fact of the girls' consent is immaterial and does not provide a defence to the charge. Equally, belief, even if reasonable, that the girl was over 13 is no defence: *R v Prince* (1875) LR 2 CCR 154.

Mode of prosecution

Class 2 offence triable on indictment.

Maximum penalty

Life imprisonment.

Punishment for attempt

By s.37 and Sched 2 para 2(b) of the Sexual Offences Act 1956, as amended by s.2 of the Indecency with Children Act 1960, the punishment for an attempt to have sexual intercourse with a girl under the age of 13 is imprisonment for not more than seven years.

Indecency with Children Act 1960

Length of imprisonment for certain offences against young girls

2.—(1) The maximum term of imprisonment to which a person is liable under the Sexual Offences Act, 1956, if convicted on indictment of an attempt to have unlawful sexual intercourse with a girl under the age of thirteen, or of an indecent assault on a girl who is stated in the indictment and proved to have been at the time under that age,—
(*a*) in the case of such an attempt, shall be seven years; and
(*b*) in the case of an indecent assault, shall be five years.

(2) In the case of a person convicted of attempted incest with a girl who is stated in the indictment and proved to have been at the time under the age of thirteen the foregoing subsection shall apply as it applies in the case of a person convicted of an attempt to have unlawful intercourse with a girl under that age.

(3) Accordingly in the Second Schedule to that Act, for the words "two years" in the third column in items 2 (*b*), 14 (*b*) and 17 (i), there shall be substituted—
(*a*) in item 2 (*b*) the words "seven years";
(*b*) in item 14 (*b*) the words "if with a girl under thirteen who is stated to have been so in the indictment, seven years; otherwise two years";
(*c*) in item 17 (i) the words "if on a girl under thirteen who is stated to have been so in the indictment, five years; othewise two years".

(4) This section shall not apply to offences committed on or before the date this Act is passed.

UNLAWFUL SEXUAL INTERCOURSE WITH A GIRL UNDER 16 YEARS

Legal source

S.6(1) Sexual Offences Act 1956; and see also ss.44 and 46 under Rape.

Sexual Offences Act 1956
Intercourse with girl between thirteen and sixteen
6.—(1) It is an offence, subject to the exceptions mentioned in this section, for a man to have unlawful sexual intercourse with a girl not under the age of thirteen but under the age of sixteen.

Who may be convicted

Any male person, except a boy under the age of 14 years.

Against whom may the offence be committed

Any female under the age of sixteen years.

Defences

Sexual Offences Act 1956
6.—(2) Where a marriage is invalid under section two of the Marriage Act, 1949, or section one of the Age of Marriage Act, 1929 (the wife being a girl under the age of sixteen), the invalidity does not make the husband guilty of an offence under this section because he has sexual intercourse with her, if he believes her to be his wife and has reasonable cause for the belief.

(3) A man is not guilty of an offence under this section because he has unlawful sexual intercourse with a girl under the age of sixteen, if he is under the age of twenty-four and has not previously been charged with a like offence, and he believes her to be of the age of sixteen or over and has reasonable cause for the belief.

In this subsection, "a like offence" means an offence under this section or an attempt to commit one, or an offence under paragraph (1) of section five of the Criminal Law Amendment Act, 1885 (the provision replaced for England and Wales by this section).

It is no defence that the girl consented; if she did not consent, it will be rape, and the defendant may be indicted accordingly. If, however, in a case where the girl did not so consent, an indictment for sexual intercourse only is preferred, the defendant may be convicted of that offence even though the facts would have justified an indictment and conviction for rape.

Mode of prosecution

Class 3 offence triable on indictment. A prosecution may not be commenced more than 12 months after the commission of the alleged offence.

Maximum penalty

Two years' imprisonment.

Punishment for attempt

Class 3 offence triable on indictment. A prosecution may not be commenced more than 12 months after the date of the alleged offence. The maximum penalty for such attempt is imprisonment not exceeding two years – Sexual Offences Act 1956 s.37, Sched 2 para 10(b).

SEXUAL INTERCOURSE WITH A DEFECTIVE

Legal source

S.7 Sexual Offences Act 1956 as amended by s.127(a) Mental Health Act 1959.

Mental Health Act 1959
Amendment of Sexual Offences Act 1956
127.—(1) The Sexual Offences Act, 1956, shall be amended as follows:—

(*a*) for section seven there shall be substituted the following section:—

Intercourse with defective

7.—(1) It is an offence, subject to the exception mentioned in this section, for a man to have unlawful sexual intercourse with a woman who is a defective.

(2) A man is not guilty of an offence under this section because he has unlawful sexual intercourse with a woman if he does not know and has no reason to suspect her to be a defective;

(*b*) for section forty-five there shall be substituted the following section:—

Meaning of 'defective'

45. In this Act 'defective' means a person suffering from severe subnormality within the meaning of the Mental Health Act, 1959;

and section eight of that Act shall cease to have effect.

Who may be convicted

Any male person except a boy under the age of fourteen.

Against whom may the offence be committed?

See s.127(1)(b) supra.

Defences

See s.127(1)(a) supra.

Mode of prosecution

Class 3 offence triable on indictment.

Maximum penalty

Two years' imprisonment – s.37 and Sched 2 para 11(a) Sexual Offences Act 1956.

Punishment for attempt

Class 3 offence triable on indictment; maximum penalty two years' imprisonment – s.37 and Sched 2 para 11(b) Sexual Offences Act 1956.

PROCUREMENT OF A DEFECTIVE

Legal source

S.9 Sexual Offences Act 1956

Sexual Offences Act 1956
Procurement of defective
9.—(1) It is an offence, subject to the exception mentioned in this section, for a person to procure a woman who is a defective to have unlawful sexual intercourse in any part of the world.

Who may be convicted

Any male person.

Against whom may the offence by committed?

Against any person suffering from severe subnormality within the meaning of the Mental Health Act 1959.

Definition

Procurement may be either by threats or intimidation, or by false pretences or false representations.

Defences

Sexual Offences Act 1956
9.—(2) A person is not guilty of an offence under this section because he procures a defective to have unlawful sexual intercourse, if he does not know and has no reason to suspect her to be a defective.

To set up the defence of absence of knowledge that the woman was a defective the defendant must establish on a balance of probabilities that he did not know that the woman was a defective – *R v Hudson* [1966] 1 QB 448. S.47 Sexual Offences Act 1956 places the burden of proving the exception to the offence on the person relying on it.

Mode of prosecution

Class 3 offence triable on indictment.

Maximum penalty

Two years' imprisonment – s.37, Sched 2 para 13(a) Sexual Offences Act 1956.

Punishment for attempt

Class 3 offence triable on indictment; maximum penalty two years' imprisonment – s.37, Sched 2 para 13(b) Sexual Offences Act 1956.

INCEST BY A MAN

Legal source

S.10 Sexual Offences Act 1956
Incest by a man
10.—(1) It is an offence for a man to have sexual intercourse with a woman whom he knows to be his grand-daughter, daughter, sister or mother.
(2) In the foregoing subsection "sister" includes half-sister, and for the purposes of that subsection any expression importing a relationship between two people shall be taken to apply notwithstanding that the relationship is not traced through lawful wedlock.

By s.37 and Sched 2 para 14(a) of the Sexual Offences Act 1956, on an indictment for incest by a man 'the jury may find the accused guilty:– (i) of intercourse with a girl under thirteen (s.5) or (ii) of intercourse with a girl under sixteen (s.6).'

Who may be convicted

Any male person except a boy under the age of fourteen years.

Against whom may the offence be committed?

Any female related to the defendant as in s.10 of the 1956 Act.

Defences

It is not a defence to show that the woman consented. The onus is on the prosecution to prove not only that the relevant relationship existed, but also that the defendant was aware of it at the time of the commission of the offence.

Mode of prosecution

Class 3 offence (unless the girl is under 13, when it is class 2) triable on indictment. A prosecution may not be commenced without the sanction of the Attorney General, except by or on behalf of the Director of Public Prosecutions – s.37(1), (2) and Sched 2 para 14(a) Sexual Offences Act 1956.

Maximum penalty

If with a girl under 13, and so charged in the indictment, life imprisonment; otherwise seven years' imprisonment.

Punishment for attempt

Class 3 offence triable on indictment, no prosecution to be commenced without the sanction of the Attorney General, except by or on behalf of the Director of Public Prosecutions. Maximum penalty two years' imprisonment. Attempted incest with girl under age 13 carries a maximum penalty of seven years (Indecency with Children Act 1960, s.2).

Power of court in case of incest with girl under 18

S.38 Sexual Offences Act 1956 (as substituted by the Guardianship Act 1973, s.17(8) and Sched 1).

Guardianship Act 1973
Provisions Substituted for Sexual Offences Act 1956 s.38

(1) On a person's conviction of an offence under section 10 of this Act against a girl under the age of eighteen, or of an offence under section 11 of this Act against a boy under that age, or of attempting to commit such an offence, the court may by order divest that person of all authority over the girl or boy.
(2) An order divesting a person of authority over a girl or boy under the foregoing subsection may, if that person is the guardian of the girl or boy, remove that person from the guardianship.
(3) An order under this section may appoint a person to be the guardian of the girl or boy during his or her minority or any less period.
(4) An order under this section may be varied from time to time or rescinded by the High Court and, if made on conviction of an offence against a girl or boy who is a defective, may, so far as it has effect for any of the purposes of the Mental Health Act 1959, be rescinded either before or after the girl or boy has attained the age of eighteen.

INCEST BY A WOMAN

Legal source

S.11 Sexual Offences Act 1956

Sexual Offences Act 1956
Incest by a woman

11.—(1) It is an offence for a woman of the age of sixteen or over to permit a man whom she knows to be her grandfather, father, brother or son to have sexual intercourse with her by her consent.
(2) In the foregoing subsection "brother" includes half-brother, and for the purposes of that subsection any expression importing a relationship between two people shall be taken to apply notwithstanding that the relationship is not traced through lawful wedlock.

Who may be convicted

Any female person over the age of sixteen years.

Against whom may the offence by committed?

Any male person related to the defendant as in s.11 Sexual Offences Act 1956.

Defences

The onus is on the prosecution to prove both the existence of the relevant relationship, and the defendant's knowledge of it.

Mode of prosecution

Class 3 offence triable on indictment. A prosecution may not be commenced without the sanction of the Attorney General, except by or on behalf of the Director of Public Prosecutions – s.37(1), (2) and Sched 2 para 15(a) Sexual Offences Act 1956.

Maximum penalty

Imprisonment for seven years.

Punishment for attempt

Class 3 offence triable on indictment, no prosecution to be commenced without the sanction of the Attorney General, except by or on behalf of the Director of Public Prosecutions. Maximum penalty is two years' imprisonment.

Power of court in case of incest with boy under 18

S.38 Sexual Offences Act 1956 as amended by Sched 1 Guardianship Act 1973 is also applicable to cases of incest by a woman against a boy under 18 years.

BUGGERY

Definition

The offence consists of sexual intercourse (per anum) by man with man or in the same manner by man with woman or by man or woman in any manner with beast (which is also referred to as bestiality): see Sir Matthew Hale (1736) *The History of Pleas of the Crown Vol 1*, 669; 1 Hawk c.4; 1 East PC 480; *Russell on Crime Vol 1* 12th edn., 735. Where the defendant forced open a child's mouth and put in his private parts, and proceeded to the completion of his lust, the judges were of opinion that this did not constitute the offence of buggery: *R v Jacobs* R&R 331. Where the offence is committed with an animal, penetration per anum is not essential – see *R v Bourne* (1952) 36 Cr App R 125, where connection per vaginam was sufficient to constitute the offence.

Legal source

S.12 Sexual Offences Act 1956.

Sexual Offences Act 1956
Buggery
12.—(1) It is felony for a person to commit buggery with another person or with an animal.
(2) Section thirty-nine of this Act (which relates to the competence as a witness of the wife or husband of the accused) does not apply in the case of this section, except on a charge of an offence with a person under the age of seventeen.
(3) For the purposes of the last foregoing subsection a person shall be presumed, unless the contrary is proved, to have been under the age of seventeen at the time of the offence charged if he is stated in the charge or indictment, and appears to the court, to have been so.

The Sexual Offences Act 1967 has narrowed the ambit of the offence of buggery by legalising homosexual acts in private between parties over 21 years of age. (See infra under *Defences*).

Parties to the offence

If the offence is committed on a boy or girl under fourteen years the agent alone is guilty, on the ground that the patient is under the age of discretion: 1 Hale 670; 3 Co Inst 59; 1 East PC 480. If the offence is committed *by* a boy under 14, the patient alone is guilty if he or she is over 14; *R v Allen* 1 Den 364. It would seem that the presumption applicable to boys under 14 applies to this offence as well as to rape where the boy is the agent.

Defences

S.1 Sexual Offences Act 1967

Sexual Offences Act 1967
Amendment of law relating to homosexual acts in private

1.—(1) Notwithstanding any statutory or common law provision, but subject to the provisions of the next following section, a homosexual act in private shall not be an offence provided that the parties consent thereto and have attained the age of twenty-one years.

(2) An act which would otherwise be treated for the purposes of this Act as being done in private shall not be so treated if done—
(*a*) when more than two persons take part or are present; or
(*b*) in a lavatory to which the public have or are permitted to have access, whether on payment or otherwise.

(3) A man who is suffering from severe subnormality within the meaning of the Mental Health Act 1959 cannot in law give any consent which, by virtue of subsection (1) of this section, would prevent a homosexual act from being an offence, but a person shall not be convicted, on account of the incapacity of such a man to consent, of an offence consisting of such an act if he proves that he did not know and had no reason to suspect that man to be suffering from severe subnormality.

(5) Subsection (1) of this section shall not prevent an act from being an offence (other than a civil offence) under any provision of the Army Act 1955, the Air Force Act 1955 or the Naval Discipline Act 1957.

(6) It is hereby declared that where in any proceedings it is charged that a homosexual act is an offence the prosecutor shall have the burden of proving that the act was done otherwise than in private or otherwise than with the consent of the parties or that any of the parties had not attained the age of twenty-one years.

(7) For the purposes of this section a man shall be treated as doing a homosexual act if, and only if, he commits buggery with another man or commits an act of gross indecency with another man or is a party to the commission by a man of such an act.

Mode of prosecution

Class 3 offence triable on indictment. Under s.8 Sexual Offences Act 1967, the consent of the Director of Public Prosecutions to proceedings is necessary in certain cases.

Sexual Offences Act 1967
Restrictions on prosecutions

8.—(1) No proceedings shall be instituted except by or with the consent of the Director of Public Prosecutions against any man for the offence of buggery with, or gross indecency with, another man, for attempting to commit either offence, or for aiding, abetting, counselling, procuring or commanding its commission where either of those men was at the time of its commission under the age of twenty-one.

Further, under s.7 of the Sexual Offences Act 1967 there is a time limit on prosecutions for any offence of buggery by a man with another man not amounting to an assault on that other man and not being an offence by a man with a boy under the age of sixteen. In such cases proceedings may not be commenced more than twelve months from the date of the commission of the offence.

Maximum penalty

For certain cases of buggery s.3(1) of the Sexual Offences Act 1967 has amended the maximum penalty of life imprisonment provided for in para 3(a) of Sched 2 of the 1956 Act.

Sexual Offences Act 1967
Revised punishments for homosexual acts

3.—(1) The maximum punishment which may be imposed on conviction on indictment of a man for buggery with another man of or over the age of sixteen shall, instead of being imprisonment for life as prescribed by para 3 of Sched 2 to the Act of 1956, be—

(*a*) imprisonment for a term of ten years except where the other man consented thereto; and

(*b*) in the said excepted case, imprisonment for a term of five years if the accused is of or over the age of twenty-one and the other man is under that age, but otherwise two years;

and the maximum punishment prescribed by that paragraph for an attempt to commit buggery with another man (ten years) shall not apply where that other man is of or over the age of sixteen.

Where the offence is committed with a boy under that age of 16, or with a woman, or with an animal, the maximum penalty continues to be life imprisonment, as laid down in s.37 and Sched 2 para 3(a).

Punishment for attempt

This is a class 3 offence triable on indictment, s.8 Sexual Offences Act 1967 (supra) requiring the Director of Public Prosecutions' consent to proceedings is also applicable. The maximum penalty for attempted buggery is ten years' imprisonment if the offence is committed with a boy under the age of 16, or with a woman, or an animal. The punishment for attempt in any other circumstances is governed by the Powers of Criminal Courts Act 1973 s.18(2): a person convicted on indictment of an attempt to commit an offence for which a maximum term of imprisonment is provided by any enactment shall not be sentenced to imprisonment for a term longer than that to which he could be sentenced for the completed offence.

GROSS INDECENCY BETWEEN MEN

Legal source

S.13 Sexual Offences Act 1956

Sexual Offences Act 1956
Indecency between men
13. It is an offence for a man to commit an act of gross indecency with another man, whether in public or private, or to be a party to the commission by a man of an act of gross indecency with another man, or to procure the commission by a man of an act of gross indecency with another man.

Definition

If there is an agreement whereby two male persons act in concert to behave in a grossly indecent manner, as, for example, to make a grossly indecent exhibition, the offence is committed even though there has been no actual physical contact, *R v Hunt* (1950) 34 Cr App R 135. An offence of indecency between men is not committed unless both men participate in the indecency. 'With another man' in s.13 cannot be construed as meaning 'against' or 'directed towards' a person who did not consent – *R v Preece and Howells* (1976) 63 Cr App R 28. Where two persons are jointly indicted for an offence under the section, one may be convicted and the other acquitted – *R v Jones* [1896] 1 QB 4; *R v Pearce* (1951) 35 Cr App R 17. It is also an offence within s.13 for a male person to procure the commission with himself of an act of gross indecency by another male person – *R v Jones* (supra); *R v Cope* (1921) 16 Cr App R 77. If a male person persuades, or attempts to persuade, a boy to handle him indecently, such person alone may be charged and convicted under this section. In a case where indecent assault may be difficult or impossible to prove, because no threat or hostile act by the defendant towards the boy can easily be established, the proper charge is that of procuring or attempting to procure, an act of gross indecency with the defendant himself – *R v Burrows* (1952) 35 Cr App R 180.

Who may be convicted

Any male person, although it seems unclear how far this applies to juveniles.

Against whom may the offence be committed?

Any male person.

Defences

This is no longer an offence where the act takes place in private and both parties consent thereto and both have attained the age of 21 years – Sexual Offences Act 1967 s.1 (supra under Buggery Defences).

Mode of prosecution

Class 4 offences, triable either on indictment or summarily – ss.16, 28 and Sched 3 to Criminal Law Act 1977.

Maximum penalty

If committed by a man over the age of 21 with a man under that age five years' imprisonment, otherwise two years.

Punishment for attempt

Class 4 offence triable either way – ss.16, 28 and Sched 3 to Criminal Law Act 1977. A letter arranging a meeting at a particular time and place, and containing terms which, in the circumstances of the case, would convey to the mind of the intended recipient an invitation to commit a gross indecency with the writer, may amount to an attempt to procure the commission of an act of gross indecency. Following *R v Bentley* [1923] 1 KB 403 it is not necessary that there should be, in the case of incitement of another to procure such an act, an ascertained person with whom the act was to be committed. If the defendant's conduct and talk were such that, although there was no specific invitation to participate in an act of indecency, they must still have conveyed to the other person his desire that they should act indecently together, such conduct and talk may be capable of being attempts to procure that person to commit an act of gross indecency with the defendant; whether they are in fact an attempt or not is a question for the jury – *R v Miskell* [1954] 37 Cr App R 214.

A conviction for attempting to commit an act of gross indecency may be maintained where one of the persons implicated alone has been charged and the other has not been charged but has been called as a witness for the prosecution and swears that he did not consent to any act of indecency – *R v Pearce* (1951) 35 Cr App R 17. The maximum penalty for attempt is imprisonment for five years if by a man over the age of 21 with another man under that age, otherwise two years' imprisonment – s.37 and Sched 2 para 16(b) of the Sexual Offences Act 1956 and s.3(4)(d) of the Sexual Offences Act 1967.

INDECENT ASSAULT ON A WOMAN

Definition

The prosecution must prove an assault, accompanied by circumstances of indecency on the part of the defendant towards the person assaulted. Kissing a girl against her will, accompanied by a suggestion that sexual intercourse or sexual activity should take place between her and the defendant is an indecent assault – *R v Leeson* (1968) 52 Cr App R 185. If that which was done to a child would have been an assault if done against her will, it would also be an assault if it was done with her consent and is of an indecent nature, since she cannot consent to an indecent assault – *Fairclough v Whipps* (1951) 35 Cr App R 138.

Legal source

S.14 Sexual Offences Act 1956

Sexual Offences Act 1956
Indecent assault on a woman
14.—(1) It is an offence, subject to the exception mentioned in subsection (3) of this section, for a person to make an indecent assault on a woman.

Who may be convicted

Any male person. Following *R v Hare* (1933) 24 Cr App R 108, it seems that a woman may also be guilty of an offence under this section.

Defences

Sexual Offences Act 1956

14.—(2) A girl under the age of sixteen cannot in law give any consent which would prevent an act being an assault for the purposes of this section.

(3) Where a marriage is invalid under section two of the Marriage Act, 1949, or section one of the Age of Marriage Act, 1929 (the wife being a girl under the age of sixteen), the invalidity does not make the husband guilty of any offence under this section by reason of her incapacity to consent while under that age, if he believes her to be his wife and has reasonable cause for the belief.

(4) A woman who is a defective cannot in law give any consent which would prevent an act being an assault for the purposes of this section, but a person is only to be treated as guilty of an indecent assault on a defective by reason of that incapacity to consent, if that person knew or had reason to suspect her to be a defective.

In *R v Donovan* [1934] 2 KB 498 it was established that consent cannot be a defence where the indecent assault consists in the infliction of blows intended or likely to cause bodily harm. A reasonable and bona fide belief that the girl upon whom the assault was committed was 16 years of age at the time of the commission of the offence is no defence – *R v Maughan* (1934) 24 Cr App R 130.

Mode of prosecution

Class 4 offence triable on indictment and, following s.16(a) of the Criminal Law Act 1977, also summarily.

Maximum penalty

On indictment – if on a girl under 13 who is stated to have been so in the indictment, five years' imprisonment, otherwise two years. On a summary conviction the maximum is provided by s.28(1) Criminal Law Act 1977, that is, six months' imprisonment, or the prescribed sum within the meaning of the section, or both.

INDECENT ASSAULT ON A MAN

Legal source

S.15(1) Sexual Offences Act 1956

Sexual Offences Act 1956
Indecent assault on a man

15.—(1) It is an offence for a person to make an indecent assault on a man.

Definition

To constitute an assault there must be a hostile act, compulsion, a threatening gesture or a threat to use violence. However, the absence of a hostile act is no defence to a charge of indecent assault on a person aged under 16 – *R v McCormack* [1969] 2 QB 442.

Who may be convicted

Any male or female person.

Defences

Sexual Offences Act 1956

15.—(2) A boy under the age of sixteen cannot in law give any consent which would prevent an act being an assault for the purposes of this section.

(3) A man who is a defective cannot in law give any consent which would prevent an act being an assault for the purposes of this section, but a person is only to be treated as guilty of an indecent assault on a defective by reason of that incapacity to consent, if that person knew or had reason to suspect him to be a defective.

(4) Section thirty-nine of this Act (which relates to the competence as a witness of the wife or husband of the accused) does not apply in the case of this section, except on a charge of indecent assault on a boy under the age of seventeen.

(5) For the purposes of the last foregoing subsection a person shall be presumed, unless the contrary is proved, to have been under the age of seventeen at the time of the offence charged if he is stated in the charge or indictment, and appears to the court, to have been so.

Where the defendant was indicted for an indecent assault on a male person, and it appeared that the person alleged to have been assaulted consented to what was done to him by the defendant, it was held that the indictment could not be sustained – *R v Wollaston* (1872) 12 Cox 180. Consent is irrelevant following s.15(2) in cases of indecent assault on a boy under the age of 16.

Victim under 16

In order to constitute an indecent assault against a child under the age of 16, the act complained of either must itself be inherently indecent, or it must be one that is hostile or threatening or an act which the child is demonstrably reluctant to accept – *DPP v Rogers* [1953] 1 WLR 1017, and *Williams v Gibbs* [1958] Crim LR 127. Although ss.14(2) and 15(2) of the 1956 Act bar the child's consent from preventing an act being an indecent assault, consent does avail to prevent the act being an assault if the act is not inherently indecent – *R v Sutton* [1977] 3 All ER 476. However the circumstances of such a case may well constitute an offence under the Indecency with Children Act 1960.

Mode of prosecution

The offence is triable both on indictment and, by virtue of s.16(2) Criminal Law Act 1977, summarily.

Maximum penalty

On indictment the maximum penalty is ten years' imprisonment. On a summary conviction, following s.28(1) of the Criminal Law Act 1977, it is either six months imprisonment, or a fine as prescribed by the section, or both.

ASSAULT WITH INTENT TO COMMIT BUGGERY

Legal source

S.16(1) Sexual Offences Act 1956

Sexual Offences Act 1956
Assault with intent to commit buggery

16.—(1) It is an offence for a person to assault another person with intent to commit buggery.

(2) Section thirty-nine of this Act (which relates to the competence as a witness of the wife or husband of the accused) does not apply in the case of this section, except on a charge of an assault on a person under the age of seventeen.

(3) For the purposes of the last foregoing subsection a person shall be presumed, unless the contrary is proved, to have been under the age of seventeen at the time of the offence charged if he is stated in the charge or indictment, and appears to the court, to have been so.

Who may be convicted

Any male person.

Against whom may the offence be committed?

Any male or female person.

Mode of prosecution

Class 3 offence triable on indictment.

Maximum penalty

Ten years' imprisonment – Sexual Offences Act s.37 and Sched 2 para 19.

ABDUCTION OF WOMAN BY FORCE OR FOR THE SAKE OF HER PROPERTY

Legal source

S.17 Sexual Offences Act 1956

Sexual Offences Act 1956
Abduction of woman by force or for the sake of her property

17.—(1) It is felony for a person to take away or detain a woman against her will with the intention that she shall marry or have unlawful sexual intercourse with that or any other person, if she is so taken away or detained either by force or for the sake of her property or expectations of property.

(2) In the foregoing subsection, the reference to a woman's expectations of property relates only to property of a person to whom she is next of kin or one of the next of kin, and "property" includes any interest in property.

Definition

It must be shown that the defendant took away or detained the woman against her will. If the woman consented initially, but afterwards refused to continue with the defendant and was then forcibly detained by him, the offence is within the statute. It is also necessary to establish that the defendant had the interest stated in the indictment from which the motives for taking the women away or detaining her may be presumed. The necessary intention may be inferred from the declarations or acts of the defendant.

Who may be convicted

Any male or presumably female person.

Against whom may the offence be committed?

Any female person, although there are separate offences for abduction of girls under the ages of eighteen and sixteen.

Mode of prosecution

Class 3 offence triable on indictment.

Maximum penalty

Fourteen years' imprisonment.

FRAUDULENT ABDUCTION OF HEIRESS

This offence which was previously contained in s.18 Sexual Offences Act 1956, has been replaced by s.11(c) of the Family Law Reform Act 1969.

ABDUCTION OF GIRL UNDER 18 YEARS OF AGE

ABDUCTION OF GIRL UNDER 16 YEARS OF AGE

Legal source

SS.19 and 20 Sexual Offences Act 1956

Sexual Offences Act 1956
Abduction of unmarried girl under eighteen from parent or guardian

19.—(1) It is an offence, subject to the exception mentioned in this section, for a person to take an unmarried girl under the age of eighteen out of the possession of her parent or guardian against his will, if she is so taken with the intention that she shall have unlawful sexual intercourse with men or with a particular man.

(2) A person is not guilty of an offence under this section because he takes such a girl out of the possession of her parent or guardian as mentioned above, if he believes her to be of the age of eighteen or over and has reasonable cause for the belief.

(3) In this section "guardian" means any person having the lawful care or charge of the girl.

Abduction of unmarried girl under sixteen from parent or guardian

20.—(1) It is an offence for a person acting without lawful authority or excuse to take an unmarried girl under the age of sixteen out of the possession of her parent or guardian against his will.

(2) In the foregoing subsection "guardian" means any person having the lawful care or charge of the girl.

'Unlawful sexual intercourse' merely means illicit intercourse – ie outside the bond of marriage – *R v Chapman* [1959] 1 QB 100.

Who may be convicted

Any male person.

Against whom may the offences be committed?

Any girl under 18 years old for s.19 and under 16 years for s.20.

Defences

It is a defence under s.19(2) if the defendant, at the time of taking the girl from lawful custody, had reasonable cause to believe that she was eighteen, although he did not inquire until after the taking – *R v Packer* (1886) 16 Cox 57. The taking need not be by force either actual or constructive, and it is immaterial whether the girl consents or not – *R v Manktelow* (1853) 6 Cox 143. The words 'taking out of the possession' and 'against the will' of the parent mean some conduct amounting to a substantial interference with the possessory relationship of parent and child – *R v Jones* [1973] Crim LR 621.

If the defendant, at the time when he took the girl away, did not know, and had no reason to know that she was under the lawful care or charge of her father, mother or some other person, he is not guilty of this offence – *R v Hibbert* LR 1 CCR 184. In the case of abduction of a girl under 16, it is no defence that the defendant did not know her to be under 16 or might suppose from her appearance that she was older, or even that the defendant bona fide believed and had reasonable grounds for believing that she was over 16 – *R v Prince* (1875) LR 2 CCR 154. (If the girl was under 14 years and was taken away by force or fraud, then the offence must be charged under s.56 of the Offences Against the Person Act 1861).

Mode of prosecution

Abduction both of a girl under 18 and of a girl under 16 is in both cases a class 3 offence triable on indictment.

Maximum penalty

In the case of abduction of a girl under 18 – two years' imprisonment – s.37 and Sched 2 para 20 Sexual Offences Act 1956. Abduction of a girl under 16 – two years' imprisonment, s.37 and Sched 2 para 21 Sexual Offences Act 1956.

Inducement

Where a man induces a girl, by promise of what he will do for her, to leave her father's house and live with him, he may be convicted, although he is not actually present or assisting her at the time when she leaves her father's house – *R v Robb* 4 F&F 59. If a girl leaves her father, without any persuasion from the defendant and only joins him afterwards, this does not constitute an offence, since the statute does not say that the defendant shall restore the girl, only that he shall not take her away. If the suggestion to go away with the defendant comes from the girl alone, and the defendant merely passively yields to her suggestion, then he should be aquitted – *R v Jarvis* (1903) 20 Cox 249.

If the defendant induced the parents, by false and fradulent representations to allow him to take the child away, then that constitutes an abduction – *R v Hopkins* C & Mar 254.

ABDUCTION OF DEFECTIVE FROM PARENT OR GUARDIAN

Legal source

S.21 Sexual Offences Act 1956

Sexual Offences Act 1956
Abduction of defective from parent or guardian
21.—(1) It is an offence, subject to the exception mentioned in this section, for a person to take a woman who is a defective out of the possession of her parent or guardian against his will, if she is so taken with the intention that she shall have unlawful sexual intercourse with men or with a particular man.

Who may be convicted

Any person – male or female.

Against whom may the offence be committed?

In the Sexual Offences Act 1956 the term 'defective' means a person suffering from severe subnormality within the meaning of the Mental Health Act 1959 – s.45 Sexual Offences Act and s.127(1)(b) Mental Health Act. In s.4(2) of the 1959 Act 'severe subnormality' means a state of arrested or incomplete development of mind which includes subnormality of intelligence and is of such a nature or degree that the patient is incapable of living an independent life or of guarding himself against serious exploitation, or will be so incapable when of an age to do so.

Defences

Sexual Offences Act 1956
21.—(2) A person is not guilty of an offence under this section because he takes such a woman out of the possession of her parent or guardian as mentioned above, if he does not know and has no reason to suspect her to be a defective.

(3) In this section "guardian" means any person having the lawful care or charge of the woman.

Mode of prosecution

Class 3 offence triable on indictment.

Maximum penalty

Two years' imprisonment – s.37 and Sched 2 para 22 Sexual Offences Act 1956.

CAUSING PROSTITUTION OF WOMAN

Legal source

S. 22 Sexual Offences Act 1956

Sexual Offences Act 1956
Causing prostitution of women
22.—(1) It is an offence for a person—
(a) to procure a woman to become, in any part of the world, a common prostitute; or
(b) to procure a woman to leave the United Kingdom, intending her to become an inmate of or frequent a brothel elsewhere; or
(c) to procure a woman to leave her usual place of abode in the United Kingdom, intending her to become an inmate of or frequent a brothel in any part of the world for the purposes of prostitution.
(2) A person shall not be convicted of an offence under this section on the evidence of one witness only, unless the witness is corroborated in some material particular by evidence implicating the accused.

'Common prostitute' includes a woman who offers her body commonly for acts of lewdness for payment although there is no act or offer of an act of ordinary sexual intercourse – *R v De Munck* [1918] 1 KB 635. It is not necessary that the woman should have submitted to acts of lewdness in a passive way. Active acts of indecency by the woman herself, eg masturbation by her of clients when acting as a masseuse will fall within the section – *R v Webb* [1964] 1 QB 357. Proof of payment for indulgence in acts of lewdness does not appear to be necessary – *Winter v Woolfe* [1931] 1 KB 549.

Who may be convicted

Any male or female person.

Mode of prosecution

Class 3 offence triable on indictment.

Maximum penalty

Two years' imprisonment – s.37 and Sched 2 para 23(a) 1956 Act.

Punishment for attempt

An attempt to commit any of the offences in s.22 Sexual Offences Act 1956 is a class 3 offence triable on indictment and is punishable by a maximum of two years – s.37 and Sched 2 para 23 (b) of the Sexual Offences Act 1956.

PROCURATION OF GIRL UNDER 21

Legal source

S.23 Sexual Offences Act 1956

Sexual Offences Act 1956
Procuration of girl under twenty-one

23.—(1) It is an offence for a person to procure a girl under the age of twenty-one to have unlawful sexual intercourse in any part of the world with a third person.

(2) A person shall not be convicted of an offence under this section on the evidence of one witness only, unless the witness is corroborated in some material particular by evidence implicating the accused.

There must be some real procuration and this may be negatived by evidence which shows that the girl was not really procured, because she needed no procuring at all, and acted of her own free will – *R v Christian* (1913) 23 Cox 321. In order to obtain a conviction under s.23(1) it is necessary to prove that unlawful sexual intercourse (ie outside the bond of marriage) actually took place.

Who may be convicted

Any person, male or female.

Defences

Where the girl acted of her own free will, then this is sufficient to negative the charge of procuration – *R v Christian* (supra).

Mode of prosecution

Class 3 offence triable on indictment.

Maximum penalty

Two years' imprisonment – s.37 and Sched 2 para 24(a) of the Sexual Offences Act 1956.

Punishment for attempt

If intercourse is not proved to have taken place, but procurement with the intention that it should take place is proved, there may be a conviction of an attempt to commit the full offence – *R v Johnson* [1964] 2 QB 404. Such an attempt is a class 3 offence triable on indictment, and is subject to the maximum penalty of two years' imprisonment – s.37 and Sched 2 para 24(b) Sexual Offences Act 1956.

DETENTION OF WOMAN IN BROTHEL OR OTHER PREMISES

Legal source

S.24 Sexual Offences Act 1956

Sexual Offences Act 1956
Detention of woman in brothel or other premises

24.—(1) It is an offence for a person to detain a woman against her will on any premises with the intention that she shall have unlawful sexual intercourse with men or with a particular man, or to detain a woman against her will in a brothel.

(2) Where a woman is on any premises for the purpose of having unlawful sexual intercourse or is in a brothel, a person shall be deemed for the purpose of the foregoing subsection to detain her there if, with the intention of compelling or inducing her to remain there, he either withholds from her her clothes or any other property belonging to her or theatens her with legal proceedings in the event of her taking away clothes provided for her by him or on his directions.

(3) A woman shall not be liable to any legal proceedings, whether civil or criminal, for taking away or being found in possession of any clothes she needed to enable her to leave premises on which she was for the purpose of having unlawful sexual intercourse or to leave a brothel.

Who may be convicted

Any person, male or female.

Mode of prosecution

Class 3 offence triable on indictment.

Maximum penalty

Two years' imprisonment – s.37 and Sched 2 para 25 Sexual Offences Act 1956.

Power to search for and remove woman detained for immoral purposes

Sexual Offences Act 1956
Power to search for and remove woman detained for immoral purposes

43.—(1) Where it is made to appear by information on oath laid before a justice of the peace by a woman's parent, relative or guardian, or by any other person who in the opinion of the justice is acting in the woman's interests, that there is reasonable cause to suspect—

(a) that the woman is detained in any place within the justice's jurisdiction in order that she may have unlawful sexual intercourse with men or with a particular man; and

(b) that either she is so detained against her will, or she is under the age of sixteen or is a defective, or she is under the age of eighteen and is so detained against the will of her parent or guardian;

then the justice may issue a warrant authorising a named constable to search for her and to take her to and detain her in a place of safety until she can be brought before a justice of the peace.

(2) A justice before whom a woman is brought in pursuance of the foregoing subsection may cause her to be delivered up to her parent or guardian, or otherwise dealt with as circumstances may permit and require.
(3) A constable authorised by a warrant under this section to search for a woman may enter (if need be, by force) any premises specified in the warrant, and remove the woman from the premises.
(4) A constable executing a warrant issued under this section shall be accompanied by the person applying for the warrant, if that person so desires, unless the justice issuing it otherwise directs.
(5) In this section "guardian" means any person having the lawful care or charge of the woman.
(6) The powers conferred by this section shall be in addition to and not in derogation of those conferred by section forty of the Children and Young Persons Act, 1933.

S.40 Sexual Offences Act 1956 sets out the powers of arrest under s.22 and s.23.

Power of arrest in case of procuration or prostitution of women
40. A constable may arrest a person without a warrant, if the constable suspects him of having committed, or of attempting to commit, an offence under section twenty-two or twenty-three of this Act, and has reasonable cause so to suspect.

PERMITTING GIRL UNDER 13 TO USE PREMISES FOR INTERCOURSE

PERMITTING GIRL UNDER 16 TO USE PREMISES FOR INTERCOURSE

Legal source

SS.25 and 26 Sexual Offences Act 1956

Sexual Offences Act 1956
Permitting girl under thirteen to use premises for intercourse
25. It is felony for a person who is the owner or occupier of any premises, or who has, or acts or assists in, the management or control of any premises, to induce or knowingly suffer a girl under the age of thirteen to resort to or be on those premises for the purpose of having unlawful sexual intercourse with men or with a particular man.

Permitting girl between thirteen and sixteen to use premises for intercourse
26. It is an offence for a person who is the owner or occupier of any premises, or who has, or acts or assists, in the management or control of any premises, to induce or knowingly suffer a girl not under the age of thirteen, but under the age of sixteen, to resort to or be on those premises for the purpose of having unlawful sexual intercourse with men or with a particular man.

'Unlawful sexual intercourse' merely means illicit intercourse, ie outside the bond of marriage – *R v Chapman* [1959] 1 QB 100.

Who may be convicted

Any owner or occupier of any premises, or any person who has, or acts and assists in, the management or control of any premises.

Against whom may the offence be committed?

As stated in the sections, any girl under the age of 13 (s.25), or under the age of 16 (s.26).

Mode of prosecution

S.25 is a class 3 offence triable on indictment. S.26 is also a class 3 offence triable both on indictment and, by virtue of ss.16 and 28 and Sched 3 of the Criminal Law Act 1977, summarily.

Maximum penalty

S.25 – imprisonment for life, s.37 and Sched 2 para 6 of the Sexual Offences Act 1956. S. 26 – imprisonment for two years – s.37 and Sched 2 para 26, Sexual Offences Act 1956.

PERMITTING DEFECTIVE TO USE PREMISES FOR INTERCOURSE

Legal source

S.27 Sexual Offences Act 1956

Sexual Offences Act 1956
Permitting defective to use premises for intercourse
27.—(1) It is an offence, subject to the exception mentioned in this section, for a person who is the owner or occupier of any premises, or who has, or acts or assists in, the management or control of any premises, to induce or knowingly suffer a woman who is a defective to resort to or be on those premises for the purpose of having unlawful sexual intercourse with men or with a particular man.

Who may be convicted

Following s.27(1), any owner or occupier of premises, or any person who assists in the management or control of any premises.

Against whom may the offence be committed?

Following s.45 Sexual Offences Act 1956 as amended by s.127(1)(b) of the Mental Health Act 1959, any person suffering from severe subnormality within the meaning of the Mental Health Act 1959.

Defences

Sexual Offences Act 1956

27.—(2) A person is not guilty of an offence under this section because he induces or knowingly suffers a defective to resort to or be on any premises for the purpose mentioned, if he does not know and has no reason to suspect her to be a defective.

Mode of prosecution

Class 3 offence, triable on indictment.

Maximum penalty

Two years' imprisonment – s.37 and Sched 2 para 27 of the Sexual Offences Act 1956.

CAUSING OR ENCOURAGING PROSTITUTION ETC. OF GIRL UNDER 16

Legal source

S.28 Sexual Offences Act 1956

Sexual Offences Act 1956

Causing or encouraging prostitution of, intercourse with, or indecent assault on, girl under sixteen

28.—(1) It is an offence for a person to cause or encourage the prostitution of, or the commission of unlawful sexual intercourse with, or of an indecent assault on, a girl under the age of sixteen for whom he is responsible.

(2) Where a girl has become a prostitute, or has had unlawful sexual intercourse, or has been indecently assaulted, a person shall be deemed for the purposes of this section to have caused or encouraged it, if he knowingly allowed her to consort with, or to enter or continue in the employment of, any prostitute or person of known immoral character.

(3) The persons who are to be treated for the purposes of this section as responsible for a girl are (subject to the next following subsection)—

(*a*) any person who is her parent or legal guardian; and

(*b*) any person who has actual possession or control of her, or to whose charge she has been committed by her parent or legal guardian or by a person having the custody of her; and

(*c*) any other person who has the custody, charge or care of her.

(4) In the last foregoing subsection—

(*a*) "parent" does not include, in relation to any girl, a person deprived of the custody of her by order of a court of competent jurisdiction but (subject to that), in the case of a girl who has been adopted under the Adoption Act, 1950, or any Act thereby repealed, means her adopters and, in the case of a girl who is illegitimate (and has not been so adopted), means her mother and any person who has been adjudged to be her putative father:

(*b*) "legal guardian" means, in relation to any girl, any person who is for the time being her guardian, having been appointed according to law by deed or will or by order of a court of competent jurisdiction.

(5) If, on a charge of an offence against a girl under this section, the girl appears to the court to have been under the age of sixteen at the time of the offence charged, she shall be presumed for the purposes of this section to have been so, unless the contrary is proved.

'Unlawful sexual intercourse' is illicit intercourse ie outside the bond of marriage – *R v Chapman* [1959] 1 QB 100.

Who may be convicted

Anyone who is 'responsible' for such a girl within s.28(3), (4).

Mode of prosecution and maximum penalty

Class 3 offence triable on indictment. Maximum penalty is two years' imprisonment – s.37 and Sched 2 para 28 of the Sexual Offences Act 1956.

CAUSING OR ENCOURAGING PROSTITUTION OF DEFECTIVE

Legal source

S.29 Sexual Offences Act 1956

Sexual Offences Act 1956
Causing or encouraging prostitution of defective
29.—(1) It is an offence, subject to the exception mentioned in this section, for a person to cause or encourage the prostitution in any part of the world of a woman who is a defective.

Who may be convicted

Any person – male or female.

Against whom may the offence be committed?

Any person suffering from severe subnormality within the meaning of the Mental Health Act 1959 – see s.45 Sexual Offences Act 1956 as amended by s.127(1)(b) Mental Health Act 1959.

Defences

Sexual Offences Act 1956
29.—(2) A person is not guilty of an offence under this section because he causes or encourages the prostitution of such a woman, if he does not know and has no reason to suspect her to be a defective.

Mode of prosecution

Class 3 offence triable on indictment.

Maximum penalty

Two years' imprisonment – s.37 and Sched 2 para 29 of the Sexual Offences Act 1956.

MAN LIVING ON EARNINGS OF PROSTITUTION

Legal source

S.30 Sexual Offences Act 1956

Sexual Offences Act 1956
Man living on earnings of prostitution

30.—(1) It is offence for a man knowingly to live wholly or in part on the earnings of prostitution.

(2) For the purposes of this section a man who lives with or is habitually in the company of a prostitute, or who exercises control, direction or influence over a prostitute's movements in a way which shows he is aiding, abetting or compelling her prostitution with others, shall be presumed to be knowingly living on the earnings of prostitution, unless he proves the contrary.

For the purpose of s.30(2) there are three ways of raising a presumption that the offence has been committed – first, proof that the accused was at the material time living with the prostitute; secondly, proof that he was habitually in her company at the material time; thirdly, proof that he exercised control, direction or influence over her movements in a way which showed him to be aiding or abetting her prostituion. The presumption thereby raised is two-sided – first, that the defendant is living on immoral earnings; and secondly, that he is doing so knowingly – *R v Clarke* (1976) 63 Cr App R 16. In the same case it was decided that it is not necessary to prove that the defendant was living with or habitually in the company of such a prostitute in a way which showed that he was aiding, abetting or compelling her prostitution with others. A man is deemed to be living on the earnings of prostitution if he receives payment, not from the prostitute herself, but from a person with whom he has arranged for he prostitution – *Calvert v Mayes* [1954] 1 QB 342.

In *R v Thomas* [1957] 1 WLR 747 it was held that if a person lets a room or a flat to a prostitute at a very inflated rent for the express purpose of her carrying on her trade therein, then a conviction for living wholly or partly on the earnings of prostitution might follow.

Prostitution is not confined to acts of sexual intercourse, but will include any form of lewdness for which a woman habitually offers herself for hire: *R v De Munck* [1918] 1 KB 635, and will include active acts of indecency performed by the woman herself, e.g. masturbation of male clients – *R v Webb* [1964] 1 QB 357. Proof of money payment does not seem to be necessary – *Winter v Woolfe* [1931] 1 KB 549.

Though a person who is paid for goods or services out of the earnings of prostitution does not necessarily commit an offence under the Act, a person does not necessarily escape from its provisions by receiving payment for the goods or services which he supplies to a prostitute. A person should be held to be living in whole or in part on the earnings of prostitution if he is paid by a prostitute for the goods or services supplied by him to her for the purpose of her prostitution which he would not supply but for the fact that she was a prostitute – *Shaw v DPP* [1962] AC 220.

In an indictment for this offence a person may be charged with having committed the offence on one specified day only – *R v Hill* [1914] 2 KB 386.

Who may be convicted

Any male person.

Mode of prosecution

Class 4 offence triable either way.

Maximum penalty

Conviction on indictment – seven years' imprisonment – s.37 and Sched 2 para 30 Sexual Offences Act 1956, as amended by s.4 of the Street Offences Act 1959. On a summary conviction the maximum penalty is six months' imprisonment.

Power of search

Sexual Offences Act 1956
Power of search in case of man living on earnings of prostitution
42. Where it is made to appear by information on oath before a justice of the peace that there is reasonable cause to suspect that any house or part of a house is used by a woman for purposes of prostitution, and that a man residing in or frequenting the house is living wholly or in part on her earnings, the justice may issue a warrant authorising a constable to enter and search the house and to arrest the man.

Power of arrest

Sexual Offences Act 1956
Power of arrest in cases of trading in prostitution, or of soliciting by men
41. Anyone may arrest without a warrant a person found committing an offence under section thirty, thirty-one, or thirty-two of this Act.

WOMAN EXERCISING CONTROL OVER PROSTITUTE

Legal source

S.31 Sexual Offences Act 1956

Sexual Offences Act 1956
Woman exercising control over prostitute
31. It is an offence for a woman for purposes of gain to exercise control, direction or influence over a prostitute's movements in a way which shows she is aiding, abetting or compelling her prostitution.

See *Man Living on Earnings of Prostitution* for details about the definition of the offence.

Mode of prosecution

Class 4 offence triable either way.

Maximum penalty

On indictment – seven years' imprisonment. On a summary conviction – imprisonment for six months – s.37 and Sched 2 para 31 Sexual Offences Act 1956 as amended by s.4 Street Offences Act 1959.

Power of arrest

S.41 Sexual Offences Act 1956 (see under *Man Living on* etc.) also applies to the offence under this section.

SOLICITATION BY MEN

Legal source

S.32 Sexual Offences Act 1956; s.1(1) Street Offences Act 1959

Sexual Offences Act 1956
Solicitation by men
32. It is an offence for a man persistently to solicit or importune in a public place for immoral purposes.

Two separate acts of importuning within the period named in the information or indictment are sufficient to render the importuning persistent – *Dale v Smith* [1967] 1 WLR 700.

In *R v Dodd* (1977) 66 Cr App R 87 a conviction was upheld under s.32 where D drove past three 14 year old girls several times in a public street inviting them in colloquial terms to have sexual intercourse with him. Not only was his behaviour immoral, but what he sought to do was criminal.

Who may be convicted

Under s.32 Sexual Offences Act 1956 any male person. Both sexes may be convicted under s.1(1) Street Offences Act 1959.

Defences

Although s.1 of the Sexual Offences Act 1967 prevents homosexual practices between consenting adults in private from being a criminal offence, the 1967 Act did not change the law to the extent of preventing approaches for such purposes from being the offence of persistently importuning for 'immoral purposes' – *R v Ford* [1978] 1 All ER 1129.

Mode of prosecution

Class 4 offence triable either way.

Maximum penalty

For a conviction on indictment – imprisonment for two years. On a summary conviction – imprisonment for six months – s.37 and Sched 2 para 32 Sexual Offences Act 1956.

Power of arrest

S.41 Sexual Offences Act 1956 (see *Man Living on* etc.) also applies to offences under s.32.

SOLICITING IN THE STREET

Legal source

S.1, Street Offences Act 1959

Street Offences Act 1959
Loitering or soliciting for purposes of prostitution

1.—(1) It shall be an offence for a common prostitute to loiter or solicit in a street or public place for the purpose of prostitution.

(3) A constable may arrest without warrant anyone he finds in a street or public place and suspects, with reasonable cause, to be committing an offence under this section.

(4) For the purposes of this section "street" includes any bridge, road, lane, footway, subway, square, court, alley or passage, whether a thoroughfare or not, which is for the time being open to the public; and the doorways and entrances of premises abutting on a street (as hereinafter defined), and any ground adjoining and open to a street, shall be treated as forming part of the street.

In *Behrendt v Burridge* (1976) 63 Cr App R 202 it was held that the fact that the defendant's conduct could not be described as an explicit form of advertising her services for prostitution did not resolve the case in her favour, under s.1(1) of the Street Offences Act 1959. Although the defendant sat motionless in the window of a house, it was clear that she was soliciting in the sense of tempting or alluring passers-by to come in for the purposes of prostitution and projecting her solicitation to such passers-by. Soliciting and advertising were held not to be mutually exclusive.

Who may be convicted

There is no statutory definition of a 'common prostitute', but two or more formally recorded police cautions for loitering or soliciting constitute *prima facie* evidence. S.2 of the Act provides a procedure for challenging such cautions at a hearing *in camera* in a magistrates' court. Since that procedure is only available to 'a woman', the substantive offence can presumably only be committed by a woman.

Mode of prosecution

Summary only.

Maximum penalty

Fine not exceeding level 2 on the standard scale, or level 3 after previous conviction. (Criminal Justice Act 1982, s.71(1).)

KEEPING A BROTHEL

Legal source

S.33 Sexual Offences Act 1956

Sexual Offences Act 1956
Keeping a brothel
33. It is an offence for a person to keep a brothel, or to manage, or act or assist in the management of, a brothel.

A brothel is a place resorted to by persons of opposite sexes for the purposes of prostitution although it is not necessary that the women using the premises are common prostitutes or that payments are made to them – *Winter v Woolfe* [1931] 1 KB 549.

By virtue of s.6 of the Sexual Offences Act 1967, the meaning of 'brothel' is extended to include premises which people resort to for the purpose of lewd homosexual practices in circumstances in which resort thereto for lewd heterosexual practices would have led to its being treated as a brothel for the purpose of ss.33 – 35 of the 1956 Act.

Mode of prosecution

This offence is punishable only summarily under Sched 2 of the Sexual Offences Act 1956.

Maximum penalty

For an offence committed after a previous conviction, six months' imprisonment, or £250 fine, or both; otherwise, three months', or £100, or both.

LANDLORD LETTING PREMISES FOR USE AS A BROTHEL

Legal source

S.34 Sexual Offences Act 1956

Sexual Offences Act 1956
Landlord letting premises for use as brothel
34. It is an offence for the lessor or landlord of any premises or his agent to let the whole or part of the premises with the knowledge that it is to used, in whole or in part, as a brothel, or, where the whole or part of the premises is used as a brothel, to be wilfully a party to that use continuing.

Mode of prosecution

Summary procedure only.

Maximum penalty

For an offence committed after a previous conviction, six months' imprisonment, or £250 fine, or both; otherwise, three months', or £100, or both.

TENANT PERMITTING PREMISES TO BE USED AS BROTHEL

Legal source

S.35 Sexual Offences Act 1956

Sexual Offences Act 1956
Tenant permitting premises to be used as brothel

35.—(1) It is an offence for the tenant or occupier, or person in charge, of any premises knowingly to permit the whole or part of the premises to used as a brothel.

(2) Where the tenant or occupier of any premises is convicted (whether under this section or, for an offence committed before the commencement of this Act, under section thirteen of the Criminal Law Amendment Act, 1885) of knowingly permitting the whole or part of the premises to be used as a brothel, the First Schedule to this Act shall apply to enlarge the rights of the lessor or landlord with respect to the assignment or determination of the lease or other contract under which the premises are held by the person convicted.

(3) Where the tenant or occupier of any premises is so convicted, or was so convicted under the said section thirteen before the commencement of this Act, and either—

(*a*) the lessor or landlord, after having the conviction brought to his notice, fails or failed to exercise his statutory rights in relation to the lease or contract under which the premises are or were held by the person convicted; or

(*b*) the lessor or landlord, after exercising his statutory rights so as to determine that lease or contract, grants or granted a new lease or enters or entered into a new contract of tenancy of the premises to, with or for the benefit of the same person, without having all reasonable provisions to prevent the recurrence of the offence inserted in the new lease or contract;

then, if subsequently an offence under this section is committed in respect of the premises during the subsistence of the lease or contract referred to in paragraph (*a*) of this subsection or (where paragraph (*b*) applies) during the subsistence of the new lease or contract, the lessor or landlord shall be deemed to be a party to that offence unless he shows that he took all reasonable steps to prevent the recurrence of the offence.

References in this subsection to the statutory rights of a lessor or landlord refer to his rights under the First Schedule to this Act or under subsection (1) of section five of the Criminal Law Amendment Act, 1912 (the provision replaced for England and Wales by that Schedule).

(For definition of 'brothel' etc see *Keeping a Brothel*.)

Who may be convicted

The tenant or occupier of any premises.

Mode of prosecution

Summarily.

Maximum penalty

For an offence committed after a previous conviction six months' imprisonment, or £250 fine, or both; otherwise, three months' imprisonment, or £100 fine, or both. A conviction of an offence punishable under s.33, 34, or 35 of the Sexual Offences Act 1956 shall be taken into account as a previous conviction in the same way as a conviction of offence punishable under s.36.

TENANT PERMITTING PREMISES TO BE USED FOR PROSTITUTION

Legal source

S.36 Sexual Offences Act 1956

Sexual Offences Act 1956
Tenant permitting premises to be used for prostitution
36. It is an offence for the tenant or occupier of any premises knowingly to permit the whole or part of the premises to be used for the purposes of habitual prostitution.

Who may be convicted

The tenant or occupier of any premises.

Mode of prosecution

Summarily.

Maximum penalty

For an offence committed after a previous conviction, six months' imprisonment, or £250 fine, or both; otherwise, three months' imprisonment, or £100 fine, or both. A conviction of an offence punishable under s.33, 34 or 35 of the Sexual Offences Act 1956 shall be taken into account as a previous conviction in the same way as a conviction of offence punishable under s.36.

STEALING CHILDREN UNDER THE AGE OF FOURTEEN YEARS

Legal source

S.56 Offences Against the Person Act 1861

Offences Against the Person Act 1861
Child-stealing, or receiving stolen child
56. Whosoever shall unlawfully, either by force or fraud, lead or take away, or decoy or entice away or detain, any child under the age of fourteen years, with intent to deprive any parent, guardian, or other person having the lawful care of charge of such child of the possession of such child, or with intent to steal any article upon or about the person of such child, to whomsoever such article may belong, and whosoever shall, with any such intent, receive or harbour any such

child, knowing the same to have been, by force or fraud, led, taken, decoyed, enticed away, or detained, as in this section before mentioned, shall be guilty of felony, and being convicted thereof shall be liable, at the discretion of the court, to be kept in penal servitude for any term not exceeding seven years . . . . —or to be imprisoned . . . . [and, if a male under the age of sixteen years, with or without whipping:] Provided, that no person who shall have claimed any right to the possession of such child, or shall be the mother or shall have claimed to be the father of an illegitimate child, shall be liable to be prosecuted by virtue hereof on account of the getting possession of such child, or taking such child out of the possession of any person having the lawful charge thereof.

It must be shown that the defendant took and enticed the child away, and that the child was under 14 years. It is not necessary to show that the defendant intended to deprive the parent permanently of the possession of the child – *R v Powell* (1914) 24 Cox 229. Following *R v Jones* [1973] Crim LR 621, the words 'taking out of the possession of her parent . . . . against her will' were construed as meaning some conduct amounting to a substantial interference with the possessory relationship of parent and child.

Who may be convicted

Any male or female person.

Against whom may the offence be committed?

Any child under the age of 14 years.

Defences

The defendant may prove that he claimed to have a right to the possession of the child, for, under s.56 such persons are specifically exempted from the operation of the section.

Mode of prosecution and maximum penalty

Class 3 offence triable on indictment. Maximum seven years' imprisonment.

SEXUAL INTERCOURSE WITH PATIENTS

Legal source

S.128(1) Mental Health Act 1959; s.1(4) Sexual Offences Act 1967

Mental Health Act 1959

Sexual intercourse with patients

128.—(1) Without prejudice to section seven of the Sexual Offences Act, 1956, it shall be an offence, subject to the exception mentioned in this section,—

(*a*) for a man who is an officer on the staff of or is otherwise employed in, or is one of the managers of, a hospital or mental nursing home to have unlawful sexual intercourse with a woman who is for the time being receiving treatment for mental disorder in that hospital or home, or to have such intercourse on the premises of which the hospital or home forms part with a woman who is for the time being receiving such treatment there as an out-patient;

(*b*) for a man to have unlawful sexual intercourse with a woman who is a mentally disordered patient and who is subject to his guardianship under this Act or is otherwise in his custody or care under this Act or in pursuance of arrangements under the National Assistance Act, 1948, or as a resident in a residential home for mentally disordered persons within the meaning of Part III of this Act.

Sexual Offences Act 1967

1.—(4) Section 128 of the Mental Health Act 1959 (prohibition on men on the staff of a hospital, or otherwise having responsibility for mental patients, having sexual intercourse with women patients) shall have effect as if any reference therein to having unlawful sexual intercourse with a woman included a reference to committing buggery or an act of gross indecency with another man.

Who may be convicted

Any hospital employee.

Against whom may the offence be committed?

Any person receiving treatment for mental disorder, either as an in- or out-patient, at the hospital or nursing home, as in s.128(1)(a) and (b) supra.

Defences

Mental Health Act 1959

128.—(2) It shall not be an offence under this section for a man to have sexual intercourse with a woman if he does not know and has no reason to suspect her to be a mentally disordered patient.

Mode of prosecution

Triable on indictment. Proceedings require DPP's consent.

128.—(4) No proceedings shall be instituted for an offence under this section except by or with the consent of the Director of Public Prosecutions.

(5) This section shall be construed as one with the Sexual Offences Act, 1956; and section forty-seven of that Act (which relates to the proof of exceptions) shall apply to the exception mentioned in this section.

Maximum penalty

Mental Heath Act 1959

128.—(3) Any person guilty of an offence under this section shall be liable on conviction on indictment to imprisonment for a term not exceeding two years.

INDECENCY WITH CHILDREN UNDER 14

Legal source

S.1(1) Indecency with Children Act 1960

Indecency with Children Act 1960
Indecent conduct towards young child

1.—(1) Any person who commits an act of gross indecency with or towards a child under the age of fourteen, or who incites a child under that age to such an act with him or another, shall be liable on conviction on indictment to imprisonment for a term not exceeding two years, or on summary conviction to imprisonment for a term not exceeding six months, to a fine not exceeding one hundred pounds, or to both.

(2) On a charge of an offence under this section, the wife or husband of the accused shall be competent to give evidence at every stage of the proceedings, whether for the defence or for the prosecution, and whether the accused is charged solely or jointly with any other person: Provided that—

(*a*) the wife or husband shall not be compellable either to give evidence or, in giving evidence, to disclose any communication made to her or him during the marriage by the accused; and

(*b*) the failure of the wife or husband of the accused to give evidence shall not be made the subject of any comment by the prosecution.

This subsection shall not affect section one of the Criminal Evidence Act, 1898, or any case where the wife or husband of the accused may at common law be called as a witness without the consent of the accused.

(3) References in the Children and Young Persons Act, 1933, except in section fifteen (which relates to the competence as a witness of the wife or husband of the accused), to the offences mentioned in the First Schedule to that Act shall include offences under this section.

(4) Offences under this section shall be deemed to be offences against the person for the purpose of section three of the Visiting Forces Act, 1952 (which restricts the trial by United Kingdom courts of offenders connected with visiting forces).

Definition

In *R v Speck* [1977] 2 All ER 859 the court held that s.1 of the Indecency with Children Act 1960 was contravened where the defendant passively permitted a child to keep her hand on his penis for so long – about five minutes – that his inactivity amounted to an invitation to her to continue the activity. If such an invitation could properly be inferred, it would constitute an 'act' within s.1(1).

Who may be convicted

Any male or female person.

Mode of prosecution

Class 4 offence triable on indictment, and also summarily. S.8 of the Sexual Offences Act 1967 which requires the consent of the Director of Public Prosecutions to any proceedings for gross indecency where any person involved is under 21 does not apply to proceedings under the Indecency with Children Act – s.48 Criminal Justice Act 1972.

Maximum penalty

On conviction on indictment – imprisonment for a period not exceeding two years. On a summary conviction – imprisonment for six months, or a fine not exceeding one hunded pounds, or both.

ACTS OUTRAGING PUBLIC DECENCY

Legal source

Common law

In general all open lewdness, grossly scandalous, and whatever openly outrages decency or is offensive and disgusting, or is injurious to public morals by tending to corrupt the mind and destroy the love of decency, morality and good order, is an offence indictable at common law – *Russell on Crime Vol 2* 12th edn, 1423. It must be proved that the act complained of was committed in public which means that more than one person must at least have been able to see it: *R v Farrell* (1862) 9 Cox 446; *R v Mayling* [1963] 2 QB 717. It is sufficient if it is proved that one person saw the act, and there is evidence that others might have witnessed it at the time: *R v Mayling* (supra), *Knuller v DPP* [1972] 3 WLR 143. Secondly, it must be proved that the act was of such a lewd, obscene or disgusting character as constitutes an outrage on public decency.

Who may be convicted

Any person, male or female.

Mode of prosecution

Offence indictable at common law.

Maximum penalty

The punishment for this offence is a fine or imprisonment or both. It would seem that there is no limit to the amount of either the fine of the imprisonment that may be imposed, provided that the sentence is not inordinate: *R v Morris* [1951] 1 KB 394.

Conspiracy

In *Shaw v DPP* [1962] AC 200 the House of Lords held that there is an offence of conspiracy to corrupt public morals. 'Corrupt' it was stated is a strong word, and should not be used interchangeably with 'leads morally astray'.

Following *Knuller v DPP* [1972] 3 WLR 143, it would seem that there is also an offence of conspiring to outrage public decency. As with the substantive offence, the circumstances must be such that the alleged outrageously indecent matter could have been seen by more than one person, even though in fact no more than one did see it. If it is capable of being seen by one person only no offence is committed. Further, 'outrage' is a very strong word and goes considerably beyond offending the susceptibilities of, or even shocking, reasonable people.

HOMOSEXUAL ACTS ON MERCHANT SHIPS

Legal source

S.2 Sexual Offences Act 1967

Sexual Offences Act 1967
Homosexual acts on merchant ships
2.—(1) It shall continue to be—

(*a*) an offence under section 12 of the Act of 1956 and at common law for a man to commit buggery with another man in circumstances in which by reason of the provisions of section 1 of this Act it would not be an offence (apart from this section); and

(*b*) an offence under section 13 of that Act for a man to commit an act of gross indecency with another man, or to be party to the commission by a man of such an act, in such circumstances as aforesaid,

provided that the act charged is done on a United Kingdom merchant ship, wherever it may be, by a man who is a member of the crew of that ship with another man who is a member of the crew of that or any other United Kingdom merchant ship.

(2) Section 11 of the Criminal Justice Act 1925 (venue in indictable offences) shall apply to an act which is an offence by virtue of this section as if it were an offence when done on land.

(3) In this section—

"member of the crew" in relation to a ship, includes the master of the ship and any apprentice to the sea service serving in that ship;

"United Kingdom merchant ship" means a ship registered in the United Kingdom habitually used or used at the time of the act charged for the purposes of carrying passengers or goods for reward.

Who may be convicted

Any man who is a member of the crew of a U.K. merchant ship.

Against whom may the offence be committed?

Any man who is a member of the crew of a U.K. merchant ship.

Mode of prosecution

Class 3 offence triable on indictment.

Maximum penalty

Where there was no consent to the act – ten years' imprisonment: s.37 and Sched 2 para 3 of the 1956 Act as amended by s.3(1) of the Sexual Offences Act 1967. Where there was consent the penalty is five years' where one man is over 21 and the other below that age; otherwise two years' imprisonment.

PROCURING OTHERS TO COMMIT HOMOSEXUAL ACTS

Legal sources

S.4 Sexual Offences Act 1967

Sexual Offences Act 1967
Procuring others to commit homosexual acts

4.—(1) A man who procures another man to commit with a third man an act of buggery which by reason of section1 of this Act is not an offence shall be liable on conviction on indictment to imprisonment for a term not exceeding two years.

(2) The Act of 1952 shall have effect as if offences under the foregoing subsection were included among those specified in paragraphs 1 to 18 of Schedule 1 to that Act (indictable offences triable summarily with the consent of the accused).

(3) It shall not be an offence under section 13 of the Act of 1956 for a man to procure the commission by another man of an act of gross indecency with the first-mentioned man which by reason of section 1 of this Act is not an offence under the said section 13.

By virtue of s.16 and Sched 13 to the Criminal Law Act 1977 this offence is now triable either on indictment or summarily.

LIVING ON EARNINGS OF MALE PROSTITUTION

Legal source

S.5 Sexual Offences Act 1967

Sexual Offences Act 1967
Living on earnings of male prostitution

5.—(1) A man or woman who knowingly lives wholly or in part on the earnings of prostitution of another man shall be liable—

(*a*) on summary conviction to imprisonment for a term not exceeding six months; or

(*b*) on conviction on indictment to imprisonment for a term not exceeding seven years.

(2) A person accused of an offence under this section cannot claim to be tried on indictment under section 25 of the Act of 1952 (right of accused to trial by jury for summary offences punishable with more than three months imprisonment).

(3) Anyone may arrest without a warrant a person found committing an offence under this section.

INCITEMENT TO COMMIT INCEST

Legal source

S.54 Criminal Law Act 1977

Criminal Law Act 1977
Inciting girl under sixteen to have incestuous sexual intercourse

54.—(1) It is an offence for a man to incite to have sexual intercourse with him a girl under the age of sixteen whom he knows to be his grand-daughter, daughter or sister.

(2) In the preceding subsection "man" includes boy, "sister" includes half-sister, and for the purposes of that subsection any expression importing a relationship between two people shall be taken to apply notwithstanding that the relationship is not traced through lawful wedlock.

(3) The following provisions of section 1 of the Indecency with Children Act 1960, namely—

subsection (2) (competence of spouse of accused to give evidence);
subsection (3) (references in the Children and Young Persons Act 1933 to the offences mentioned in Schedule 1 to that Act to include offences under that section);
subsection (4) (offences under that section to be deemed offences against the person for the purpose of section 3 of the Visiting Forces Act 1952),

shall apply in relation to offences under this section.

Formerly, a father could not be guilty of inciting his daughter to commit incest with him if she was under the age of 16 (see s.11(1) of the Sexual Offences Act 1956), or over the age of 14 (s.1 of the Indecency with Children Act 1960 applies to children under 14). Nor could a father be guilty of inciting his daughter to aid and abet him in the commission of incest: the purpose of s.11 is to protect girls under 16 from criminal liability. This lacuna in the law was revealed in *R v Whitehouse* (1977) 65 Cr App R 33, and was filled by s.54 Criminal Law Act 1977.

Mode of prosecution

Class 4 offence triable either way.

Maximum penalty

Criminal Law Act 1977

54.—(4) A person guilty of an offence under this section shall be liable—

(*a*) on summary conviction, to imprisonment for a term not exceeding six months or to a fine not exceeding £1,000, or both;

(*b*) on conviction on indictment, to imprisonment for a term not exceeding two years.

PUBLIC NUISANCE – PUBLICLY EXPOSING PERSON

Legal Source

Common law: *R v Sidley* 1 East PC 3; *R v Newcastle-upon-Tyne Justices* 1 B&Ad 933; *R v Rowed* (1842) 3 QB 180. Also see s.4 Vagrancy Act 1842.

Definition

Publicly exposing the naked person. An indecent exposure which is seen, and is capable of being seen, by only one person, is not indictable as a common nuisance. *R v Rentegard* (1830) T&M 25; *R v Watson* (1847) 2 Cox CC 376; *R v Webb* (1848) 3 Cox CC 183; *R v Farrell* (1862) 9 Cox CC 446; *R v Mayling* [1963] 2 QB 717. (But, see s.4 infra). 'Public place' has been held, on a charge of indecent exposure, to include the roof of a private house, in view of the back windows of other houses, but not visible from the street: *R v Thallman* (1863) 9 Cox CC 388; and a field, out of sight of a public footpath, but into which the public were in the habit of going, although with no legal right to do so: *R v Wellard* (1884) 14 QBD 63.

S.4 Vagrancy Act 1824 provides that a man who 'wilfully, openly, lewdly and obscenely' exposes his person with the intent to insult a female, is guilty of a summary offence. The word 'person' in the section, following *Evans v Ewels* [1972] 1 WLR 671, means 'penis'. If such an act takes place in a private room and is only witnessed by a female in the same room, then that is sufficient for the purposes of the section 4 offence – *Ford v Falcone* [1971] 2 A11 ER 1138.

Method of Prosecution

Offence triable on indictment at common law; however, it is now usually tried summarily under s.4 Vagrancy Act 1824.

Maximum Punishment

Fine, and/or imprisonment.

'PEEPING TOMS' – EAVESDROPPING

Being a 'peeping Tom' used to constitute the offence of eavesdropping contrary to s.4 Vagrancy Act 1824, until the passage of the Criminal Law Act 1967, which abolished the offence in s.13(1).

Abolition of certain offences, and consequential repeals

13.—(1) The following offences are hereby abolished, that is to say—

(*a*) any distinct offence under the common law in England and Wales of maintenance (including champerty, but not embracery), challenging to fight, eavesdropping or being a common barrator, a common scold or a common night walker; . . .

APPENDIX II

Tables

Table 1:
Persons sentenced in 1982 for indictable sexual offences – by offence

Offence	*No. sentenced*		%	
Indecent assault on female	2261		34.2	
Indecency between males	1144	1930	17.3	29.2
Solicitation by males	786		11.9	
Indecent assault on male	622		9.4	
Unlawful sexual intercourse (USI) with a girl under 16	417		6.3	
Rape	403		6.1	
Procuration	330		5.0	
Gross indecency with children	233		3.5	
Buggery	209		3.2	
Incest	100		1.5	
USI with a girl under 13	71		1.1	
Bigamy	22		0.3	
Abduction	17		0.3	
	6615		100	

Table 2: Persons sentenced in 1982 for indictable sexual offences – sentences passed by offence (percentages)

Offence	*Fine or Discharge*	*Probation or Supervision*	*Custodial Sentence*	*Suspended Sentence*	*Other*	*TOTAL (No)*
Indecent assault on female	36	25	21	12	6	100 (2261)
Indecency between males } Solicitation by males	92	4	2	2	1	100 (1930)
Indecent assault on male	32	29	20	14	4	100 (622)
Unlawful sexual intercourse (USI) with a girl under 16	50	12	20	12	6	100 (417)
Rape	1	1	94	3	1	100 (403)
Procuration	55	4	24	16	2	100 (330)
Gross Indecency with children	26	36	18	16	4	100 (233)
Buggery	10	11	59	17	3	100 (209)
Incest	4	13	73	9	1	100 (100)
USI with a girl under 13	10	23	42	18	7	100 (71)
Bigamy	68	5	14	14	–	100 (22)
Abduction	6	6	41	41	6	100 (17)
All indictable sexual offences	50	15	22	9	4	100 (6615)

Table 3: Persons sentenced in 1982 for indictable sexual offences – length of prison sentences

Offence	*Up to 6 months*	*over 6 months to 2 years*	*over 2 years to 5 years*	*over 5 years*	*TOTAL*
Indecent assault on female	198	175	38	–	411
Rape	1	46	182	80	309
Buggery	4	48	54	15	121
Indecent assault on male	47	45	17	7	116
Procuration	32	34	10	1	77
Unlawful sexual intercourse (USI) with a girl under 16	48	26	(1)*	–	75
Incest	2	41	27	1	71
Gross indecency with children	26	12	(1)*	–	39
Indecency between males } Solicitation by males }	17	8	3	–	28
USI with a girl under 13	1	10	14	2	27
Abduction	1	2	1	1	5
Bigamy	3	–	–	–	3
All indictable sexual offences	380 (29.6%)	447 (34.9%)	348 (27.1%)	107 (8.3%)	1282 (100%)

*Misrecorded

References

Abel, G. G., Becker, J. V., Blanchard, E. B. and Djenderedjian, A. (1978) 'Differentiating sexual aggressiveness with penile measures', *Criminal Justice and Behavior 5*, 315–332

Abel, G. G., Becker, J. V., Murphy, W. D. and Flanagan, B. (1981) 'Identifying dangerous child molesters'. In R. Stuart (ed.) *Violent Behavior.* New York: Brunner/Mazel

Adams, M. S. and Neel, J. V. (1967) 'Children of incest', *Pediatrics 40*, 56–62

Advisory Council on the Penal System (1978) *Sentences of Imprisonment: A review of maximum penalties.* London H.M.S.O.

Amir, D. and Amir, M. (1979) 'Rape crisis centres: An arena for ideological conflicts', *Victimology 4*, 247–257

Archbold (1982) (41st Edn.) *Pleading, Evidence and Practice in Criminal Cases.* London: Sweet and Maxwell

Ariès, P. (1962) *Centuries of Childhood*, (translated). London: Jonathan Cape

Bailey, V. and Blackburn, S. (1979) 'The Punishment of Incest Act 1908: A case study of law creation', *Criminal Law Review* (Nov), 708–718

Bailey, V. and McCabe, S. (1979) 'Reforming the law of incest', *Criminal Law Review* (Dec), 749–764

Bancroft, J. (1974) *Deviant Sexual Behaviour: Modification and Assessment.* Oxford: Clarendon Press

Bander, K., Fein, E., and Bishop, G. (1982) 'Child sex abuse: some barriers to program operation', *Child Abuse and Neglect 6*, 185–191

Barlow, D. H. and Wincze, J. P. (1980) 'Treatment of sexual deviations'. In S. R. Leiblum and L. A. Pervin (eds.) *Principles and Practice of Sex Therapy.* London: Tavistock

Bart, P. B. (1981) 'A study of women who both were raped and avoided rape', *Journal of Social Issues 37*, 123–137

Becker, J. V., Abel, G. G. and Skinner, L. J. (1979) 'The impact of sexual assault on the victim's sexual life', *Victimology 4*, 229–235

Becker, J. V. *et al* (1982) 'The effects of sexual assault on rape and attempted rape victims', *Victimology 7*, 106–113

Bell, A. P., Weinberg, M. S. and Hammersmith, S. K. (1981) *Sexual Preference.* Bloomington: Indiana University Press

Bender, L. and Grugett, A. E. (1952) 'A follow-up report on children who had atypical sexual experience', *American Journal of Orthopsychiatry 22*, 825–837

Berlin, F. S. and Meinecke, C. F. (1981) 'Treatment of sex offenders with antiandrogenic medication', *American Journal of Psychiatry 138*, 601–607

Besharov, D. J. (1981) 'Report from Amsterdam: The 3rd International Congress on Child Abuse and Neglect', *The Family Law Reporter Monograph 3, 9 June*

Bissett, J. (1982) 'Child sexual abuse within the family – Confidentially, a police view', In Dundee Coordinating Committee for the Care of the Abused Child. *Proceedings of the Conference on Sexual Abuse: The Child Victim* (Sept)

Bluglass, R. (1980) 'Indecent exposure in the West Midlands'. In D. J. West (ed.) *Sex Offenders in the Criminal Justice System.* (Proceedings of the 12th Cropwood Conference.) Cambridge: University Institute of Criminology

Bluglass, R. (1982) 'Assessing dangerousness in sex offenders'. In J. R. Hamilton and H. Freeman (eds.) *Dangerousness: Psychiatric Assessment and Management.* London: Gaskell (for The Royal College of Psychiatrists)

Bowden, P. (1978) 'Men remanded in custody for medical reports', *British Journal of Psychiatry 133*, 320–338

Bowker, L. H. (1979) 'The criminal victimization of women', *Victimology 4*, 371–384

Box-Grainger, J. (1983) 'Employers' attitudes to ex-offenders', *Personnel Management* (Nov), 32–35

Brecher, E. M. (1978) *Treatment Programs for Sex Offenders.* U.S. Dept. of Justice, Washington D.C.: Govt. Printing Office

Brodsky, S. L. (1980) 'Understanding and treating sexual offenders', *Howard Journal 19*, 102–115

Brodsky, S. L. and West, D. J. (1981) 'Life-skills treatment of sex offenders', *Law and Psychology Review 6*, 97–168

Brody, S. J. (1976) *The Effectiveness of Sentencing.* Home Office Research Study No. 35. London: H.M.S.O.

Brody, S. and Tarling R. (1980) *Taking Offenders Out of Circulation.* Home Office Research Study No. 64. London: H.M.S.O.

Burgess, A. W. and Holstrom, L. L. (1974) *Rape: Victims of Crisis.* Bowrie, Md: Brady

Burgess, A. W., Groth, A. N., Holstrom, L. L. and Sgrol, S. M. (1978) *Sexual Assault on Children and Adolescents.* Toronto: Lexington Books

Burgess, A. W., Groth, A. N. and McCausland, M. P. (1981) 'Child sex initiation rings', *American Journal of Orthopsychiatry 51*, 110–119

Burton, L. (1968) *Vulnerable Children.* London: Routledge and Kegan Paul

Byles, J. A. (1980) 'Adolescent girls in need of protection', *American Journal of Orthopsychiatry 50*, 264–278

Cahill, K. M. (ed.) (1984) *The AIDS Epidemic.* London: Hutchinson

Callahan, E. J. and Leitenberg, H. (1973) 'Aversion therapy for sexual deviation: contingent shock and covert sensitisation', *Journal of Abnormal Psychology 81*, 60–73

Canada, Law Reform Commission of (1978) *Report on Sexual Offences.* Ottawa: Law Reform Commission

Chambers, G. and Millar, A. (1983) *Investigating Sexual Assault.* (A Scottish Office Social Research Study.) Edinburgh: H.M.S.O.

Chappell, D. and Singer, S. (1977) 'Rape in New York City: a study of material in the police files and its meaning'. In D. Chappell, R. Geis and G. Geis (eds.) *Forcible Rape.* New York: Columbia University Press

Christiansen, K. O. *et al* (1965) 'Recidivism among sexual offenders', *Scandinavian Studies in Criminology Vol 1*, London: Tavistock

Christiansen, K. O. (1983) 'Factors influencing recidivism'. In F. Ferracuti and M. E. Wolfgang (eds.) *Criminal Diagnosis: An International Perspective.* Lexington, Mass: D. C. Heath

Coggan, G. and Walker, M. (1982) *Frightened for My Life: An Account of Deaths in British Prisons.* London: Fontana

Cohen, M. L., Garotalo, R., Bouscher, R. and Seghorn, T. (1971) 'The psychology of rapists', *Seminars in Psychiatry 3*, 307–327 (Reprinted in Chappell and Geis, 1977, *op cit*)

Constantine, L. L. and Martinson, F. M. (eds.) (1981) *Children and Sex: New Findings, New Perspectives*. Boston: Little, Brown

Constantine, L. L. (1981) 'The effects of early sexual experience'. In L. L. Constantine and F. M. Martinson (eds.) *Children and Sex*. Boston: Little, Brown

Cook, M. and Howells, K. (eds.) (1981) *Adult Sexual Interest in Children*. London: Academic Press

Cooper, I. (1984) – personal communication.

Cormier, B. M. and Cooper, I. (1982) *Incest in Contemporary Society: Legal and Clinical Management*. Montreal: McGill Forensic Clinic

Council for Science and Society (1981) *Treating the Troublesome*. London: CSS

Courtois, C. A. (1980) 'Studying and counselling women with past incest experience', *Victimology 5*, 332–334

Courtois, C. A. (1979) 'The incest experience and its aftermath', *Victimology 4*, 337–347

Crane, P. (1982) *Gays and the Law*. London: Pluto Press

Crawford, D. A. (1981) 'Treatment approaches with paedophyles'. In M. Cook and K. Howells (eds.) *Adult Sexual Interest in Children*. London: Academic Press

Crawford, D. A. and Allen, J. V. (1979) 'A social skills training programme with sex offenders'. In M. Cook and G. Wilson (eds.) *Love and Attraction: Proceedings of an International Conference*. Oxford: Pergamon

Criminal Law Revision Committee (1980) *Working Paper on Sexual Offences* London: H.M.S.O.

Criminal Law Revision Committee (1982) *Working Paper on Offences Relating to Prostitution*. London: H.M.S.O.

Criminal Law Revision Committee (1984) *Fifteenth Report: Sexual Offences* Cmnd 9213. London: H.M.S.O.

Currier, R. L. (1981) 'Juvenile sexuality in global perspective'. In L. L. Constantine and F. M. Martinson (eds.) *Children and Sex*. Boston: Little, Brown

Davies, W. (1982) 'Violence in prisons', In P. Feldman (ed.) *Developments in the Study of Criminal Behaviour Vol 2, Violence*. Chichester: Wiley

De Francis, V. (1971) 'Protecting the child victim of sex crimes committed by adults'. *Federal Probation 3* 15–20

Delin, B. (1978) *The Sex Offender*. Boston: Beacon Press

De Mause, L. (1974) (ed.) *The History of Childhood*. New York: Psychohistory Press

Densen-Gerber, J. and Hutchinson, S. F. (1978) 'Medical-legal and societal problems involving children – child prostitution, child pornography and drug-related abuse; recommended legislation'. In S. M. Smith (ed.) *The Maltreatment of Children*. Lancaster: M.T.P. Press

Desroches, F. (1974) 'The April 1971 Kingston Penitentiary riot', *Canadian Journal of Criminology and Corrections 16*, 317–331

Dietz, P. E. (1978) 'Social factors in rapist behaviour'. In R. T. Rada (ed.) *Clinical Aspects of the Rapist*. New York: Grune & Stratton Inc

Ditton, J. & Duffy, J. (1983) 'Bias in the newspaper reporting of crime news', *British Journal of Criminology 23*, 159–165.

Doek, J. E. (1978) 'Child abuse in the Netherlands: the medical referee', *Chicago-Kent Law Review 54*, 785–826

Dörner, G. (1976) *Hormones and Brain Differentiation*. Amsterdam: Elsevier

Doshay, L. J. (1943) *The Boy Sex Offender and his Later Criminal Career*. New York: Grune and Stratton

Downes, D. (1982) 'The origins and consequences of Dutch penal policy', *British Journal of Criminology 22*, 325–362

Ellis, E. M. (1983) 'A review of empirical rape research: Victim reactions and response to treatment', *Clinical Psychology Review 5*, 475–490

Farrell, C. and Kellaher, L. (1978) *My Mother Said: The Way Young People Learned about Sex and Birth Control*. London: Routledge and Kegan Paul

Feldman, P. and MacCulloch, M. (1980) *Human Sexual Behaviour*. Chichester: J. Wiley, Ch. 6.

Finch, S. M. (1973) 'Adult seduction of the child: Effects on the child', *Medical Aspects of Human Sexuality* 7, 170–187

Finkelhor, D. (1979) *Sexually Victimised Children*. New York: Free Press

Finkelhor, D. (1983) 'Removing the child – prosecuting the offender in cases of sexual abuse: evidence from the national reporting system for child abuse and neglect', *Child Abuse and Neglect* 7, 195–205

Fisher, S. (1973) *The Female Orgasm: Psychology, Physiology, Fantasy*. New York: Pergamon

Floud, J. and Young, W. (1981) *Dangerousness and Criminal Justice*. London: Heinemann

Fluker, J. L. (1981) 'Homosexuality and sexually transmitted diseases', *British Journal of Hospital Medicine 26*, 265–269

Ford, C. S. and Beach, F. A. (1952) *Patterns of Sexual Behaviour*. London: Eyre and Spottiswoode

Forman, B. D. (1982) 'Reported male rape', *Victimology* 7, 235–236

Foucault, M. (1979) *History of Sexuality Vol 1* (translated). London: Allen Lane

Fox, C. A. (1980) 'The non-violent sex offender. Alternatives to present provisions and practices'. In D. J. West (ed.) *Sex Offenders in the Criminal Justice System*. (Proceedings of the 12th Cropwood Conference.) Cambridge: University Institute of Criminology

Freeman, M. D. A. (1979) 'The law and sexual deviation'. In I. Rosen (ed.) *Sexual Deviation*. London: Oxford University Press

Freund, K. (1974) 'Male homosexuality: An analysis of the pattern'. In J. A. Loraine (ed.) *Understanding Homosexuality*. Lancaster: Medical and Technical

Freund, K. (1981) 'Assessment of paedophilia'. In M. Cook and K. Howells (eds.) *Adult Sexual Interest in Children*. London: Academic Press

Freund, K., McKnight, C. K., Langevin, R. and Cibiri, S. (1972) 'The female child as surrogate object', *Archives of Sexual Behavior 2*, 119–133

Gagnon, J. H. (1965) 'Female child victims of sex offenses', *Social Problems 13*, 176–192

Galloway, B. (ed.) (1983) *Prejudice and Pride: Discrimination against Gay People in Modern Britain*. London: Routledge and Kegan Paul

Gebhard, P. H. Gagnon, J. H., Pomeroy, W. B. and Christenson, C. V. (1965) *Sex Offenders: An Analysis of Types*. New York: Harper and Row

Geis, R., Wright, R. and Geis, G. (1978) 'Police surgeons and rape: A questionnaire survey', *The Police Surgeon (*No 14 Oct*)* 7–14

Gelder, M. (1979) 'Behaviour therapy for sexual deviations'. In I. Rosen (ed.) *Sexual Deviations*. London: Oxford University Press

Giarretto, H. (1981) 'A comprehensive child sexual abuse treatment program'. In P. B. Mrazek and C. H. Kempe (eds.) *Sexually Abused Children and their Families*. Oxford: Pergamon

Gibbens, T. C. N. and Prince, J. (1963) *Child Victims of Sex Offences*. London: Inst for the Study of Treatment of Delinquency

Gibbens, T. C. N., Soothill, K. L. and Pope, P. J. (1977) *Medical Remands in the Criminal Court*. London: Oxford University Press

Gibbens, T. C. N., Soothill, K. L. and Way, C. K. (1981) 'Sex offences against young girls: a long-term record study', *Psychological Medicine 11*, 351–357

Giese, H. (1964) (2nd Edn.) *Der homosexuelle Mann in der Welt*. Stuttgart: F. Enke

Gittleson, N. L., Eacott, S. E. and Mehta, B. M. (1978) 'Victims of indecent exposure', *British Journal of Psychiatry 132*, 61–66

Goodwin, J. (1981) 'Suicide attempt in sexual abuse victims and their mothers', *Child Abuse and Neglect 5*, 217–221

Goodwin, J. (1982) *Sexual Abuse: Incest Victims and their Families*. Boston: J. Wright

Gosselin, C. and Wilson, G. (1980) *Sexual Variations*. London: Faber

Green, J. and Miller, D, (1983) 'AIDS in Europe', *British Medical Journal 287*, 1715–1716

Greenland, C. (1977) 'Psychiatry and the dangerous sexual offender', *Canadian Psychiatric Association Journal 22*, 155–159

Greenland, C. (1983) 'Sex law reform in an international perspective: England and Wales and Canada', *Bulletin of the American Academy of Psychiatry and Law 11*, 309–330

Greenland, C. (1984) 'Dangerous sexual offender legislation in Canada, 1948–1977: An experiment that failed', *Canadian Journal of Criminology 26*, 1–12

Groth, A. N. (1979) *Men Who Rape: The Psychology of the Offender*. New York: Plenum

Groth, A. N. and Birnbaum, H. J. (1978) 'Adult sexual orientation and attraction to underage persons', *Archives of Sexual Behavior 7*, 175–181

Groth, A. N., Longo, R. E. and McFadin, J. B. (1982) 'Undetected recidivism among rapists and child molesters', *Crime and Delinquency 28*, 450–458

Gruber, K. J. (1981) 'Does sexual abuse lead to delinquent behaviour? A critical look at the evidence', *Victimology 6*, 85–91

Hackett, T. P., Saber, F. A., and Curran, W. J. (1980) 'Exhibitionism'. In W. J. Curran *et al* (eds.) *Modern Legal Medicine, Psychiatry and Forensic Medicine*. Philadelphia: F. A. Davis

Halleck, S. L. (1971) *Psychiatry and the Dilemmas of Crime*. Los Angeles: University of California Press

Hall-Williams, J. E. (1974) 'The neglect of incest', *Medicine, Science and the Law 14*, 64–67

Hamilton, G. V. (1929) *A Research in Marriage*. New York: A. and C. Boni

Hawton, K. (1983) 'Behavioural approaches to the management of sexual deviations', *British Journal of Psychiatry 143*, 248–255

Herman, J. L. (1981) *Father-Daughter Incest*. Cambridge, Mass.: Harvard University Press

Home Office (1975) *Report of the [Butler] Committee on Mentally Abnormal Offenders*. Cmnd 6244. London: H.M.S.O.

Home Office Policy Advisory Committee on Sexual Offences (1979) *Working Paper on the Age of Consent in relation to Sexual Offences*. London: H.M.S.O.

Home Office Policy Advisory Committee on Sexual Offences (1981) *Report on the Age of Consent in Relation to Sexual Offences*. Cmnd 8216. London: H.M.S.O.

Home Office (1981) *Report of H.M. Chief Inspector of Prisons.* Cmnd 8532. London: H.M.S.O.

Home Office (1982) *Report of an Inquiry by the Regional Director of the South East Region of the Prison Department.* (H.C. 199) London: H.M.S.O.

Home Office (Annually) *Criminal Statistics, England and Wales.* London: H.M.S.O.

Home Office Law Officers' Dept. (1983) *An Independent Prosecution Service for England and Wales.* Cmnd 9074. London: H.M.S.O.

Home Office (1984) *Statistical Bulletin no. 5/84*, 15th March, 1984. 'Notifiable offences recorded by the police in England and Wales 1983.' London: Home Office

Home Office (1984) *Cautioning by the Police: A Consultative Document.* London: Home Office

Honoré, T. (1978) *Sex Law*. London: Duckworth

Hough, M. and Mayhew, P. (1983) *The British Crime Survey*. Home Office Research Study No. 76. London: H.M.S.O.

Humphreys, L. (1970) *Tearoom Trade*. London: Duckworth; Chicago: Aldine

Hursh, C. J. and Selkin, J. (1974) *Rape Prevention Research Project*. (Annual Report of the Violence Research Unit) Denver: Division of Psychiatric Service, Dept of Health

Ingram, M. (1979) 'The participating victim: A study of sexual offences against pre-pubertal boys'. In M. Cook and K. Howells (eds.) *Adult Sexual Interest in Children*. London: Academic Press

Jackson, S. (1982) *Childhood and Sexuality*. Oxford: Blackwell

James, J. and Meyerding, J. (1978) 'Early sexual experience as a factor in prostitution', *Archives of Sexual Behavior 7*, 31–42

Jones, J. H. and Frei, D. (1977) 'Provoked anxiety as a treatment of exhibitionism', *British Journal of Psychology 131*, 295–300

Jones, M. (1974) *Justice and Journalism*. Chichester: Barry Rose

Jones, M. (1980) *Crime, Punishment and the Press*. London: National Association for the Care and Rehabilitation of Offenders

Justice (1970) *The Prosecution Process in England and Wales*. (Chairmen L. Hawser and B. Wigoder.) London: Justice Educational and Research Trust

Justice (1980) *Breaking the Rules* (Chairman P. Sieghart) London: Justice Educational and Research Trust

Katz, S. and Mazur, M. A. (1979) *Understanding the Rape Victim: A Synthesis of Research*. New York: Wiley

Kaufman, A., Divasto, P., Jackson, R., Voorhees, D. and Christy, J. (1980) 'Male rape victims: non-institutionalised sexual assault', *American Journal of Psychiatry 137*, 221–223

Keefe, M. L. and O'Reilly, H. T. (1976) 'Police and rape victims in New York', *Victimology 1*, 272–283

Kiersch, T. A. (1983) – personal communication. Atascadero State Hospital, California

Kilpatrick, D. G., Resick, P. A. and Veronen, L. J. (1981) 'Effects of a rape experience: a longitudinal study', *Journal of Social Issues 37*(4), 105–122

King, H. E. and Webb, C. (1981) 'Rape crisis centres: progress and problems', *Journal of Social Issues 37*(4), 93–104

Kirchoff, G. F. and Thelen, C. (1976) 'Hidden victims of sex offenders in Germany'. In E. C. Viano (ed.) *Victims and Society*. Washington: Visage Press

Knopp, F. H. (1983) *Remedial Intervention in Adolescent Sex Offences: Nine Program Descriptions*. New York: Safer Society Press

Koss, M. P. and Oros, C. J. (1982) 'Sexual experiences survey: A research instrument investigating sexual aggression and victimisation', *Journal of Consulting and Clinical Psychology 50*, 455–457

Kraemer, W. (ed.) (1976) *The Forbidden Love: The Normal and Abnormal Love of Children*. London: Sheldon Press

Landis, J. T. (1956) 'Experiences of 500 children with adult sexual deviants', *Psychiatric Quarterly Supplement 30*, 91–109

Langevin, R. (1983) *Sexual Strands: Understanding and Treating Sexual Abnormalities in Men*. Hillsdale, N.J.: Erlbaum

Langfeldt, T. (1981) 'Sexual development in children'. In M. Cook and K. Howells (eds.) *Adult Sexual Interest in Children*. London: Academic Press

Law Society (1983) *Prostitution and Allied Offences*. Memorandum by the Society's Standing Committee on Criminal Law. London: Law Society

Laws, D. R. and Holmen, M. L. (1978) 'Sexual response faking by paedophiles', *Criminal Justice and Behavior 5*, 343–356

Lawson, C. (1978) *The Probation Officer as Prosecutor: A Study of Proceedings for Breach of Requirement in Probation*. Cambridge: Institute of Criminology

Levine, S. and Koenig, J. (eds.) (1982) *Why Men Rape: Interviews with convicted rapists*. London: W. H. Allen

Lewis, P. (1980) *Psychiatric Probation Orders: Roles and Expectations of Probation Officers and Psychiatrists*. Cambridge: Institute of Criminology

Libai, D. (1980) 'The protection of the child victim of a sexual offence in the criminal justice system'. In L. G. Schultz (ed.) *The Sexual Victimology of Youth*. Springfield, Ill: C. C. Thomas

Lisners, J. (1983) *House of Horrors*. London: Corgi Books

Lockwood, D. (1980) *Prison Sexual Violence*. New York: Elsevier

London Rape Crisis Centre Reports (1977, 1978, 1982) P.O. Box 69, London WC1X 9NJ

MacLean, N. M. (1979) 'Rape and false accusations of rape'. *The Police Surgeon 15*, 29–40

Maisch, H. (1973) *Incest*. London: Deutsch

Malamuth, N. M. (1981) 'Rape proclivity', *Journal of Social Issues 37*(4), 138–157

Malamuth, N. M. and Check, J. V. P. (1983) 'Sexual arousal to rape depictions. Individual differences', *Journal of Abnormal Psychology 92*, 56–57

Manchester, A. H. (1978) 'Incest and the law'. In J. M. Eckelaar and S. N. Katz (eds.) *Family Violence*. Toronto: Butterworths

Marsh, J. C., Geist, A. and Caplan, N. (1982) *Rape and the Limits of Law Reform*. Boston, Mass: Auburn House

Marshall, W. L. and Barbaree, H. E. (1978) 'Reduction of deviant sex arousal: satiation treatment for sexual aggressors'. *Criminal Justice and Behavior 5*, 294–303

Marshall, W. L., Williams, S. M. and Christie, M. M. (1977) 'The treatment of rapists'. In C. B. Qualls (ed.) *Perspectives on Rape*. New York: Pergamon

Masters, W. H. and Johnson, V. E. (1979) *Homosexuality in Perspective*. Boston: Little, Brown

Mawby, R. I. (1979) 'Policing the age of consent', *Journal of Adolescence 2*, 41–9

Mazelan, P. M. (1980) 'Stereotypes and perceptions of the victims of rape', *Victimology 5*, 121–132

Meiselman, K. (1978) *Incest: A Psychological Study of Cause and Effects*. San Francisco: Jossey Bass

Meldrum, J. and West, D. J. (1983) 'Homosexual offences as reported in the press', *Medicine, Science and the Law 23*, 41–53

Miller, B. and Humphreys, L. (1980) 'Lifestyles and violence: Homosexual victims of assault and murder', *Journal of Qualitative Sociology 3*, 169–185

Mohr, J. W., Turner, R. E. and Jerry, M. B. (1964) *Pedophilia and Exhibitionism.* Toronto: Toronto University Press

Money, J., Cawte, J. E., Bianchi, G. N. and Nurcombe, B. (1977) 'Sex training and traditions in Arnhem Land'. In J. Money and H. Musaph (eds.) *Handbook of Sexology*. Amsterdam: Elsevier/North-Holland Biomedical Press

Moody, S. R. and Tombs, J. (1982) *Prosecution in the Public Interest*. Edinburgh: Scottish Academic Press

Mrazek, P. Beezley and Kempe, C. H. (eds.) (1980) *Sexually Abused Children and their Families*. New York: Pergamon

Mrazek, P. B., Lynch, M. A. and Bentovim, A. (1983) 'Sexual abuse of children in the United Kingdom', *Child Abuse and Neglect* 7, 147–153

Nadelson, C. C. *et al* (1982) ' A follow-up study of rape victims', *American Journal of Psychiatry 139*, 1266–1270

Nash, C. L. and West, D. J. (1985) 'Sexual Molestation of Young Girls'. In D. J. West (ed.) *Sexual Victimisation*. Aldershot: Gower

National Council for One Parent Families (1979) *Pregnant at School*. London: National Council

Newton, D. E. (1978) 'Homosexual behaviour and child molestation: A review of the evidence', *Adolesence 13*, 29–54

O'Carroll, T. (1980) *Paedophilia: The Radical Case*. London: Peter Owen

Olsen, J. (1974) *The Man with the Candy*. New York: Simon and Schuster

O'Reilly, H. (1982) In S. Levine and J. Koenig (eds.) *Why Men Rape*. London: W.H. Allen

Ortmann, J. (1980) 'The treatment of sexual offenders: Castration and antihormone therapy', *International Journal of Law and Psychiatry 3*, 443–451

Osborne, K. (1982) 'Sexual violence'. In M. P. Feldman (ed.) *Developents in the Study of Criminal Behavior* Vol 2. Chichester: J. Wiley

Otterbein, K. F. (1979) 'A cross-cultural study or rape', *Aggressive Behavior 5*, 425–435

Panton, J. H. (1978) 'Personality differences appearing between rapists of adults, rapists of children and non-violent sexual molesters of female children', *Research Communications in Psychology, Psychiatry and Behavior 3*(4), 385–393

Perkins, D. (1982) 'The treatment of sex offenders'. In M. P. Feldman (ed.) *Developments in the Study of Criminal Behaviour*. Chichester: Wiley

Perkins, D. E. (1983) 'The psychological treatment of offenders in prison and the community'. Paper read at a conference on *Options for the Mentally Abnormal Offender*. Wolfson College, Oxford

Peters, J. J. (1975) 'Social, legal and psychological effects of rape on the victim'. *Pennsylvania Medicine 78*,34–36

Peters, J. J. and Roether, H. A. (1968) 'Group psychotherapy for the sex offender', *Federal Probation 32*(3), 41–45

Phipps-Yonas, S. (1980) 'Teen-age pregnancy and motherhood: A review of the literature', *American Journal of Orthopsychiatry 50*, 403–431

Plummer, K. (1981a) 'Paedophilia: Constructing a sociological baseline'. In M. Cook and K. Howells (eds.) *Adult Sexual Interest in Children*. London: Academic Press

Plummer, K. (1981) (ed.) *The Making of the Modern Homosexual*. London: Hutchinson

Porter, R. (1984) (ed.) *Child Sexual Abuse within the Family*. London: Tavistock for C.I.B.A. Foundation

Porteus, H. (1972) *Sex and Identity: Your Child's Sexuality*. New York: Bobbs-Merrill

Powell, G. E. and Chalkley, N. J. (1981) 'The effects of paedophile attention on the child'. In B. Taylor (ed.) *Perspectives on Paedophilia*. London: Batsford

Prins, H. A. (1976) 'Remands for psychiatric reports', *Medicine, Science and the Law 14*, 129–138

Quinsey, V. L. (1984) 'Sexual aggression: Studies of offenders against women'. In D. Weisstub (ed.) *International Yearbook on Law and Mental Health 1*. New York: Pergamon

Quinsey, V. L., Chaplin, T. C. and Carrigan, W. F. (1980) 'Biofeedback and signalled punishment in the modification of inappropriate sexual age preferences'. *Behavior Therapy 11*, 567–576

Quinsey, V. L. and Chaplin, T. C. (1982) 'Penile responses to non-sexual violence among rapists', *Criminal Justice and Behavior* 372–381

Radizinowicz, L. (1957) *Sexual Offences*. London: Macmillan

Reiber, I. and Sigusch, V. (1979) 'Psychosurgery on sex offenders and sexual "deviants" in West Germany', *Archives of Sexual Behavior 8*, 523–7

Reifen, D. (1973) 'Court procedures in Israel to protect child-victims of sexual assaults'. In I. Drapkin and E. Viano (eds.) *Victimology: A New Focus Vol 3*. Lexington, Mass: D. C. Heath

Rossman, G. P. (1979) *Sexual Experience Between Men and Boys*. London: Temple Smith

Royal Commission on Criminal Procedure (1978) *Written Evidence of the Director of Public Prosecutuions*. Memorandum

Royal Commission on Criminal Procedure (1979) *Memorandum VI: Cautioning by the Police*. London: Home Office

Royal Commission on Criminal Procedure (1981) *Report*. Cmnd 8092. London: H.M.S.O. Ch. 7

Rush, F. (1980) *The Best Kept Secret: Sexual Abuse of Children*. Engelwood Cliffs, N. J.: Prentice-Hall

Russell, D. E. H. (1982) 'The prevalence and incidence of forcible rape and attempted rape of females', *Victimology* 7, 81–93

Russell, D. E. H. (1983) 'The incidence and prevalence of intrafamilial and extrafamilial sexual abuse of female children', *Child Abuse and Neglect* 7, 133–146

Salem, S. (1983) – personal communication based on Cambridge Institute of Criminology Psychiatric Remands Research Project

Sanday, P. R. (1981) 'The socio-cultural context of rape: A cross-cultural study', *Journal of Social Issues 37* (4), 5-27

Sanders, W. B. (1980) *Rape and Woman's Identity*. Beverly Hills: Sage

Sandfort, T. (1982) *The Sexual Aspect of Paedophile Relations*. Amsterdam: Pan/Spartacus

Saylor, M. (1980) 'A guided self-help approach to the treatment of the habitual sex offender'. In D. J. West (ed.) *Sex Offenders in the Criminal Justice System*. Cropwood Conference Series No. 12. Cambridge: Institute of Criminology

Scacco, A. M. (1975) *Rape in Prison*. Springfield, Ill: C. C. Thomas
Schofield, M. (1965) *The Sexual Behaviour of Young People*. London: Longmans
Schultz, L. G. (1980) 'The age of consent: fault, friction, freedom'. In L. G. Schultz (ed.) *The Sexual Victimology of Youth*. Springfield: C. C. Thomas
Scott, G. D. (1982) *Inmate: The Casebook Revelations of a Canadian Penitentiary Psychiatrist*. Montreal: Optimum Publishing International
Scottish Home and Health Department (1975) *Criminal Procedure in Scotland*. (2nd Report. Chairman Lord Thompson) Cmnd 6218. Edinburgh: H.M.S.O.
Sechrest, L., White, S. O. and Brown, E. D. (eds.) (1979) *The Rehabilitation of Criminal Offenders: Problems and Prospects*. Washington, D. C.: National Academy of Sciences
Seemanova, E. (1971) 'A study of children of incestuous matings'. *Human Heredity 21*, 108–128
Serber, M. (1970) 'Shame aversion therapy', *Journal of Behavior Therapy and Experimental Psychiatry 1*, 217–226
Serber, M. and Keith, C. G. (1974) 'The Atascadero Project: Model of a sexual retraining program for incarcerated homosexual pedophiles', *Journal of Homosexuality 1*, 87–97
Shaffer, D., Pettigrew, A., Wolkind, S. and Zajicek, E. (1978) 'Psychiatric aspects of pregnancy in schoolgirls: a review', *Psychological Medicine 8*, 119–130
Shaw, R. (1978) 'The persistent sexual offender – control and rehabilitation', *Probation Journal 25*, 9–13, 61–63
Silbert, M. H. and Pines, A. M. (1981) 'Sexual child abuse as an antecedent to prostitution', *Child Abuse and Neglect 5*, 407–411
Silbert, M. H. and Pines, A. M. (1982) 'Victimisation of street prostitutes', *Victimlogy 7*, 122–133
Smith, D. (ed.) (1979) *Life Sentence Prisoners*. Home Office Research Study 51. London: H.M.S.O.
Soothill, K. L. and Gibbens, T. C. N. (1978) 'Recidivism of sexual offenders: a re-appraisal', *British Journal of Criminology 18*, 267–276.
Sparrow, G. (1966) *Satan's Children*. London: Odhams
Speijer Committee (1969) *Report Concerning Homosexual Relations with Minors*. Netherlands: Council of Health
Stafford, A. (1964) *The Age of Consent*. London: Hodder and Stoughton
Stewart, C. H. (1981) 'A retrospective survey of alleged sexual assault cases', *Police Surgeon (*Nov*)*, 28–32
Stone, W. G. (1982) *The Hate Factory*. (As told to I. Hirliman.) Agoura, Ca: Paisano
Sturup, G. K. (1972) 'Castration: The total treatment'. In H. L. P. Resnik and M. E. Wolfgang (eds.) *Sexual Behaviors: Social, Clinical and Legal Aspects*. Boston: Little, Brown
Swanson, D. W. (1968) 'Adult sexual abuse of children: The man and circumstances'. *Diseases of the Nervous System 29*, 677–683
Sykes, G. M. (1971) *The Society of Captives*. Princeton: Princeton University Press
Taylor, B. (1981) (ed.) *Perspectives on Paedophilia*. London: Batsford
Thomas, D. A. (1979) *Principles of Sentencing*. London: Heinemann
Tindall, R. H. (1978) 'The male adolescent involved with a pederast becomes an adult', *Journal of Homosexuality 3*, 373–382
Tolsma, F. J. (1957) *De betekenis van de verleiding in homofiele ontwikkelingen*. Amsterdam: Psychiatric Juridical Society

Toner, B. (1982) *The Facts of Rape.* (2nd Edn.) London: Arrow

Topper, A. B. and Aldridge, D. J. (1981) 'Incest: Intake and investigation'. In P. B. Mrazek and C. H. Kempe (eds.) *Sexually Abused Children and their Families.* Oxford: Pergamon

Trenchard, L. and Warren, H. (1984) *Something to Tell You.* London Gay Teenage Group

United Nations (1980) *The Effect of Islamic Legislation on Crime Prevention in Saudi Arabia.* Rome: United Nations Social Defence Research Institute

Virkkunen, M. (1975) 'Victim-precipitated paedophilia offences', *British Journal of Criminology 15*, 175–180

Wald, M. S. (1982) 'State intervention on behalf of endangered children – a proposed legal response', *Child Abuse and Neglect 6*, 3–45

Walmsley, R. (1978) 'Indecency between males and the Sexual Offences Act 1967', *Criminal Law Review (July)*, 400–407

Walmsley, R. and White, K. (1979) *Sexual Offences, Consent and Sentencing.* Home Office Research Study No. 54. London: H.M.S.O.

Walmsley, R. and White, K. (1980) *Supplementary Information on Sexual Offences and Sentencing.* Research Unit Paper 2. London: Home Office

Walters, D. R. (1975) *Physical and Sexual Abuse of Children.* Bloomington: Indiana University Press

Ward, E. (1982) 'Rape of girl children by male family members', *Journal of Australian and New Zealand Criminology 15*, 90–99

Weiss, C. and Friar, J. (1975) *Terror in the Prisons: Homosexual Rape and Why Society Condones It.* New York: Bobbs-Merrill

Weiss, J., Rogers, E., Darwin, M. R., and Dutton, C. E. (1955) 'A study of girl sex victims', *Psychiatric Quarterly 29*, 1–27

Wells, N. H. (1958) 'Sexual offences as seen by a woman police surgeon', *British Medical Journal (2)*, 1404–1408.

West, D. J., Roy, C. and Nichols, F. (1978) *Understanding Sexual Attacks.* London: Heinemann

Wickramasekera, I. (1976) 'Aversive behavioral rehearsal for sexual exhibitionism', *Behavior Therapy 7*, 167–176

Williams, E. (1967) *Beyond Belief: A Chronicle of Murder and Its Detection.* London: Hamish Hamilton

Williams, E. and Holmes, K. A. (1981) *The Second Assault: Rape and Public Attitudes.* Westport, Connecticut: Greenwood Press

Wilson, G. D. (1978) *The Secrets of Sexual Fantasy.* London: Dent

Wilson, G. D. and Cox, D. N. (1983) *The Child Lovers.* London: Peter Owen

Wilson, P. R. (1981) *The Man they called a Monster.* North Ryde, Australia: Cassell

Wright, M. (1982) *Making Good: Prisons, Punishment and Beyond.* London: Hutchinson

Wright, R. (1980) 'Rape and physical violence'. In D. J. West (ed.) *Sexual Offenders in the Criminal Justice System.* (Proceedings of the 12th Cropwood Conference.) Cambridge: University Institute of Criminology

Wright, R. and West, D. J. (1981) 'Rape – A comparison of group offences and lone offences', *Medicine, Science and the Law 21*, 25–30

Yates, A. (1978) *Sex Without Shame.* London: Temple Smith

Young, M. de (1982) *The Sexual Victimization of Children.* Jefferson, N. C.: McFarland

Zangwill, O. L. (Chairman) (1980) *Behaviour Modification: Report of a Joint Working Party to Formulate Ethical Guidelines for the Conduct of Behaviour Modification Programmes in the National Health Service.* London: H.M.S.O.

Index of Names and Cases

Subject Index

Also published by Waterlows

Legal and Social Policy Library:

Pornography and Politics *by A. W. B. Simpson*
Fair Charges *by M. R. Ludlow*

Waterlow's Business Library:

Understanding Computer Contracts *by Martin Edwards*
Understanding Insurance *by Gwilym Williams*
Understanding Business Taxation *by A. D. Preston*
Understanding Commercial and Industrial Licensing *by Brendan Fowlston*
Understanding Recruitment Law *by David Newell*
Understanding Dismissal Law *by Martin Edwards*

Practitioners' Library:

Estate Conveyancing *by P. M. A'Court*
Consumer Credit Agreements *by Jan Karpinski and Stephen Fielding*
The Law of Co-Operatives *by Ian Snaith*

And:

Marketing Legal Services *edited by S. C. Silkin*
The Layman's Dictionary of English Law *by Gavin McFarlane*

UNLAWFUL SEX